Inflation-Linked Products

Inflation-Linked Products

A Guide for Investors and Asset & Liability Managers

Edited by Brice Benaben

Published by Risk Books, a Division of Incisive Financial Publishing Ltd

Haymarket House
28–29 Haymarket
London SW1Y 4RX
Tel: +44 (0)20 7484 9700
Fax: +44 (0)20 7484 9800
E-mail: books@riskwaters.com
Sites: www.riskbooks.com
        www.incisivemedia.com

ISBN 1 904339 60 3

British Library Cataloguing in Publication Data
A catalogue record for this book is available from the British Library

Managing Editor: Laurie Donaldson
Development Editor: Vasuki Balasubramanian
Designer: Rebecca Bramwell

Typeset by Mizpah Publishing Services Private Limited, Chennai, India

Printed and bound in Spain by Espacegrafic, Pamplona, Navarra

Contents

About the Editor

Brice Benaben is the global head of inflation structuring at ABN AMRO. His team have been structuring a wide range of inflation-linked products and innovative solutions for hedge funds, pension funds, corporates, financial institutions, and project finances both in Europe and the USA. He was initially involved in linkers trading as a portfolio manager in the International Finance Corporation (World Bank group) in Washington DC. Then, as head of fixed income and portfolio strategies in Crédit Agricole Indosuez (Calyon), he worked with sophisticated investors on risk budgeting frameworks, focusing particularly on inflation strategies within fixed income portfolios. He also advised major European sovereign issuers on various debt management issues; this includes optimising the funding strategies for debt portfolio, mixing nominal and inflation-linked bonds with risk-adjusted cost quantitative models.

Brice speaks regularly at conferences and has co-written various papers on asset management and debt management with inflation-linked products. Brice is a graduate of Oxford University, where he studied applied mathematics.

List of Contributors

Markus Aakko is vice president and head of the fixed income manager selection and risk management teams. He is responsible for identifying, evaluating, and monitoring managers across all aspects of fixed income investment management, and for building the risk management capabilities of the fixed income team. As head of risk management, he oversees the team's equity and fixed income portfolio risk management. He joined the investment management division of Goldman Sachs in 2000 from the Treasury of the International Finance Corporation of the World Bank Group. He received his masters of science in finance from the Helsinki School of Economics in 1998.

Valdimar Armann has worked at ABN AMRO, as a senior inflation structurer, since 2003. His role focuses particularly on structuring a wide range of inflation assets for financial institutions and private investors. Previously, Valdimar was involved in the oldest inflation market, the Icelandic linkers, as a derivatives structurer at Kaupthing bank. Valdimar is quoted in expert financial papers, is a speaker at inflation conferences and has written several papers on inflation products. He holds an MSc in financial engineering and quantitative analysis from the ISMA Centre, University of Reading.

Nabyl Belgrade is currently a member of the fixed income quantitative research team at IXIS CIB. He is currently finishing his PhD thesis on "Modelling Inflation in Mathematical Finance" at Paris1 Pantheon-Sorbonne University and he holds a DEA (European post masters degree) in stochastic calculus from the same university. His main works are on inflation derivatives:

❏ valuation of inflation European vanillas: swaps, floors;
❏ valuation of exotic inflation swaptions and hybrid options on forward real yield; and
❏ seasonality modelling and estimating and its impact on the pricing of inflation derivatives.

Eric Benhamou is a principal at Pricing Partners. Previously, he was the global head of quantitative research at IXIS CIB for fixed income, inflation, foreign exchange, hybrids and funds derivatives for Europe and Asia.

He has senior experience in developing new pricing models and risk management tools and has worked, among others, for banks such as Goldman Sachs, Commerzbank, Société Générale, and Crédit Lyonnais. A former alumnus of the Ecole Polytechnique and the French National School of Statistics (E.N.S.A.E), he holds a D.E.A. in stochastic calculus from University Paris VI (Jussieu), and a PhD in financial mathematics from the London School of Economics.

Daniel S. Bernstein is the director of research at Bridgewater Associates, Inc and is responsible for co-supervising Bridgewater's research effort. He has been with Bridgewater since 1988. Dan specialises in inflation-indexed bond market research. He has co-authored several papers on inflation-linked bonds and is responsible for implementing the real return strategies of the inflation-linked bond portfolios. Dan graduated in 1987 from Dartmouth College with a BA in economics.

David Bieber joined ABN AMRO in London, in 2001. He initially worked as a quantitative analyst in an interest rate risk advisory team before moving into the inflation products team in 2004. He is now responsible for structuring ALM inflation solutions for both corporates and pension funds. Prior to this David had a spell as a development senior engineer in a biotech start-up company. David graduated from Oxford University in 1997, with a PhD in physics.

Benoît Coeuré is the deputy chief executive of France's debt management office, Agence France Trésor (AFT). Priori to joining AFT, he was an economist at the French statistical institute (INSEE) and at the French Treasury, where he was involved in international and European policy issues. He has previously been the chief economic adviser to the director of the French Treasury, and the head of foreign exchange and economic policy. Benoît teaches macroeconomics and economic policy at École polytechnique in Paris. He has written on exchange rates, international monetary issues and European policy and has published two books, *Economie de l'Euro* and *Politique Economique*.

Raymond T. Dalio is the president and chief investment officer of Bridgewater Associates, Inc. Raymond's lifetime economic research has concentrated on global credit and currency markets. In 1975, Raymond formed the company and, as CIO, he heads the senior investment team that directs the firm's research effort. Prior to founding Bridgewater, he was director of commodities at Dominick and Dominick, a Wall Street brokerage house and subsequently joined Shearson Hayden Stone, where he was in charge of the Institutional Futures Department. He graduated with an MBA degree in finance from Harvard Business School in 1973.

Sébastien Goldenberg is head of trading for inflation products at ABN AMRO in Amsterdam. His team trades all inflation-linked products, such as inflation-linked bonds, swaps and options in EUR, USD and GBP. He joined ABN AMRO in the summer of 2003 to set up the inflation-linked trading desk. He has more than six years experience in the inflation market. Before joining ABN AMRO, he was in charge of inflation trading at Crédit Agricole Indosuez in Paris (CALYON). Previously, Sébastien worked at Crédit Industriel et Commercial where he built a solid experience in fixed income trading. He has been involved recently in a number of publications and is a regular speaker at major inflation products conferences in Europe. Sébastien holds a masters degree in applied mathematics and finance from Université Paris Dauphine and from the French business school, ESSEC.

John Hancock is head of the economic value management department at Swiss Reinsurance Company. Previously, he was deputy head of Swiss Re's risk management methods group. Prior to joining Swiss Re in 1998, John worked for the World Bank and RFA as a consultant to the banking industry on credit risk management issues. John holds PhD and BA degrees from the University of Pennsylvania, where he specialised in finance, and an MA in economics from Georgetown University.

Alan James is a director and head of inflation-linked research at Barclays Capital. He is responsible for coordinating Barclays Capital's global inflation-linked research, and writing reports on all the major inflation-linked bond and derivatives markets. Prior to joining Barclays Capital in August 2003, Alan spent six years at Credit Suisse First Boston, working on European fixed income strategy and global strategy. Alan holds an MA in economics from Cambridge University.

Stuart Jarvis is a senior strategist in the liability-driven investment team at Barclays Global Investors (BGI), based in London. He is responsible for developing techniques for analysing clients' asset/liability profiles, working with clients to manage their interest rate and inflation rate risks and helping them to design portfolios to generate returns efficiently. Stuart is a qualified actuary, and prior to joining BGI in 2004, he worked as a consultant at Hewitt Associates (formerly Bacon & Woodrow). He holds a BA mathematics degree from Cambridge University and a DPhil from Oxford University. He was a research fellow for three years at Oxford prior to joining Bacon & Woodrow.

Theo Kocken is a partner and CEO at Cardano Risk Management. He graduated from The Hogeschool Eindhoven with a degree in business administration and is a *cum laude* graduate of Tilburg University, with a masters degree in econometrics. He has conducted research on risk management and asset and liability management at the Bank Nederlandse Gemeenten in The Hague and headed, among others, the market risk department at ING Barings in Amsterdam and Rabobank International in Utrecht. In 2000, he founded Cardano Risk Management in Rotterdam. He is the co-author of various books and articles in the area of risk management, with a research focus on the strategic application of derivatives in asset and liability management.

Etienne Koehler is head of quantitative risk analysis at Natexis BP. He validates internal or external valuation and hedging models for all products in the bank. He also works on VAR developments. Previously, Etienne was global head of research and development (credit derivatives, interest and FX rates) at IXIS CIB, Credit Agricole Indosuez and Credit Lyonnais. He is also associate professor at Paris1 Pantheon-La Sorbonne University. Etienne is a former alumnus of Ecole Normale Supérieure. He holds an "Aggregation of Mathematics", a DEA (post masters degree) of mathematics and an MBA from INSEAD. He has published various articles, including one in *Risk* magazine. He is a regular speaker at quantitative finance conferences.

Bruno Lambert leads the fixed income arbitrage desk of CM-CIC group and is the investment adviser of Cigogne Fund, a Luxembourg-based hedge fund. He began as a proprietary trader on government bonds and fixed income derivatives at banque CIAL in 1995. He has been actively trading inflation-linked products worldwide on a relative value perspective since 1998.

Oliver Letzgus graduated with a degree in economics in 1992. As a scientific assistant for the Institute of Economics, University of Stuttgart-Hohenheim, he focused on public finance, monetary theory and economic policy. In 1998, he completed his doctorate in public finance. In the same year, Oliver became a public relations consultant at Dirk Bläse Public Relations in Stuttgart, responsible for the PR of several Swiss banks. In April 2001, he joined Union Investment, one of Germany's major asset management groups. Working on the fixed income side, he is responsible for fundamental portfolio and market research.

Bob Litterman is the director of quantitative resources within the investment management division of Goldman Sachs. He is the co-developer, along with the late Fischer Black, of the Black-Litterman Global Asset

Allocation Model, a key tool in the division's asset allocation process. Over his 19 years at Goldman Sachs, Bob has also headed the firm-wide risk department and has been co-director, with Fischer Black, of the research and model development group within the Fixed Income Division's research department. Bob has authored or co-authored many papers on risk management, asset allocation, and the use of modern portfolio theory.

Adam Michaels MA, FIA is an investment consultant at Lane, Clark & Peacock LLP. His work includes providing investment advice to pension schemes, researching UK investment managers offering liability-driven investment and other structured solutions, and economic research. His main area of focus is on investment strategy. Previously, at the UK Government actuary's department, he worked first in pensions policy and demography, and then as a pensions actuary. He has written articles for a range of publications, including *Professional Pensions* and *The Actuary*.

Dariush Mirfendereski is the managing director and head of inflation-linked trading at UBS Investment Bank in London. Prior to joining UBS in early 2004, Dariush was head of inflation derivatives trading at Barclays Capital. He has traded inflation-linked products since 1998. Dariush is a co-author of the book *Inflation-Indexed Securities: Bonds, Swaps, and Other Derivatives, 2nd Ed.*, published in January 2004. He has been an invited speaker at numerous international conferences and has over a dozen conference papers and journal publications in the fields of micro-electro mechanical engineering, catastrophe insurance loss modelling, option pricing, and inflation derivatives dating from 1991 to present. Dariush obtained his BSc and MSc degrees from UCL and Imperial College, London and, subsequently, a PhD in engineering from the University of California at Berkeley.

Stanley Myint is a director in the corporate risk solutions group at the Royal Bank of Scotland (RBS). Stanley's responsibilities include advising clients on risk management issues, including IAS39 and portfolio analysis, and he is a frequent speaker at the events organised by RBS. Stanley joined RBS in 2002 from McKinsey & Company, where he was a consultant in their risk management practice. Prior to this, he was an executive director at the Canadian Imperial Bank of Commerce. Stanley obtained a PhD in physics from Boston University.

Nicolas Sagnes is head of research and strategy at the French debt management office, Agence France Trésor. He is also a teacher at ENSAE, which trains statistics, economic and financial specialists. Prior to this, Nicolas worked as an economist for the Treasury. Nicolas has published several papers in academic and professional journals. He graduated from

Ecole Polytechnique and ENSAE and holds a masters degree in pure mathematics from Paris 7 University.

Hidesaka Taki is a quantitative strategist at BNP Paribas Japan, where he is responsible for analysing hybrid flow products, such as CMT/CMS-linked products or inflation-linked products. The inflation trading team at BNP Paribas Tokyo is one of the pioneers of the Japanese inflation-linked market. Hidesaka, who has a masters degree in engineering from the University of Tokyo (where he focused on time-series analysis in the crude oil future markets), began his professional career as a bond fund manager with Merrill Lynch Investment Managers in 2001. His areas of interest/expertise include yield curve or volatility curve strategies from a quantitative viewpoint, and portfolio allocation and model tracking.

Jeroen van der Hoek is a senior consultant and project manager at Cardano Risk Management, where he has worked since 2000. He is responsible for the implementation of derivatives strategies with pension funds and insurance companies. Previously, he worked at Rabobank International, where he was a risk manager, responsible for several projects in the field of risk management and treasury. Jeroen holds a masters degree in applied mathematics.

Jörg Warncke is a senior fund manager at Union Investment, one of Germany's largest asset management companies. In this capacity, he is responsible for managing a number of mutual funds and institutional mandates with a focus on European fixed income. He develops yield-enhancing strategies and supervises a team of fund managers. His core product areas include government bonds, inflation-linked bonds, covered bonds, and derivatives. Jörg started his career in 1994 as a quantitative analyst at DIT and moved to DWS in 1996 as a fund manager. In 2001 he joined Union in his current position. He holds a degree in physics from Johann Wolfgang Goethe-University in Frankfurt and a CEFA diploma from the German Association for Fund Management and Asset Allocation.

Introduction

Brice Benaben

ABN AMRO

The idea of linking financial asset returns to the price of goods is not recent. According to the authors of "Inflation-indexed Securities",[1] the first indexation can be tracked back to the 18th century; the State of Massachusetts issued bills linked to the cost of silver. The silver price increased more quickly than general prices, causing economic losses for the issuer. This bad experience discouraged others to issue such products for many years.

A more and maybe the most successful story can be found in recent history with the unprecedented growth of inflation-linked debt. Yet the paradox is why this has occurred at a time when the major economies have experienced low and stable inflation rates.

On one side, in the world's largest economies, the inflation level has rarely been so low. Most of these economies (England, European Monetary Union, Canada, Australia and Sweden) have adopted inflation targeting which, to some extent, has contributed to this inflation environment. Even the USA, which has no explicit inflation-targeting mandate (there is debate about whether they should adopt one),[2] has seen their inflation rate stabilising at around 2%. Japan is the extreme example, as its economy has been in deflation for almost eight years.

On the other side, the inflation product market is developing at an unprecedentedly rapid pace, even in Japan. The liquid sovereign debt market capitalisation has been growing exponentially. It amounts today to EUR578bn in terms of market capitalisation and represents 6.1% of nominal dept of government regular linkers

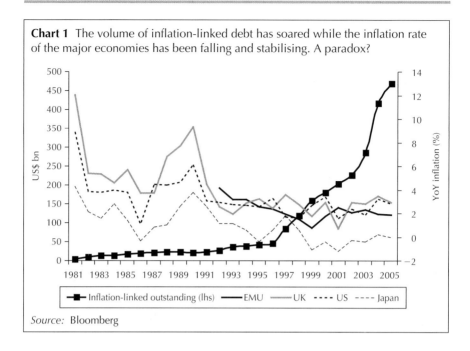

Chart 1 The volume of inflation-linked debt has soared while the inflation rate of the major economies has been falling and stabilising. A paradox?

Inflation-linked outstanding (lhs) — EMU — UK ---- US ---- Japan

Source: Bloomberg

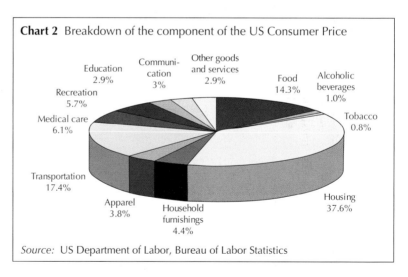

Chart 2 Breakdown of the component of the US Consumer Price

Education 2.9%
Communication 3%
Other goods and services 2.9%
Food 14.3%
Alcoholic beverages 1.0%
Recreation 5.7%
Medical care 6.1%
Tobacco 0.8%
Transportation 17.4%
Apparel 3.8%
Household furnishings 4.4%
Housing 37.6%

Source: US Department of Labor, Bureau of Labor Statistics

issuers. This development is not a local but a global phenomenon; recently Japan joined the club of sovereign issuers and Germany is expected to step in soon; as a result, all major economies will have issued inflation-linked bonds. In parallel, the market has reached

Table 1 Standardisation and globalisation of the sovereign inflation-linked bond market

Issuer	Year of first issue	Amount outstanding €(bn)	Inflation adjusted amount outstanding €(bn)	Longest maturity	Structure	Floor	Indexation lag	Inflation index
US	1997	219	241	15-Apr-32	Multiplicative	Y	2–3M	US CPI Urban consumers
France	1998	91	97	25-Jul-32	Multiplicative	Y	2–3M	EMU HICP Ex tobacco & FR CPI Ex tobacco
UK	1981	70	144	26-Jan-35	Multiplicative	N	8M[1]	UK RPI all items
Italy	2003	34	36	15-Sep-35	Multiplicative	Y	2–3M	EMU HICP Ex tobacco
Sweden	1994	21	24	01-Dec-28	Multiplicative	Y/N[2]	2–3M	Swedish CPI
Canada	1991	13	16	01-Dec-36	Multiplicative	Y	2–3M	Canadian CPI
Japan	2004	11	11	10-Jun-15	Multiplicative	N	2–3M	Japan CPI Ex fresh food
Greece	2003	5	5	25-Jul-25	Multiplicative	Y	2–3M	EMU HICP Ex tobacco
Iceland	1964	5	5	15-Jun-44	Annuity	Y	1M[3]	Iceland CPI
Australia	1985	4	5	20-Aug-20	Multiplicative	Y	9–12M[4]	Australian CPI
Poland	2004	1	1	24-Aug-16	Multiplicative	Y	2–3M	Polish CPI
		474	583					

Notes:
1 All new bonds issued after June 05 will have the standard 3M interpolated indexation lag.
2 In 1999 Swedish National Debt Office reformed the inflation-indexed bond market and a deflation floor on principal repayment was also introduced.
3 Interpolation between last month's CPI and current month's CPI using current month's CPI forecast from Central Bank of Iceland until actual CPI is published.
4 Average percentage change in the CPI over the two quarters prior to that in which the next interest payment falls.

Source: Bloomberg

an unprecedented level of standardisation in terms of the index and the structure. In addition, regulatory barriers, which have prevented some investors from purchasing inflation-linked products, have been lifted or are in the process of being removed.[3] It seems that everything is set up for the sustainable growth of this market.

And yet the paradox remains – the purpose of inflation products is to protect investors from rising prices, which reduce their investment return. In other words, inflation products prevent a deterioration of the purchasing power of the investors. So why should investors purchase inflation-protected instruments if inflation is stabilised at a low level?

An answer might be found in the definition of inflation. Inflation is a generic term referring to a multitude of macro-economic measures.[4] The best known measure is the Consumer Price Index (CPI), which tracks prices of selected goods and services purchased by an average consumer. It is published monthly and in the EMU it is standardised to enable country comparison.[5] Inflation targeting regimes have adopted this index. However, the targeted CPI inflation may be poorly correlated to the inflation that some pension funds or insurance companies would like to hedge. Therefore, even if monetary policy inflation rates were stabilised, it would not imply that these specific inflation rates would be. Then the question becomes whether the financial market can provide these specific inflation-hedging products. Most liquid inflation products are also linked to CPI but, interestingly, new products linked to less conventional indices are developing even if their liquidity remains limited, at least so far.

Another answer is the imperfect relationship between monetary cycle and inflation cycle. Multiple reasons can explain it, such as the granularities in the transmission of monetary policy into the economy, the unpredictability of short-term inflation shocks (oil price shocks, fiscal shocks…) and so on. This creates difficulties for the central banks in controlling CPI inflation. For instance, the inflation reports from Sveriges Riksbank or the Bank of England depict a probability distribution of the inflation path over the coming years. However, what is striking to the reader is the wide range of reasonably possible inflation scenarios that the central banks expect. This can also cast doubts about the efficiency of monetary policy in maintaining inflation targets and their long-term sustainability.

These effects contribute to the weak and unstable correlation between the return of inflation linked and nominal bonds. As a result a growing number of investors consider inflation-linked bonds as a separate asset class.

This paradox should also be seen in the context of the fundamental imbalance between inflation-linked assets and liabilities rather than simply as a function of inflation levels. Inflation-linked liabilities exceed by far the existing asset base. Two important drivers have stimulated the growth in liabilities:

❑ The growing awareness of inflation risk and tougher regulations on pension liabilities encourage or force the hedging of inflation risk embedded in these liabilities. This has been, and will remain, an important driver of the inflation market.
❑ The return of the French tax exempted saving accounts (livret "A") was linked partially to inflation in 2003. This added a EUR175bn pool of liabilities linked to French inflation, while the EMU inflation bonds amounted to only 75bn! Such a "regulation shock", which boosted the potential demand for products paying inflation, may be a one-off event but its amplitude has long-term consequences.

The sovereign issuers have been the first "inflation payers" driven by the desire to capture this rising demand. In addition, inflation-funding programmes create advantages to the issuer, such as stabilisation and reduction of their financial costs. The commitment for a linkers programme by sovereign issuers has created a sort of virtuous circle, which led rapidly to growing supply and (even quicker) growing demand. At present the scene is set for the inflation market to move into new dimensions. Inflation "payers" and "receivers" are multiplying, inflation products are more sophisticated and their use is broadening into most areas of finance.

This gives an idea of the breadth of the inflation subject area, which has been building around the early inflation market where sovereign issuers "pay" inflation (by issuing inflation-linked bonds) to long-term investors who "receive" this inflation (to hedge liabilities). This book aims to explore the different dimensions of the inflation market, from the investors', issuers' and asset/liability managers' perspectives. Leading inflation experts from different segments of the industry (asset management, hedge funds, bank trading and structuring, bank and academic research, pension funds, insurance companies) will outline how and why they use inflation products.

The first section covers inflation products, both bonds and derivatives from the investment angle. It explains the mechanics of inflation products and how they fit within a portfolio for a broad range of users. For the asset manager, it details the current investment strategies used by the industry, such as the basic carry trades, sophisticated inflation convergence plays and the diversification benefit of using linkers within a global portfolio. For the quantitative modeller and bank trading desks, it looks at the new generation of inflation products, the current state of the art in inflation modelling and the associated challenges.

The second section outlines how inflation products fit within an asset-liability framework. On the issuer side it looks at why sovereign and corporate borrowers use inflation products and how they can be used to create value for taxpayers and shareholders. From the standpoint of natural receivers, such as pension funds and insurance companies, the book covers themes of how to quantify and hedge their inflation risk.

1 For a complete historical perspective and detailed analysis of the of inflation linked bond markets: "Inflation-indexed Securities; Bonds, Swaps & Other Derivatives", Second edition, Mark Deacon, Andrew Derry and Dariush Mirfendereski.
2 Remarks by Governor Edward M. Gramlich at the Euromoney Inflation Conference, Paris, France, May 26th, 2005.
3 For more information: "Inflation-linked products in the Euro area: An AMTE working group to standardise, develop and promote the asset class", June 2005.
4 Some classic measures are the Producer Price Index, which covers only the consumer goods (manufacturers prices) and capital equipment. The broadest inflation measure is probably the Gross Domestic Product Deflator. It covers, among other things, consumer goods and services, housing and capital equipments.
5 This effort of standardisation has been important in the European Union; Eurostat has developed a common methodology to compute a Harmonised Index of Consumer Price (HICP) for each European country. As a result the HICP of each European Monetary Union (EMU) countries are aggregated based on their household final monetary consumption expenditure to give the EMU HICP.

Section 1

Understanding and Investing in Inflation-Linked Products

An Asset Manager's Approach to Real Yield Management

Jörg Warncke and Oliver Letzgus

Union Investment

INTRODUCTION

Real return bonds (linkers) are gaining increasing importance in fixed-income fund management. In contrast to traditional bonds, where coupons and the repayment amount are established in advance, these measures depend on the inflation level. The inflation hedge here results on the basis of officially determined price increases. As a basic principle, price setting for linkers takes place in an analogous manner to nominal return bonds. Break even inflation (BEI) plays a central role when comparing the performance of both bond types. If, at bullet maturity, the BEI is below the actual inflation rate measured, then investing in real return bonds is more advantageous than investing in nominal return bonds with the same maturity. However, in practice, the comparison is complicated by the existence of an inflation risk premium that is hard to quantify. The tried and tested concepts of duration and convexity are used as risk measures. In this case duration is a measure of price changes in *real* interest rates. As a general rule it can be said that the price volatility of linkers is lower than that of nominal return bonds. This is often reflected in lower beta values. Seasonal factors play a decisive role in the short-term valuation of linkers due to significant fluctuations in the monthly inflation rate. In particular, carry considerations, that is, the exploitation of the interest differential between the forward and spot market, are thereby impacted decisively. We further analyse during which economic phases real return bonds tend to be advantageous, and how yield and BEI curves change according to what is the ideal type during the economic cycle. The closing section of this chapter illustrates what additional sources of performance and what diversification potential for portfolio management can be gained from intermarket trading.

REAL RETURN BONDS IN FUND MANAGEMENT: SOME PRELIMINARY REMARKS

Inflation-indexed bonds – linkers for short – represent a bond class with a steadily growing significance for issuers and investors. With the exception of Germany, all G7 countries have already issued inflation-indexed bonds. Germany in all likelihood will follow in the autumn of 2005. This is important because German government bonds represent the benchmark for the nominal bond market of the Eurozone. Assuming that, as is the case in France, the proportion of inflation-indexed government bonds is approximately 20% of the issuing volume, this corresponds to €30 billion per annum.

Apart from increasing investor pressure, issuer self-interests play an important role here. First, with the issuance of linkers, countries (or companies) can reduce costs, especially the inflation risk premium, which is implicitly demanded by investors holding nominal bonds where the real value is decreased by inflation. Second, the liability portfolio can be better structured. From the issuers' point of view, a mixed liability portfolio – with real return bonds and nominal return bonds – represents an insurance against inflationary and deflationary shocks. Finally, the investor base can be diversified by the issuance of linkers.*

Although there are currently no inflation-indexed *Bundesanleihen* in Germany, recently numerous fixed-income funds, based on linkers, have developed, which provide cheap and simple access for both private as well as institutional investors to these market segments. The products can be differentiated according to the assumed benchmark as well as the concrete market and currency allocations. Thus there are products that are structured without foreign currency risk and also those that can utilise the opportunities in the international inflation market. Other fund providers target

*For good surveys see Hammond (2002), Kaufmann (2004), DZ BANK (2003) or Shen (1995). For more detailed information see Deacon/Derry/Mifrendereski (2004) or Barclays Capital (2002).

a certain annual performance that corresponds to at least the inflation rate plus a certain margin.

Furthermore, real return bonds are gaining increasing popularity as off-benchmark additions to traditional fixed-income funds. This no longer presents a problem from a regulatory point of view; although, until 2003 in Germany, this was a legal grey area, this has since been resolved by BaFin (the German Financial Supervisory Authority) in that it explicitly classified real return bonds as an approved financial innovation. The consideration of whether to add these bonds is driven by relative value aspects. For this reason, they represent an additional source for active management contributions. The average holding period would probably be less than one year, so that in most cases tactical considerations determine their implementation. The particular risk characteristics of this asset class also play a role in absolute return funds (funds with capital preservation) and also in total return funds (funds without benchmark orientation with the target to maximise the risk–reward ratio). Fund of funds managers use dedicated real return funds, in addition to many other products, in the same way that fund managers use conventional fixed-income funds with individual real return bonds.

Last but not least, linkers also show some characteristics that are particularly significant in fixed-income fund management. First, linkers serve as an important information tool. Their traded prices correspond to an assured real interest rate at bullet maturity. Comparing the real interest rates of different countries and different residual maturities provides valuable information for the analysis of international bond markets. Second, comparing real and nominal interest rates also provides conclusions regarding the relative value of the two asset classes. The nominal interest rate of two countries may be almost identical, yet the real interest rates can vary noticeably, which points to significant differences in the market's inflation expectations for these two countries. We will set out these themes more fully in the following sections and will then go into detail regarding their implementation in trading strategies.

Overall, the fund industry in Germany contributes to the rapid prevalence of real return bonds. The following sections discuss the characteristics, valuation, risks and the application of real return bonds primarily in fund management.

REGARDING THE CHARACTERISTICS OF REAL RETURN BONDS
Protection against inflation

Linkers offer protection against loss of purchasing power caused by inflation. The size of the repayments to the investor depends on changes in the underlying price index. In concrete terms, the payments on most bonds consist of regular inflation-adjusted coupons and a redemption payment on maturity, which is likewise adjusted to the inflation rate. To illustrate this, the following example assumes a 10-year bond with a nominal value of €100 and a basis coupon of 3% with annual payment, as well as a constant annual inflation rate of 2%. After the first year, the coupon payment is €3.06 (= $100 \times 0.03 \times 1.02$), after the second year the payment is €3.12 (= $100 \times 0.03 \times 1.02 \times 1.02$) etc. On the due date, the bond holder receives the final coupon of €3.66 (= $100 \times 0.03 \times 1.02^{10}$) plus the repayment of €121.90 (= 100×1.02^{10}), which is €125.56 in total (see Figure 1). This multiplicative structure of indexing is applied to the vast majority of government linkers.

Other indexing structures are additive. These are favoured by corporate issuers and are sometimes used for medium-term notes. In this structure, the bond pays back at par and the total compensation for inflation of the latest coupon period is added to the coupon. In contrast to the multiplicative structure, which better

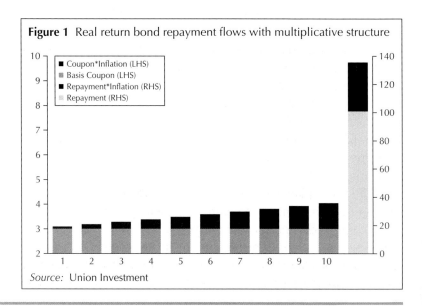

Figure 1 Real return bond repayment flows with multiplicative structure

- Coupon*Inflation (LHS)
- Basis Coupon (LHS)
- Repayment*Inflation (RHS)
- Repayment (RHS)

Source: Union Investment

meets the needs of long-term investors who are looking for long-term purchasing power protection, the additive method offers more timely inflation cashflows in the form of higher coupons and therefore mitigates the risk of default. It also provides a better hedge for corporates with inflation-linked revenues.

Indexing

The exact indexing, that is the compensation for price increases, is one of the more important technical details of these instruments. Eurozone linkers are linked either to the Harmonised Indices of Consumer Prices excluding tobacco (HICP ex tobacco[1]) or, in the case of French inflation-linked government bonds (OATi), to the French consumer price index excluding tobacco prices using the multiplicative structure. The method described below is the same also for US Treasury Inflation Protected Securities (TIPS), Canadian, Swedish and Japanese linkers, and is known as "Canadian style".

Since it concerns effective prices with interest accrued calculated on a daily basis, the linkers' nominal value must be continually adjusted for inflation. However, the problem here is that the official inflation figures are released only after a significant time lag and, in addition, are fixed only once a month. To overcome this problem, one can, first, decide against using the current inflation rate but agree, instead, to build in a two-month delay. Second, in order to take into account that the price index is fixed only on a monthly cycle, an individual reference index, DIR_t, is assigned that is derived from the linear interpolation of the two monthly values for the preceding three and two months, respectively. Thus, for example, the reference index for the 15th January 2005 is 14/31 of the inflation index for November 2004 plus 17/31 of the October 2004 value (see also Panel 1 in this regard). Figure 2 clarifies this time lag in fixing the inflation rate. The indexing method has a direct short-term impact on the coupon and repayment calculation.

For long-term protection against inflation, this two-month delay does not play a significant role since the price change for a basket of goods within two months is generally insignificant compared to price changes over many years. Nevertheless, the "inflation lag" has a significant impact on the price determination of traded linkers. Due to this lag, the course of the inflation reference can be calculated for a few days, so that the publication of a new

PANEL 1 CALCULATING INTEREST ACCRUED, COUPON AND REPAYMENT (CANADIAN STYLE)

The daily inflation reference index DIR_t for any date in January, for example, is derived from the October and November values according to the following formula. It is also officially fixed and published.[3]

$$\text{Daily Inflation Reference } = DIR_t = CPI_{m-3} + \frac{nds-1}{nd_m}\left(CPI_{m-2} - CPI_{m-3}\right)$$

with CPI_{m-3} price index of month $m-3$
    CPI_{m-2} price index of month $m-2$
    nds number of days since start of month
    nd_m number of days in month m

The quotient from the latest daily inflation reference value DIR_t and the basis index DIR_0 (the inflation reference value at bond issue) is the measure for the cumulated price increase since the issue, and is indicated as IR_t (the inflation ratio). This value is needed to calculate the accumulated interest accrued since the last coupon payment and the repayment on the due date:

$$IR_t = \frac{DIR_t}{DIR_0}$$

The interest entitlement accrued since the last coupon payment is the product of the basis coupon, the number of days since the last payment divided by the exact number of days in the coupon period, and the nominal and the inflation quotients IR_t.

accrued interest in % at time $t = AI_t^{\%}$

$$= \frac{\text{days of accrued interest}}{\text{days in coupon period}} \cdot \text{basis coupon}$$

accrued interest at time $t = AI_t^{\%} \cdot \text{nominal} \cdot IR_t$

On the coupon date the same procedure is followed. The coupon paid is the product of the basis coupon, the inflation ratio IR_{t_C} and the nominal:

$$\text{coupon at payment day } t_c = \text{coupon}_{real} \cdot IR_{t_C} \cdot \text{nominal}$$

The repayment on the due date is also the product of the $IR_{\text{on repayment date}}$ and the nominal:

$$\text{repayment} = IR_{\text{on repayment date}} \cdot \text{nominal}$$

This ensures that each payment increases by the same amount as the price increase, which is measured in the form of the inflation index for the holding period. That this involves accepting a two-month delay in the inflation index is a concession to the availability of inflation data and, at most, only marginally impacts the success of the direct protection against inflation. As a market convention, rounding of *DIR* and *IR* includes five decimals, so that rounding starts to impact invoice amounts beyond a notional 100.000 units of a currency.

Figure 2 At the current point *t* the DIR is derived from the interpolation of previous monthly inflation data. The result is included in the coupon and repayment calculation

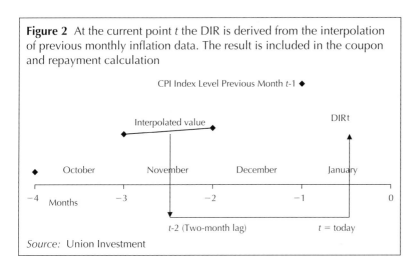

Source: Union Investment

monthly inflation figure has a noticeable impact on the repayment amount.[2]

The quotation of traded linkers

Linkers are quoted in real terms. The price determination ensues as a percentage of the notional amount (generally 100% in the case of new issues) without indexing. This practice allows for the simple calculation between price and yield according to the well-known equation that is also used with nominal bonds:

$$P(r) = \sum_{i=1}^{n} \frac{C}{(1+r)^i} + \frac{100}{(1+r)^n}$$

where P is the clean price, C the basis coupon, r the real yield and n the number of annual coupon payments. In contrast, in the case of conventional nominal bonds r represents the nominal yield. In simple terms the bond price is the present value of all future cashflows, which consist of the coupon payments and the redemption amount.

The settlement and day count conventions applied to local nominal bonds are also used with real return bonds. In the Eurozone these are three-day settlement and actual/actual interest accrued settlement. The amount to be paid I_t (the invoice) when concluding a buy order consists of the clean price P_t and the accumulated interest accrued since the last coupon payment AI_t. Both components are then multiplied by the total inflation since the launch of the bond IR_t,

$$I_t = (P_t + AI_t) \cdot IR_t$$

(see calculation example in Panel 2).

Total return breakdown

The components of the total return of investments in inflation-indexed bonds correspond to those of conventional bonds. They include coupon income and the bond's increase in value. However, the return of both components also depends on the inflation level.

PANEL 2 CALCULATION EXAMPLE FOR THE PURCHASE OF THE OATI 3% 25TH JULY 2009

We buy a nominal of €1 million on Friday 21st January 2005 with settlement $T + 3$, thus on Wednesday 26th January 2005. The agreed price is €109.591, which corresponds to a real yield of 0.82%. What is the effective price?

The inflation index in October 2004 is 109.90 and that in November is 110.00. The reference value DIR is 109.98065 on 26th January 2005.

The basis value of the inflation index at the bond's launch on 25th July 1998 was 100.17406. This produces an inflation quotient IR of 1.09790.

It is 185 days since the last coupon payment. The current coupon period has 365 days. Thus the real interest accrued is $3\% \times 185/365 = 1.521\%$.

The amount to be paid is then

$$\text{Invoice} = (109.591 + 1.521) \times 1.0979 \times 1,000,000/100$$
$$= €1,219,898.65.$$

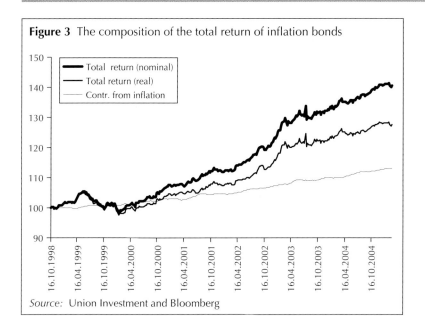

Figure 3 The composition of the total return of inflation bonds

Source: Union Investment and Bloomberg

Figure 3 shows the total return for the OATi 3% 25th July 2009, the real return and the contribution from inflation.

The performance of the bond in Figure 3 fluctuated during the time period observed, largely due to the real return. Inflation, on the other hand, had a relatively constant impact on the total return. It has to be said that the price level changes during the time period observed, but also in the preceding years, were almost always positive. In contrast, deflation phases with declining price levels were rare. However, these cannot generally be ruled out.

What is the impact of inflation on the volatility of the total performance of an inflation-indexed bond? Real yields and inflation are generally positively correlated.[4] However, the effect on the performance of real return bonds is in the opposite direction. Their price falls as real yields rise, whereas the price rises as inflation rises so that there is at least some compensatory effect on the performance. However, since the bond's real price generally fluctuates more than the inflation contribution and both components do not necessarily develop in opposite directions in each phase, a market risk also remains for the linkers' total performance (see Panel 3).

PANEL 3 THE PERFORMANCE OF LINKERS

The absolute return R of an investment in inflation-indexed bonds between time t and $t-1$ results from the difference of the invoice amounts $I_t - I_{t-1}$ plus a contingent coupon payment $C_t \cdot IR_t$. Assuming that the coupon at time t is reinvested in the bond, the return is

$$R_t = R_{t-1} + I_t - I_{t-1} + C_t \cdot IR_t$$

The performance is the investment's percentage increase in value,

$$Perf_T = \frac{R_T - R_0}{R_0} - 1$$

VALUATION ANGLES

The valuation of Euro real return bonds requires a benchmark. In general, nominal return bonds, assets such as stocks, real estate and commodities (eg, gold), economic fundamental data and also real return bonds in other currencies are considered. However, traditional government bonds, based on nominal interest rates, undoubtedly head the list.

On the other hand, the performance of real return bonds is also an important reference point, particularly for long-term asset allocation decisions. From the investor's point of view, saving is not usually an end in itself but is aimed at a clearly defined saving target, which generally relates to a specific real increase in purchasing power.[5] Real return bonds occupy a privileged position in this regard. No other investment instrument can achieve such a real increase in purchasing power – with regard to a representative basket of goods – with such high reliability as inflation-indexed bonds. However, due to their brief history and their relatively minor prevalence, many market participants are less familiar with them than they are with traditional nominal return bonds. As a result, real return bonds have not yet succeeded in establishing a firm reference magnitude. However, this appears only to be a question of time when looking at the growth rates of this bond sector.

Comparing nominal and real return bonds: the concept of breakeven inflation

Traditional and inflation-indexed bonds differ with regard to the size of the repayment amount as well as the nominal and real revenues. Whereas in the former case, the repayment amount and the coupon are established in advance, with linkers these measures depend on the inflation level. In contrast, the linkers' real return at maturity is already determined at the time of investment, whereas with nominal return bonds the inflation rate has a decisive impact.

It is now possible to calculate the correct inflation rate that would be required until the real return bond reaches bullet maturity in order to generate the same nominal return as a conventional bond with the same maturity. This inflation rate is known as breakeven inflation (BEI) and serves as a gauge of the market's inflation expectations. If the actual inflation level measured until bullet maturity exceeds BEI, then an investment in real return bonds is more advantageous than that in nominal return bonds; in this case, the investor is compensated for actual inflation, whereas at the time of purchase he/she only paid for the lower BEI. In the opposite scenario when BEI exceeds actual inflation, an investment in nominal return bonds would be more favourable. With nominal return bonds a fixed inflation rate to bullet maturity is earned that is priced in at the time of purchase, whereas the inflation income from real return bonds is the actual, and in this case lower, inflation rate itself.

Apart from credit risks, fixed-income investments, in principle, offer the certainty of bullet maturity yields. As shown in Figure 4,

Figure 4 A comparison of nominal return and real return bonds

	Cash flow	Nominal return	Real return
Nominal return bond	Known	Known	**Depends on inflation**
Inflation-indexed bond	Depends on inflation	Depends on inflation	**Known**

Source: Union Investment

both the nominal yield as well as the real yield are known in the market so that an element of uncertainty becomes apparent in BEI that is based, first, on uncertain inflation expectations and, second, on a risk premium whose level is hard to determine.

The Fisher equation as a starting point

The Fisher equation, named after the American economist Irving Fisher, establishes the formal link between nominal return bonds and inflation bonds. It breaks down the nominal yield into the real yield and inflation expectations, plus a risk premium. This risk premium is based on the assumption that investors, seen as generally risk averse, want to be refunded for the inflation risks assumed with nominal return bonds.[6]

The Fisher equation represents the correlation between nominal yields, real yields, inflation expectations and the risk premium:

$$(1 + n) = (1 + r) \cdot (1 + f) \cdot (1 + rp)$$

(where n = nominal yield, r = real yield, f = inflation expectation (until maturity), rp = risk premium).

BEI is thus the inflation rate at which the return on a real return bond equals that of a comparable nominal return bond over the remaining time to maturity:

$$(1 + n) = (1 + r) \cdot (1 + BEI)$$

whereby

$$(1 + BEI) = (1 + f) \cdot (1 + rp)$$

BEI therefore represents the link between the nominal and real interest rates. However, at the present state of scientific knowledge, it is impossible to give an exact split into both components, namely inflation expectations and risk premium. From an empirical point of view, the question of a fair BEI is thus often answered with the aid of inflation expectations derived from surveys plus a constant assumed risk premium.[7]

In practice, with small values one often uses the approximation derived from the equation

$$n = r + BEI$$

For this reason, BEI does not have an impact on the total return of real return bonds and is thus also no measure of their absolute value. Their performance depends exclusively on the development of real interest rates and actual inflation.

BEI is decisive for relative performance compared to traditional nominal return bonds. To the extent that BEI exceeds expected average inflation plus a risk premium until the bond reaches maturity, real return bonds are more expensive than conventional bonds. The real interest rate is too low in this case and the expected total return is less than with nominal return bonds (see Figure 5).

Figure 5 The progression of BEI from French OAT 4% April 2009 nominal yield minus OATi 3% July 2009 real yield, the real yield of OATi 2009 and year-on-year French headline inflation excluding tobacco since inception of the real bond. The actual year-on-year inflation adds to the past performance of a linker, but it must not correspond closely to BEI, which is forward looking in nature. The real yield came down significantly during most of the period, whereas inflation and BEI were bound to a narrow range. It is worth mentioning that over time the initial maturity of the bonds used has decreased from ten to only four years

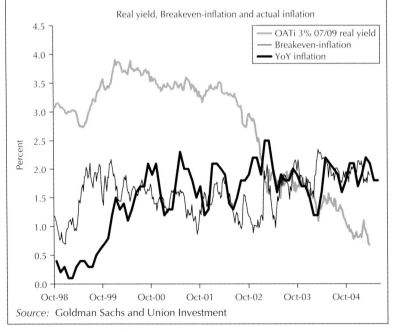

Source: Goldman Sachs and Union Investment

In practice, BEI is actively traded. This occurs in the form of over- and underweighting linkers in investment funds, financing real return bonds by short-selling nominal bonds on a bank's book and by hedge funds, as well as with the help of inflation swaps, which will be explained in a later chapter of this book.

The Great Unknown: regarding the significance of the inflation risk premium

It is generally assumed in the bond market that the revenue from a nominal return bond also includes an inflation premium. This reflects uncertainty over future inflation performance. The inflation premium's level is proportional to the risk that the overall price increase will reduce the real value of the conventional bond's nominal return. This is supposed to compensate the investor for the inflation risk assumed.[8] However, market participants, analysts and monetary policy makers also deliver valuable information regarding its level. From the issuer's perspective, the inflation premium level is an indicator of the potential interest cost saving of substituting nominal bonds with real return bonds. For their part, central banks can read how credible their promise to maintain long-term monetary stability is with the market. However, measuring the inflation premium runs into considerable difficulties.

According to the prevailing market wisdom, BEI – in simple terms the difference between observed nominal and real yields – is a measure of expected inflation until a bond's maturity. However, this is only half the story. It also includes a risk premium, which is determined by the uncertainty over future inflation and serves to compensate the investor in nominal bonds for the risk assumed. In practice, it is extremely hard to quantitatively break down BEI into the two components of inflation expectations and risk premium.

Changes to the risk premium

Assuming rational expectations, the risk premium is nothing more than the difference between BEI and expected inflation with regard to a bond's maturity. In other words, the inflation risk premium refers to the cumulated inflation over the bond's maturity and not to the year-on-year inflation rate. With a concrete investment decision, from the investor's point of view, a below-average risk premium would favour the purchase of a real return bond, whereas an above-average risk premium would favour the purchase of a nominal return bond. As simple as it is to formulate this sentence in theory, it is just as hard to convert this into practice.

Determining the risk premium assumes knowledge of inflation expectations traded in the market. In practice, one is partially assisted either by surveys ("inflation consensus") or the central bank's inflation target. Both methods, however, can deliver only an approximate value for inflation expectations.

Thus, more intuitive considerations replace an exact derivation of the risk premium, where the following considerations are at the fore.

❑ The risk premium should, as a rule, be positively correlated to a bond's *residual maturity* for two reasons. First, it is more difficult to deploy a somewhat reliable inflation forecast for a longer time period than for a shorter time period. Second, the consequences of an inflation surprise have a more serious impact on long-term bonds than on short-term bonds (Shen 1998). Put another way, the risk premium curve shows a positive gradient.

❑ The risk premium depends not least on inflation volatility. For this reason, it is closely correlated to the *monetary policy credibility* of the respective central bank. An explicit inflation target should reduce market participants' uncertainty over future inflation performance and thereby ensure somewhat lower risk premiums. In the opposite case, when the central bank is seen to be unreliable on monetary policy issues, this would probably lead to rising risk premiums.[9] However, in a democratic society, even a formally autonomous central bank with strong monetary policy credibility depends on public support. Long-term forecasts on the importance with which society regards the price level, however, are flawed by many factors that increase uncertainty. These include, for example, demographic changes, the creditor–debtor structure or public debt. Thus, an analysis of the risk premium level must also rest on sustainable assumptions regarding these factors.

❑ However, it seems, generally speaking, not too far-fetched to assume a high positive correlation between *inflation expectations* and the risk premium. Accordingly, rising inflation expectations result in higher risk premiums and declining inflation expectations in lower risk premiums. Therefore, increasing risk premiums should also lead to higher BEI (Deutsche Bank 2005). Exceptions to this rule are possible. Low inflation expectations could accompany high risk premiums. When inflation expectations are low in an economy the short-term efficiency of expansive monetary policy will rise (eg, to cut unemployment via a reduction in real wages). In other words, with general low inflation expectations there is, from a political point of view, a specific incentive to generate inflation. This could justify a higher inflation risk premium.

❑ In addition, growing demand for protection against inflation could increase risk premiums of nominal return bonds. In particular, the foreseeable transition of the baby boomer generation into retirement should lead to a noticeable increase in demand. Furthermore, stronger shifts in demand and supply between real return and nominal return bonds could lead to market disequilibria, and thus have a lasting impact on risk premiums.

Estimates on risk premiums levels have resulted, in part, in strongly diverging outcomes. Several long-term surveys for the USA produced risk premiums of between 50 and 100 basis points for the mid- to long-term maturity segment (5 to 10 years). In contrast, econometric simulations based on long-term BEI rates produced risk premiums that, over time, fluctuated around the 40 basis points level (ABN AMRO 2005).

In contrast to nominal return bond investors, the buyers of real return bonds relinquish this risk premium in exchange for protection against inflation. Their returns are constantly adjusted to the actual inflation level, so that real revenue is guaranteed at maturity. For this reason, real return bonds have an inbuilt insurance against one of the key systematic risks in the bond market. From the point of view of the issuer of real return bonds, the omission of the risk premium signifies an expected cost saving; however, this is pitted against the abandonment of a possible inflation of interest payments and the repayment amount.

As practice reveals, negative inflation risk premiums are also possible. In this case, BEI is below general inflation expectations. Expressed differently, in this case the issuer of a real return bond – contrary to the usual assumption that no risk premium is due with the launch of a real return bond – nevertheless offers the investor a premium. One reason for this could be that the issuer of an infla-tion-indexed bond expects noticeably lower inflation than the mar-ket. In this case, the cost savings from reduced coupon payments to the investors overcompensate for the risk premium. Another reason for this could be, for example, that the issuer, with regard to his asset liability management, deliberately wants to diversify his fixed-income portfolio towards a higher proportion of inflation-indexed bonds. From the investor's point of view, under some cir-cumstances, the motivation to subscribe to real return bonds may not be sufficient due to the lower liquidity of this market segment. The issuer could probably offer potential investors an additional buying incentive to compensate for this disparity. This could play an appreciable role, particularly when real return bonds are intro-duced to the market for the first time.

However, in general it is safe to assume that the inflation pre-mium in the bond market is a positive sign and therefore repre-sents a cost advantage for the issuer of real return bonds compared to the issuers of nominal return bonds. An exact rule is not gener-ally possible due to the difficulties described.

A somewhat alternative point of view: the currency analogy

The link between the real and the nominal interest rate worlds via the price indexing mechanism contains an informative parallel to the relationships between two nominal bond markets denomi-nated in different currencies. The following comparison should also clarify the methodical approach to evaluating their relative value.

Assuming free arbitrage, a domestic currency bond investment should produce the same return as a fixed rate investment in a foreign currency with subsequent re-exchange into the domestic currency at the valid forward exchange rate. This procedure is represented on the left-hand side of Figure 6.

Following the two paths in the left-hand figure from $t = 0$ to T along the arrow produces the following equation:

$$(1+n)^T = Fx \cdot (1+f)^T \cdot \frac{1}{Fx_T}$$

where Fx is the spot exhange rate, Fx_T is the forward exhange rate, n is the domestic yield, f is the foreign yield and T is the time of deposit.

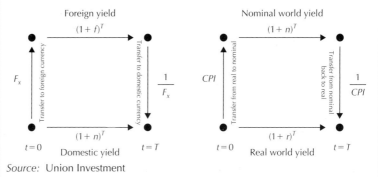

Figure 6 The cross-country valuation of yield and exchange rate in nominal space (left-hand side) and the valuation of a nominal and a real yield world with forward inflation (right-hand side)

Source: Union Investment

The forward exchange rate is thus the result of the interest relation and the exchange rate. If the actual exchange rate is below the forward exchange rate at point T, that is, the foreign currency unexpectedly appreciates, then an investment in the foreign currency without a forward exchange hedge would be more advantageous. The difference between the forward exchange rate and the (subjectively or generally) expected exchange rate is a risk premium for unavoidable fluctuations, and is thus a measure for the relative value of both interest rates. The higher risk of the foreign currency investment is compensated by a higher premium.

In the same way, we now proceed with the real interest rate investment swap into the nominal world and a re-exchange at point T into the real world. Refer to the right-hand side of Figure 6. Following the arrows one obtains the same equation as above, only with different designations:

$$(1+r)^T = CPI \cdot (1+n)^T \cdot \frac{1}{CPI_T}$$

where CPI is the consumer price index, CPI_T is the forward consumer price index, n is the nominal yield, r is the real yield and T is the time of deposit.

Exchange rates have now been replaced by price indices. If the realised price index at point T is below the forward price index CPI_T, then the investment in the nominal interest rate without inflation hedge (that is, the sale of forward inflation) would have been more advantageous. The nominal interest rate then contains sufficient buffer compared to the real interest rate to at least generate the same increase in real purchasing power. Using equation $(1 + n) = (1 + r) \cdot (1 + BEI)$, we can deduce that the BEI corresponds exactly to the inflation hedge:

$$(1+BEI)^T = CPI_T \Big/ CPI$$

Now it is really evident that the difference between the realised price index at point T and the forward price index CPI_T is a measure for the realised risk premium from the Fisher equation.[10]

Here, the analogy between price indices and exchange rates is largely limited to the formal aspects. Empirically, however, there are noticeable differences.

❑ Exchange rate swings are generally much larger than changes in price indices.
❑ In contrast to most foreign currency additions that tend to increase the risk in bond portfolios, the combination of real and nominal interest investments tends to reduce risk.
❑ While key central banks have similar core inflation targets, which they have generally achieved for some time, the same harmony is not given in foreign exchange policy. Efforts to devalue one currency can only be successful at the price of the appreciation of other currencies. Thus, by definition, this already rules out any harmony.
❑ As a result, the nominal interest rate regularly exceeds the real interest rate, whereas the interest differential of two countries can easily be positive or negative. Thus, since 1984 the yield differential of 10-year US Treasuries and the yields of 10-year German government bonds (*Bundesanleihen*) has frequently changed sign, whereas the respective nominal interest rates constantly exceeded real interest rates.

RISK MEASURES FOR INFLATION-INDEXED BONDS
Duration and convexity
The interest risk measure of modified duration, which is well known in the world of nominal bonds, can also be used in the same

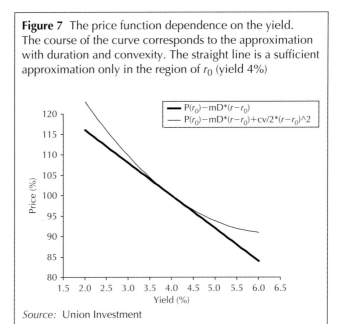

Figure 7 The price function dependence on the yield. The course of the curve corresponds to the approximation with duration and convexity. The straight line is a sufficient approximation only in the region of r_0 (yield 4%)

Legend:
$P(r_0) - mD*(r-r_0)$
$P(r_0) - mD*(r-r_0) + cv/2*(r-r_0)^\wedge 2$

Source: Union Investment

way to derive the price formula to calculate the real yield. In concrete terms: when real yields increase by 1% the percentage loss in value with reference to the linker's dirty price [(traded price + interest accrued) × inflation rate] roughly corresponds to the modified duration value. However, this only applies to small interest rate changes since this concerns the linear approximation of the price, which is dependent on the yield. Figure 7 demonstrates the price's actual interest rate dependence, as well as the initial approximation with modified duration.

In contrast, larger interest rate changes demand either an exact price calculation or a second approximation term, also known as convexity (see Panel 4). In turn, the half convexity is the percentage value of the dirty price, by which the modified duration overestimates the loss in value when interest rates increase by 1%. In general, the higher the convexity, the better it is for the investor. When yields decline, the price increases disproportionately, whereas it falls less then proportionately when the interest rate increases.

PANEL 4 THEORY REGARDING DURATION AND CONVEXITY

The formulaic correlation between price, yield, modified duration and convexity results from the so-called Taylor development of price function to the second degree. Thus,

$$P(r) = P(r_0) + \frac{dP(r_0)}{dr}(r - r_0) + \frac{1}{2}\frac{d^2P(r_0)}{dr^2}(r - r_0) + \text{other terms}$$

with $\dfrac{dP(r_0)}{dr} = -mD$ (modified duration)

and $\dfrac{d^2P(r_0)}{dr^2} = cv$ (Convexity)

In the case of real return bonds r is the real interest rate. The same formula applies to nominal bonds where r is the nominal interest rate. Thus, with real return bonds, modified duration is the price sensitivity in relation to changes in the real interest rate.

The product of modified duration and instantaneous changes in BEI gives the initial approximation for the performance difference between a linker and a conventional bond with comparable modified duration. When looking at this over a longer time period, the current returns, which deviate from one another, must also be taken into account. In the case of real return bonds these are subject to greater fluctuations in value. We will explore this in more detail in the section "Seasonality and carry".

The greater real interest rates fluctuate in the market, the more important convexity becomes. Real return bonds usually have a greater convexity than nominal return bonds with the same maturity. In contrast, nominal yields often fluctuate more strongly than real yields. Depending on the precise relationships, the convexity of real return bonds can have some additional basis points of value that are concealed in the BEI rate. Accordingly, BEI contains not only an inflation expectation and a risk premium, but also a convexity component. This plays only a subordinate role in practice. Even when evaluating BEI, an exact correction for the convexity proportion is unnecessary given the inaccuracies, in principle, of the other terms.

However, when evaluating the interest rate risk of inflation-indexed bonds compared to nominal return bonds, a comparison of the respective modified duration is not necessarily suitable here. In contrast to nominal return bonds, where the size of the payment flows is known in advance, with linkers the future cashflows depend on the inflation level. In an initial approximation, linker prices alter according to the product of modified duration and the change in the real interest rate, as illustrated above. However, real interest rate changes are generally lower than the corresponding nominal interest rate changes, so that the price volatility between the two instruments also differs. The example in Figure 8 should illustrate this more clearly. The two French government bonds OAT 4% 25th October 2009 and OATi 3% 25th July 2009 have almost the same residual maturity and duration over a specific period of time. The price fluctuations, measured as rolling volatilities, proceed very differently. The volatility of the real return bond is usually noticeably lower than the nominal bond. However, there have also been phases of equal volatility. In principle, even phases of higher volatility cannot be ruled out.

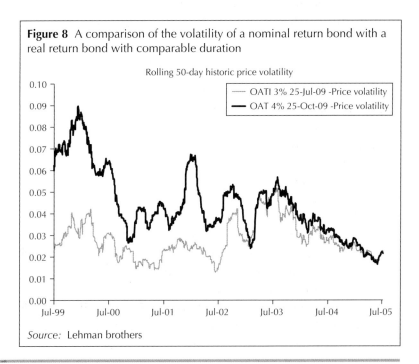

Figure 8 A comparison of the volatility of a nominal return bond with a real return bond with comparable duration

Rolling 50-day historic price volatility

OATI 3% 25-Jul-09 -Price volatility
OAT 4% 25-Oct-09 -Price volatility

Source: Lehman brothers

We can derive from this that the calculated duration in both cases represents a different interest risk measure. In the linker's case, it is a measure of the price change when real interest rates change. In the case of nominal bonds, it is a measure of the price change when nominal interest rates change.

The beta concept

A portfolio with linkers and nominal return rate bonds frequently requires an interest rate risk indicator for the entire portfolio. This indicator actually serves only to gain a better overview and is at the expense of accuracy. Since most fund managers grew up in the nominal bond world and have become accustomed to duration as a measure for parallel interest rate risk changes, they adapt the real interest rate duration to that of the nominal interest rate duration with the simple equation

$$\Delta r = \beta \cdot \Delta n + \Delta \varepsilon$$

where Δr is the real interest rate change, Δn the nominal interest rate change, β the coefficient and $\Delta \varepsilon$ the residual value. Thus, beta reflects the relationship in which the nominal and the real yield oscillate towards one another. It is determined by the correlation or synchronisation of the yields and the ratio of their standard deviation (see Panel 5).

Beta can be ascertained only statistically and is by no means stable or identical for all maturities. For this reason, it is of only limited value. Figure 9 shows the beta's progression for two sets of bonds, both averaged over 3 months.

We refer here to beta instability because historically calculated values depend on the time frame for which they were calculated. Averages over longer periods are naturally more reliable than shorter averages. However, even beta values for two disjunctive longer time periods can vary greatly.

The first phase of the development of the Eurozone linker market between 1998 and 2002 was characterised, for example, by low beta values up to 0.5. When this was followed by declining nominal interest rates at the same time as a movement sideways in inflation rates – roughly in line with the central bank target – a higher proportion of the swings in the nominal interest rate were due to real interest rate swings. This led to a distinct increase in beta (see Figure 10).

PANEL 5 THE THEORETICAL BASIS OF THE BETA CONCEPT

The link between beta β, the correlation $\rho_{r,n}$ of the nominal interest rate n and the real interest rate r as well as the standard deviations σ can be theoretically derived by deploying a diffusion equation for the dynamic of r and n respectively:

$$dr = r \cdot dt + \sigma_r \cdot d\xi_r \text{ and}$$

$$dn = n \cdot dt + \sigma_n \cdot d\xi_n$$

where $d\xi$ r/n are the respective probabilities. For the covariance of yields this produces

$$\langle dr, dn \rangle = \rho_{r,n} \cdot \sigma_r \cdot \sigma_n$$

where $\rho_{r,n}$ is the correlation between r and n. If we now use the beta relationship

$$dr = \beta \cdot dn + d\varepsilon$$

in which $d\varepsilon$ are the uncorrelated residuals to calculate the covariance

$$\langle dr, dn \rangle = \langle \beta \cdot dn + d\varepsilon, \ dn \rangle = \beta \langle dr, dn \rangle + \langle d\varepsilon, dn \rangle = \beta \cdot \sigma_n^2$$

then, equating this with the above equation, we have

$$\beta = \rho_{r,n} \cdot \frac{\sigma_r}{\sigma_n}$$

Beta is thus proportional to the relationship between the standard deviations and the correlation between real and nominal interest rates.

Ultimately, the BEI dynamic is decisive for beta values. If one fails to capture beta over one or more complete BEI cycles, then this value cannot properly represent the future statistical correlation for the interest rate dependence.[11]

Various cases for beta changes are helpful for this observation.

1. When the nominal bond market is rising, even though inflation is not declining and real return bonds have a superior carry, beta increases. The decline in nominal yields is even exceeded by real yields.

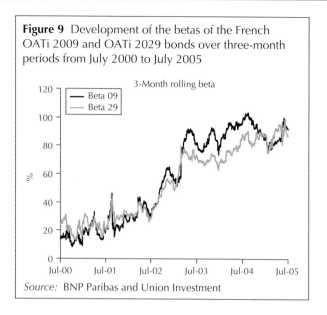

Figure 9 Development of the betas of the French OATi 2009 and OATi 2029 bonds over three-month periods from July 2000 to July 2005

Source: BNP Paribas and Union Investment

Figure 10 The sensitivity of real yield changes in comparison to nominal yield changes correlates well with the level of nominal yields ($R^2 = 0.86$). The data used is from the French OATi and OAT 2009 in the period from October 1998 to July 2005. The triangle depicts the latest point in time

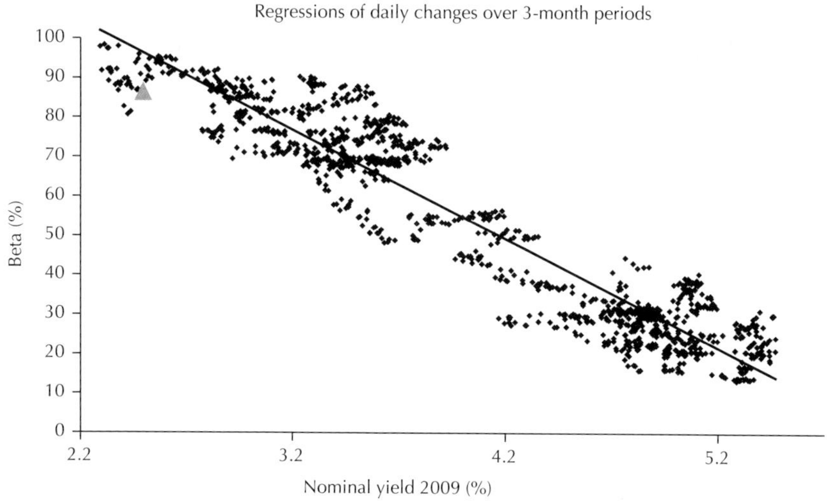

Regressions of daily changes over 3-month periods

Source: BNP Paribas and Union Investment

2. In the case of a sell-off of nominal return bonds the beta would likewise increase – despite falling inflation and the negative carry of real return bonds compared to nominal bonds. In this case, real return bonds demonstrate a weaker performance than nominal bonds.

3. The more common case with a sell-off is, however, one with rising inflation and positive relative carry. In such a scenario, beta would decline. The defensive character of real return bonds thus emerges.

4. Even when the market performs well (nominal bond rally), because inflation is declining and relative negative carry dominates, beta would decline. In this scenario, linkers loose performance relative to nominal bonds.

In conclusion, one can stress that realised inflation and changes in inflation expectations decisively influence the relative interest rate sensitivity of linkers and conventional bonds. For this reason, when evaluating total interest rate risks, one should aim to observe scenarios that contain explicit assumptions regarding inflation and real interest rates.

SEASONALITY AND CARRY
Seasonality

As a rule of thumb, inflation indices that form the basis for European and US real return bonds are not seasonally adjusted. However, over the course of the year, inflation data is subject to regular patterns that are, in part, attributable to normally predictable price volatility, for example, in food or in energy. In Figure 11, the trend in the monthly change of the inflation rate is shown, using the HICP ex tobacco, between 1998 and 2003. It can be seen in the chart that there was considerably higher inflation in December, on average, than in January.

Nevertheless, time and again the seasonal pattern is superimposed by unpredictable effects. During some months of 2004, for example, some extraordinary outliers were observed. Moreover, seasonality itself cannot be assumed to remain constant in perpetuity. Instead, it also changes over a longer period of time.

Interestingly, exactly the opposite relationship is true for US inflation data seasonality in December and January. This is possibly

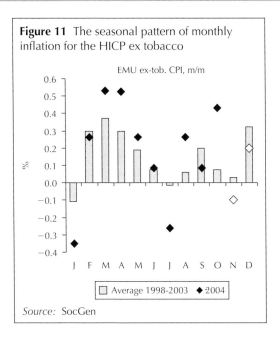

Figure 11 The seasonal pattern of monthly inflation for the HICP ex tobacco

EMU ex-tob. CPI, m/m

Source: SocGen

related to differing consumption and competitive habits (eg, sales discount policies), as well as differing compilation methodologies.

It can generally be said, however, that the seasonal development of inflation indices definitely has a direct impact on BEI and can, therefore, not be disregarded. Seasonal patterns play an important role, in particular, in making tactical investment decisions, for example in the short-term overweighting or underweighting of linkers in a mixed portfolio. Nevertheless, regular seasonal patterns can be overridden. The strong increase in the price of oil during the run-up to the Iraq war can be cited as exemplary of this. It is precisely politically-vulnerable energy prices that can thwart regular trends.

Considerations on carry

In conjunction with real return bonds, carry aspects play a particularly important role due to the high *monthly* volatility of the inflation rate. While the seasonal pattern of the much-cited *annual* change in the rate of inflation is not meaningful, it is particularly relevant in the short-term valuation of real return bonds. Both the coupon and the repayment vary from month to month with the monthly change in the rate of inflation, due to indexation. Inflation volatility is thereby extremely pronounced and can – especially with respect to linkers with short maturities – cause considerable valuation volatility relative to nominal return bonds.

The exact and generally applicable calculation for interest carry is derived from the difference between the forward interest rate and the spot interest rate:

$$Carry_{nominal} = n_T - n$$

$$Carry_{real} = r_T - r$$

It shows to what degree the bond interest rate must change in order for the investment return that results from this to be identical to a time deposit over the same investment horizon. In other words: the carry shows whether a long position in a bond, financed by a collateralized loan, produces a profit or a loss. If interest rates do not change by this date, this difference represents the advantage in holding bonds versus time deposits.

The advantage in holding real return bonds versus nominal return bonds corresponds to the difference between nominal interest carry and the real interest carry and is named as breakeven carry:

$$Carry_{BEI} = Carry_{real} - Carry_{nominal}$$

In line with this definition, a positive breakeven carry indicates, that in the case of unchanged yields until the end of the holding period, by purchasing an inflation-indexed bond and selling a nominal return bond you could earn a return equal in size to the breakeven carry. In other words, until the end of the holding period, the breakeven carry could fall by the absolute value before you lose money with this trade.

The example in Panel 6 also makes clear that the impact of inflation volatility is dampened by the lever of modified duration. Long-term bonds are less "carry volatile".[12] BEI, especially with regard to shorter maturities, is somewhat carried along, because the demand for these bonds will probably rise in times of high carry. This means that the bonds become more expensive relative to nominal return bonds whose carry is not impacted by the price index. The gap between nominal interest rates and real interest

PANEL 6 CARRY IN PRACTICE

We assume that inflation rises by 0.6% month-on-month (as in March 2004), which is equivalent to an annual rate of 7.2% (0.6% $\times$ 12 months). Moreover, we assume that the constant inflationary adjustment of the nominal return bond (or BEI) is at 2%. If the real return bond is now compared with the nominal return bond, then the projected advantage of holding (carry) is 5.2% (7.2% − 2%) for the year and 0.43% for a holding period of one month as an approximation.

A linker with a 5-year maturity and a 4.7% modified duration is therefore able to bear a 9.2 basis point (43/4.7) increase in the real interest rate, versus the nominal interest rate, before the position loses money. These 9.2 basis points are termed breakeven carry, because BEI can sink so low without the position losing money.

A linker with a 30-year maturity and 24% modified duration has only about 1.8 basis points of breakeven carry under the same assumptions.

PANEL 7 CALCULATION OF THE FORWARD RATE

The forward rate is derived from equating earnings from time deposits and from bonds. The invoice amount I_0 is invested at the time deposit rate r_F for the duration of T and should be equal to the invoice amount I_T of the bond at the end:

$$I_T = I_0 \cdot (1 + r_F)^T$$

The approach for linkers and nominal bonds is identical up to this point. However, there are differences in the calculation of the invoice amounts due to indexation. The revenues from the bond are made up of the clean price P_T, the coupons K which are possibly paid in the interim K and the interest accrued AI_T. The invoice amount of linkers is additionally raised further by the inflation ratio IR_T. This results in the following equation:

$$I_T = [P(r_T) + K + AI_T] \cdot IR_T$$

From the bond's clean price function, we can now calculate the forward rate with a numerical method. The possibly paid coupon is treated here as if it were re-invested at the time deposit rate. For the time horizon T that extends beyond the known inflation ratio's time period, a forecast for inflation's monthly rate of change must be made. Through this, the carry from linkers, in contrast to nominal bonds, ultimately becomes dependent on forecasts.

rates increases, which is identical to a rise in the inflation expectation that is displayed in BEI.

An additional effect is thereby made apparent. Because the BEI rates of shorter maturities react more strongly than those with longer maturities, the steepness of the BEI curve changes with increasing carry. These effects should be taken into account when BEI is used as a measure for the long-term use of real return bonds versus other bonds.*

Carry and inflation forecasts

Assumptions over the progression of the inflation index are necessary to calculate carry. The time lag in indexation displayed in the section on "Indexation" permits a purely mathematical derivation of carry in the Eurozone and in the United States of between something like 15 and 45 days. The exact numbers depend on the number of days between succeeding monthly publications of consumer prices indices (CPIs). Additional assumptions on the progression of inflation are required for the time horizon that extends beyond this, which means that it is subject to forecasting error. As an illustration, the French inflation rate FRCPIX, in 2004, is displayed up to the measured November value in Figure 12. The November number is usually not published until mid-December. The daily inflation ratio DIR, up to the end of January, can be calculated with certainty from this rate. So, right after the publication of the November CPI in December, there is mathematical certainty about the DIR for the rest of December and all of January, which amounts to about 45 days. The day before the November CPI is fixed in December, the certainty about DIR lasts only until the end of December or about 15 days. Surprises in the reported monthly CPI data will find their way into the pricing of linkers almost immediately under normal circumstances because they will affect the carry for a limited period with certainty. CPI monthly data assumptions for December and January are necessary for carry until the end of March.

A practical approach to forecasting the inflation path comes from the long-term fundamentally based trend, seasonal factors and foreseeable technical distortions such as a VAT hike or announced changes to the weightings of the CPI. In the example

*With regard to the calculation of the forward rate see Panel 7.

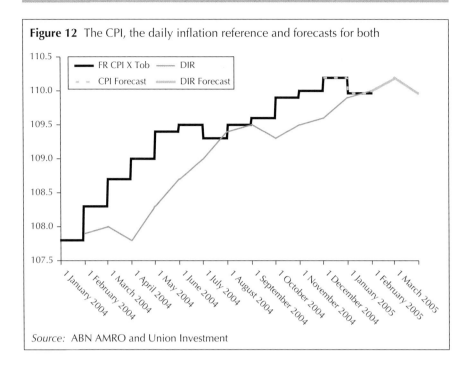

Figure 12 The CPI, the daily inflation reference and forecasts for both

Source: ABN AMRO and Union Investment

referred to, the current month is December 2004 and we expect a deflationary trend for the following year, 2005. The annual inflation rate falls from its previous rate of 2.3% in November 2004 to 1.8% in November 2005. The decline is distributed evenly and its seasonal rate is added on every month. The result is displayed in the table below. The seasonal rate in December is rising considerably and surpasses the slight decline in the annual trend. Only with the January value does the sinking of the *DIR*, and therefore the carry as of March, begin to take effect (see Table 1).

Carry's influence on BEI rates

BEI rates fluctuate due to various influences on nominal and real interest rates. In months with strongly rising interest rates, the breakeven rate tends to rise (and *vice versa*) as can be seen in Figure 13 in the example with OATi 3% 2009. An overshooting or undershooting of BEI is probably the result of trends in the direction of positive and negative carry. However, a high forecast for inflation, alone, is not a sufficient criterion for successful trading strategies between real and nominal bonds. It is more important to estimate when

Table 1 Measured CPI numbers until the end of November 2004. Thereafter the CPI path is governed by fundamental medium-term drift and superimposed seasonal effects. The second column with the monthly CPI changes is necessary to calculate carry. The third column displays the path of future year-on-year CPI changes, which is displayed only for reference to this common measure in economic analysis

	CPI	CPI MoM	CPI YoY	
31.08.2005	111.5	0.13	1.84	based on monthly CPI forecasts
31.07.2005	111.4	−0.13	1.9	
30.06.2005	111.5	0.15	1.85	
31.05.2005	111.4	0.24	1.79	
30.04.2005	111.1	0.29	1.91	
31.03.2005	110.8	0.43	1.9	
28.02.2005	110.3	0.29	1.83	
31.01.2005	110.0	−0.21	2.01	
31.12.2004	110.2	0.17	2.03	
30.11.2004	110.0	0.09	1.95	based on measured monthly CPI numbers
31.10.2004	109.9	0.27	1.67	
30.09.2004	109.6	0.09	1.48	
31.08.2004	109.5	0.18	1.77	
31.07.2004	109.3	−0.18	1.86	
30.06.2004	109.5	0.09	1.96	
31.05.2004	109.4	0.37	2.05	
30.04.2004	109.0	0.28	1.49	
31.03.2004	108.7	0.37	1.12	
29.02.2004	108.3	0.46	1.12	
31.01.2004	107.8	−0.19	1.41	
31.12.2003	108.0	0.09	1.6	

Source: Union Investment

demand waxes or wanes due to generally expected carry. This is because seasonal patterns are known to all informed investors. This means that some begin to invest in months with negative carry in order to then fully exploit the expected increase in BEI. At this point, speculation over the behaviour of the players sets in, along with all of the difficulties inherent in rationally handling the irrationalities of the market. This is reflected in all areas of trading.

THE TERM STRUCTURE OF INFLATION AND REAL YIELD
So far we have considered only yields and BEI for individual residual maturities. However, analysing the yield and BEI curves can also be of considerable benefit when managing real return bonds. In Figure 14 we have demonstrated the correlation between

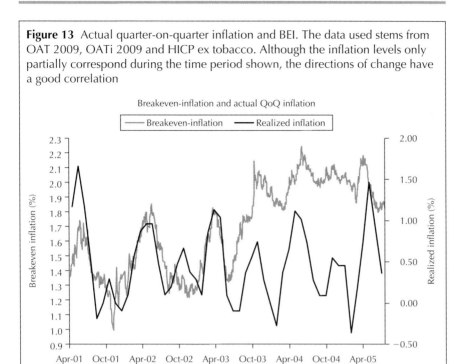

Figure 13 Actual quarter-on-quarter inflation and BEI. The data used stems from OAT 2009, OATi 2009 and HICP ex tobacco. Although the inflation levels only partially correspond during the time period shown, the directions of change have a good correlation

Source: Goldman Sachs, Bloomberg and Union Investment

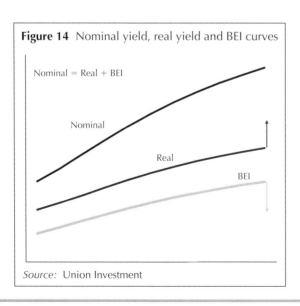

Figure 14 Nominal yield, real yield and BEI curves

Source: Union Investment

nominal yield, real yield and BEI curves. According to the Fisher equation, the nominal yield curve is the sum of the real yield and the BEI curve. Thus, at any time, the third curve can be determined from the other two curves.

As the steepness of the real yield curve increases and the nominal yield curve remains unchanged, the BEI curve has to flatten. This is indicated by the arrows. Aligning the real yield curve with the economic cycle, potential growth and the key interest rate, on the one hand, and comparing the BEI steepness, inflation risk premium and the level of inflation, on the other, permits a step-by-step approach to the nominal return curve. Anomalies, exaggerations or special characteristics of the nominal yield curve can be assigned to the other two curves, and thus help to identify their causes.

The change in the steepness of the real yield curve and the BEI curve is positively correlated, as a rule. Accordingly, the nominal yield curve is also positively correlated to the nominal curve as can be seen in Figure 15.

The reasons for this lie in the, historically well-proven, parallel course between real growth and inflation, as well as its impact on

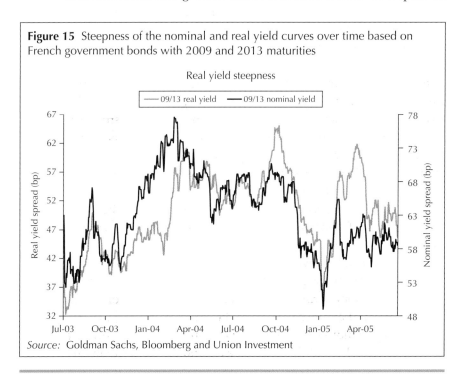

Figure 15 Steepness of the nominal and real yield curves over time based on French government bonds with 2009 and 2013 maturities

Source: Goldman Sachs, Bloomberg and Union Investment

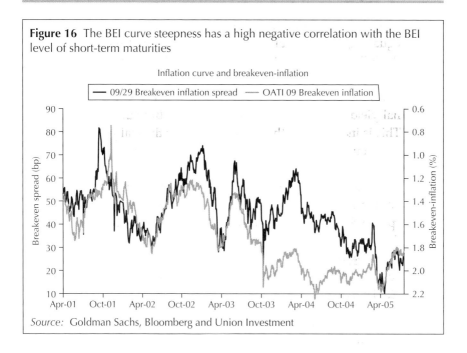

Figure 16 The BEI curve steepness has a high negative correlation with the BEI level of short-term maturities

Inflation curve and breakeven-inflation

—— 09/29 Breakeven inflation spread —— OATI 09 Breakeven inflation

Source: Goldman Sachs, Bloomberg and Union Investment

forming expectations. The anticipation of higher growth is generally accompanied by expected higher prices and increasing uncertainty over future inflation. The economic cycle has greater impact here on short-term rather than on long-term maturities. In some cases, long-term maturities encompass several economic cycles that the market partly averages out. Therefore, long-term yields and BEI should orientate more strongly towards an economy's structural characteristics and should fluctuate less than short-term maturities, which are strongly dependent on expectations regarding short-term central bank actions. Here monetary policy is subject, at least in part, to the impact of short-term changes in economic and inflation data. This relationship is clarified in Figure 16, where the BEI steepness and the level of short-term real yields, which have a negative correlation, are shown.

In this context, however, it is worth taking a closer look at the impacting factors on long-term yields: Is there an internal logic that explains why long-term bonds react to cyclical environmental changes? Or, put another way, why should, for example, average inflation expectations for the next 30 years increase simply because an unusually high monthly price increase update was announced?

Contrary to intuition, there is in fact a directionality, that is, a parallel, if somewhat diversely impacting, change on the yields in all maturities. In the current extremely low interest rate environment, for example, the market tends to reinterpret long-term magnitudes, such as potential growth or expected inflation uncertainty. The current condition "felt" is then embraced as the dominant condition over the long term. Many are unable to easily withdraw from this feeling in favour of a rational evaluation. As a result, short-term fundamental data have an – albeit frequently weakened – impact on the long end of the term structure curve.

To systemise the behaviour of yields and the different curves involved, we construct an ideal type model for a complete economic cycle. Based on this simplified demonstration, we want to identify phases with rising and falling yields, as well as steeper and flatter curves. The model cycle should be characterised by a harmonious oscillation of the output gap. In addition, we assume for the BEI that the phases adjust at a quarter of the regular cycle. This assumption is based on the empirical finding that inflation reacts with a certain time lag to changes in an economy's capacity utilisation, and that expectations, in turn, correspond to measured inflation. We divide the cycle into four sections and obtain the pattern for the nominal yield level

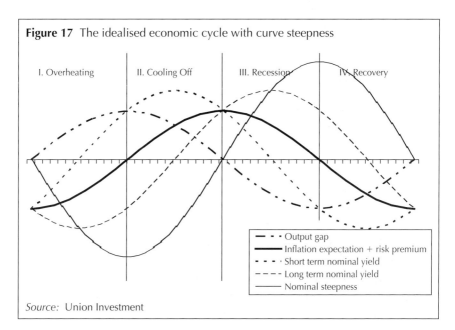

Figure 17 The idealised economic cycle with curve steepness

I. Overheating   II. Cooling Off   III. Recession   IV. Recovery

- · · Output gap
— Inflation expectation + risk premium
· · · · Short term nominal yield
- - - - Long term nominal yield
—— Nominal steepness

Source: Union Investment

Table 2 The advantage of real return and nominal return bonds within the economic cycle

Economic cycle	Inflation expectation + inflation risk premium (lag of a quarter cycle)	Central bank action	Effects on bond markets?	Nominal or real bonds?
I. Overheating	Low, but increasing		Negative	Real bonds
II. Cooling off	Overshooting	Interest rate hike by the central bank	Less negative	Real bonds
III. Recession	High, but decreasing		Positive	Nominal bonds
IV. Recovery	Undershooting	Interest rate cut by the central bank	Less positive	Nominal bonds

Table 3 The impact of the economic cycle on yields and inflation expectations

Economic cycle	Short-term nominal yield	Real curve	BEI curve	Nominal curve
I. Overheating	Low, but increasing	Bear flattening	Flat	Bear flattening
II. Cooling off	High, but decelerated increasing, then decreasing	Change from bear flattening into bull flattening	Flat to inverse	Change from bear flattening into bull flattening
III. Recession	High, but strongly decreasing	Bull steepening	Again steeper	Bull steepening
IV. Recovery	Low, but decelerated decreasing, then increasing	Change from bull steepening into bear steepening	Steep	Change from bull steepening into bear steepening

and the curve steepness as demonstrated in Figure 17. Tables 2 and 3 describe the pattern for all constituents and allow us to derive an ideal type investment strategy regarding asset class and maturity.

In practice, of course, we observe that developments deviate from this model world. So, for example, there are situations where the real yield curve is steep despite a flat BEI curve. Figure 18 shows the yield and BEI curves at a time when the central bank interest rate of 2% appeared to be too low measured against a

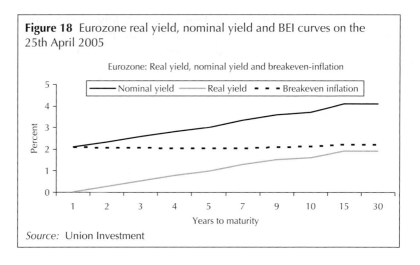

Figure 18 Eurozone real yield, nominal yield and BEI curves on the 25th April 2005

Eurozone: Real yield, nominal yield and breakeven-inflation

Source: Union Investment

general expectation of 2.2% real potential growth and a central bank inflation target of just under 2%. In this environment, market participants were surprised by a series of comparatively high monthly inflation rates. Inflation was generally expected to be lower due to high unemployment and the liberalisation of Eurozone job markets. Market participants reacted to the altered situation with a greater demand for short-term real bonds in order to earn the higher breakeven carry compared to nominal bonds. As a result, the BEI curve flattened (due to a rise in short-term maturities) at the same time as nominal yields were generally falling, and thus the real yield curve steepened. The combination of a low central bank interest rate, temporary higher inflation together with generally lower inflation risks produced a steep real yield curve with a flat inflation curve.

Low central bank interest rates tend to ensure a steep real yield curve. Low inflation and high inflation risk premiums, for their part, ensure a steep BEI curve. In contrast, high inflation and low inflation risk premiums produce a flat or even inverse BEI curve. Without declining all possible theoretical combinations at this point, it is nevertheless apparent that, of course, correlations between curves can develop that cannot be captured by our cycle systematically.

For the success of actual curve trades in the portfolio, on a bank's book or in hedge funds, timing plays an important role, as does the forecast on future curve changes. This is because the real yield and

Table 4 Linkers as an information tool. Data from July 2005 for some of the international linker markets with 10-year maturity. It helps to identify value within a market with respect to the nominal bonds (BE–CPI), equity dividend yields or money market real yields. If a real bond compares favourably to these, this particular real yield bond market could be more valuable than others

International Overview		US	UK	Eurozone	Sweden	Canada
	IL maturity	Jan 15	Jul 16	Jul 15	Dec 15	Dec 21
Conventional bond yield	(%)	4.221	4.29	3.238	3.052	4.185
Real bond yield	(%)	1.87	1.63	1.22	1.42	1.79
Inflation YoY	(%)	2.5	2	2	0.6	1.7
Short-rates (three month)	(%)	3.21	4.52	2.002	1.47	2.7
Equity dividend yield	(%)	1.99	3.27	2.90	2.75	1.59
	Index	S&P 500	FTSE 100	Euro STOXX 50	OMX 30	S&P/TSX Composite
BE inflation	(%)	2.35	2.66	2.02	1.63	2.40
BE – CPI	(%)	−0.15	0.66	0.02	1.03	0.70
Money market real yield	(%)	0.71	2.52	0.00	0.87	1.00
Real yield – equity spread	(%)	−0.13	−1.64	−1.68	−1.33	0.20

Source: HSBC and Union Investment

inflation carry gain significance as a position's holding period increases. A duration-neutral real yield rate steepener has, for example, greater prospect of success during times of high inflation carry than at other times.

CROSS COUNTRY CONSIDERATIONS AND INTERMARKET TRADING

In this section, we want to consider what insights can be gained by comparing national real return bond markets. Nominal yield spreads between two countries can, along the lines of nominal yield analysis in a closed currency environment, be separated into the components of the Fisher equation already demonstrated. Roughly speaking, the international yield differential can thus be ascribed to differences in traded real yields *and* diverging inflation expectations (BEI spreads).

Although the inflation level, economic momentum and the economic cycle of the major economic blocks deviate in part substantially from each other, for some time there has been a surprisingly strong correlation between nominal yields. This would seem to suggest that real yields are likewise strongly correlated. However, deriving the development of real yields from the market for inflation-indexed bonds runs into considerable difficulties. Due to their much lower volume compared to conventional nominal return markets, real return markets are distinctly more vulnerable to demand and supply shocks. In addition, national real return bonds show marked differences with regard to the buyer structure. In the United States, for example, a few dominant investors exercise a noticeable impact on market performance with their investment decisions. In contrast, the Eurozone real return bond market, with its deeper inflation swap market and a broader number of buyers, exhibits a more diverse structure.

From a portfolio aspect, the trade in real return bonds between individual markets can represent an additional source of performance largely uncorrelated to the general market direction, and thereby offers an additional source of diversification. This offers the opportunity to generate additional income for active fixed-income fund management. In contrast, the single currency curve trades described earlier are frequently encumbered with higher market directionality.

Fund managers constrained to domestic inflation-indexed bond markets are abandoning not only the higher liquidity associated with international diversification but they also depriving themselves of investment opportunities, which result from the differences between the individual markets. Variations of real returns, long-term BEI and seasonal patterns in the inflation trends and temporary market distortions in individual markets provide opportunities to generate additional income. Moreover, several studies on volatility show a general risk-reducing effect of international diversification. Furthermore, country- or market-specific risks arising from long-term structural changes (eg, demographic trends, choice of currency regime) could be better absorbed.

Even within asset liability management, where liabilities are typically hedged against inflation in the same market (eg, liabilities of French corporates are hedged against inflation in France), there is nothing to be said against international diversification with inclusion of a currency hedge. Over the past few years an increasing correlation of the inflation trends between the industrialised countries can be seen. The absolute difference in the inflation rate tends to be compensated by the currency hedge, provided the underlying nominal short-term rates reflect the inflation expectations, which is normally true. To summarise, international diversification offers additional opportunities for active fixed-income fund management.

Intermarket trading

Comparing the prices of real return bonds of different currencies and maturities can be carried out using the respective performance and risk expectations. A linker's absolute nominal performance depends on the development of real yields and inflation. The forecasts for these magnitudes for a due date T must be compared to the relevant forward rates, which can deviate substantially from spot rates. In this regard, it is useful to concentrate on real yield and inflation spreads.

The minimum level that these spreads need to achieve for a successful trade at the end of the holding period is derived from the following approach.

Assuming constant yield curves over time, the (nominal) return R of a fixed-income investment is generally identical to the return of a time deposit investment n_F plus the carry from the bond[13],

$$R \simeq n_F \cdot T + Carry_{Bond}$$

since, as already described, the carry reflects the advantage of holding a fixed-income investment compared to a time deposit. We now buy a foreign currency bond (US$), sell a domestic bond in exchange (€) and hold the position for T years. The carry of the total position is then

$$Carry_{Trade} = n_F^{US\$} \cdot T + Carry_{US\$} - (n_F^{€} \cdot T + Carry^{€})$$

The differential between the two time deposits corresponds exactly to the costs of a currency hedge on the due date T. In this example we ignore currency speculation and then receive

$$Carry_{Trade} = Carry_{US\$} - Carry_{€}$$

To generate a profit from the intermarket trading, the differential between the realised yields (indicated with a *) must be lower than the differential between the forward yields:

$$r_*^{US\$} - r_*^{\epsilon} < r_T^{US\$} - r_T^{\epsilon}$$

If we now want to attach linkers to the position, we need forecasts for the development of real yields in both countries in order to judge the profitability. Explicit forecasts for real yields are, however, rather unusual on the whole. The larger nominal yield market sets the tone. Since seasonality and the inflation lag also have a major impact on short-term BEI changes (refer to the section "Carry and seasonality"), in analogy to the Fisher equation, we substitute r with $n - BEI$,

$$(n_*^{US\$} - n_*^{\epsilon}) - (BEI_*^{US\$} - BEI_*^{\epsilon}) < (n_T^{US\$} - n_T^{\epsilon}) - (BEI_T^{US\$} - BEI_T^{\epsilon})$$

If the differential between nominal yield spreads and BEI spreads at the end of the holding period (left-hand side of the equation) is below the forward spread differentials (right-hand side of the equation), then the trade was successful.

The successful trades have coordinates above the breakeven line in Figure 19. The coordinates of this line correspond to the right-hand side of the preceding equation, that is, the differential between the forward spreads of nominal yields and BEIs.

In addition to comparing one's own views with the forwards, in actual cases one should naturally also observe the technical details of individual bonds, that is, rating, credit spread, liquidity, portion of possible tax gains, inter-correlation and the respective volatilities.

Following the same analysis, it can be rewarding to finance the purchase of a long-term foreign currency real return bond with the sale of a short-term domestic bond. The success of such panel trades ultimately depends, as described above, on the yields and BEI rates relative to their forward rates. The question of whether, and to what extent, currency hedging is carried out must be decided based on the currency forecasts relative to the time deposit differential between the countries and the additional currency risk.

If we finance the purchase of a real bond in the same currency by short-selling a nominal bond, only the profit or loss of the

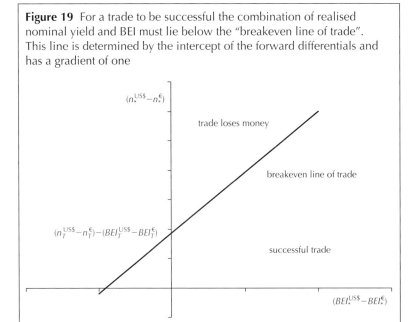

Figure 19 For a trade to be successful the combination of realised nominal yield and BEI must lie below the "breakeven line of trade". This line is determined by the intercept of the forward differentials and has a gradient of one

$(n_*^{US\$} - n_*^{€})$

trade loses money

breakeven line of trade

$(n_T^{US\$} - n_T^{€}) - (BEI_T^{US\$} - BEI_T^{€})$

successful trade

$(BEI_*^{US\$} - BEI_*^{€})$

combination is exposed to currency shifts and currency hedging could be obsolete. Nevertheless, in many fund legislations short-selling is not allowed. This shortcoming can be circumvented by the use of inflation swaps, which allows for the direct trading of BEI without the use of cash instruments. This and many other features of the inflation swap market will be treated in a later chapter of this book.

1   The HICP is determined by Eurostat. Detailed information on the composition according to country and components is published on the Internet at http://epp.eurostat.cec.eu.int/portal.
2   See the section "Seasonality and carry" for a detailed presentation.
3   The French Ministry of Economy and Finance publishes the individual latest daily inflation references on the Internet at www.francetresor.gouv.fr.
4   This statement can be derived from the economic cycle. During boom phases real interest rates will rise due to their close correlation with economic growth. At the same time, inflation rates are expected to rise due to high capacity utilisation.
5   This aspect plays an increasingly important role, particularly in regard to private pension provision.
6   Strictly speaking, the risk premium of nominal return bonds includes, in addition to inflation risk, compensation for other risks (eg, liquidity risk, default risk). In the following, however, we assume that this is either very minor or stable over time and therefore can be ignored. Furthermore, it is the case that these other risks also apply to real return bonds and therefore, *a priori*, can be removed when comparing both bonds.
7   Refer to the following section in this regard.

8 A negative risk premium compensates analogously for the deflation risk assumed by the bond issuer. The following reflections concentrate on the case where the inflation premium is positive.

9 This is based on the monetary assumption that inflation always represents a monetary phenomenon in the long term, and for this reason also determines monetary policy. However, you have to take into account the fact that for central banks it is in many cases easier to achieve a long-run inflation target than a short-run inflation target.

10 Since inflation expectations will generally deviate from realised inflation, this cannot be used to circumscribe the unrealised risk premium.

11 In the section on "Carry and Seasonality" the historical pattern of progression of BEI in connection with actual inflation is clarified using the example of the French OATi (Figure 13).

12 We will show later that BEI itself is influenced by the carry situation.

13 For greater clarity we linearise the time deposit: $(1 + n_f)^T - 1 \simeq n_f \cdot T$. Here T is a fraction of a year.

REFERENCES

Axel, R., D. Johnson, A. Reyfman, and P. Vankudre, 1998, "Valuing the Real Yield Curve", *Lehman Brothers Fixed Income Research*.

Barclays Capital, 2002, *Inflation-linked Bonds A User's Guide* (London).

Baz, J., J. Dumas, N. Firoozye, R. Lumsdaine, P. Mussche, and J. Saragoussi, 2004, "Inflation-linked Bonds", *Deutsche Bank Fixed Income Research Series*.

Benaben, B., A. Arman, L. Jelinnek, P. Conyers, and C. Carrillo, 2005, "Mastering Inflation-Linked Products", *AMRO Global Inflation Research*.

Challande, P., V. Wellmann, and H. Cros, 2004, *The Global Inflation Market* (BNP PARIBAS).

Deacon, M., A. Derry and D. Mifrendereski, 2004, *Inflation-indexed Securities: Bonds, Swaps and Other Securities*, 2nd edn (London).

Deutsche Bank, 2005, *Fixed Income Weekly: Linkers Update*, 28th January.

DZ BANK EURO Rentenmärkte, 2003, *TIPS für Investoren – Indexierte Anleihen als Alternative?*

Hammond, P. B., 2002, "Understanding and Using Inflation Bonds", *TIAA-CREF Institute Research Dialogue*, No. 73, September.

Kaufmann, P., 2004, *Inflation-linked Bonds* (Bern Stuttgart Wien).

Jellinek, Luca and Valdimar Armann, 2005, *ABN AMRO Advanced Topics in IL Markets* (ABN AMRO).

Nannizzi, S., 2004, *Framework for Analysis and Active Management of Inflation and Inflation-linked Products* (Goldman Sachs).

Nannizzi, S., and E. Sitruk, 2003, *Introduction to Inflation* (Goldman Sachs).

Schaffrik, P., and D. Pfaendler, 2005, "Ein Modell für die Breakeven-Inflation", in *Ahead of the Curve* (DRKW).

Shen, B. P., 1995, "Benefits and Limitations of Inflation Indexed Treasury Bonds", *Federal Reserve Bank of Kansas City, Economic Review* 3rd Quarter, pp 41–56.

Shen, B. P., 1998, "How Important is the Inflation Risk Premium?", *Federal Reserve Bank of Kansas City, Economic Review* 4th Quarter, pp 35–47.

2

The Benefits of Global Inflation-Indexed Bonds

Raymond T. Dalio and Daniel S. Bernstein

Bridgewater Associates, Inc

Many investors have embraced the idea that incorporating inflation-indexed (I/I) bonds into a portfolio results in numerous benefits and, ultimately, a more efficient portfolio. This is evidenced by
the large number of institutional and retail investors that have
made an explicit allocation to I/I bonds in recent years and by the
accelerating growth in the demand for I/I bonds.

The best way to further improve the allocation to I/I bonds is to
diversify the portfolio by investing in global I/I bonds hedged to
the local currency. A currency-hedged portfolio of global I/I bonds
preserves all of the benefits of a domestic portfolio and provides
some additional advantages. The purpose of this paper is to fully
explore the advantages of a global I/I bond portfolio relative to a
domestic-only portfolio.

To sum it up, a global I/I bond portfolio, currency hedged, maintains the most attractive features of a domestic portfolio, specifically:

❏ competitive returns;
❏ low risk;
❏ high correlation to inflation;
❏ low correlation to traditional asset classes.

In addition, a global portfolio provides the following incremental
advantages:

❏ lower risk;
❏ better diversification;

❑ improved liquidity;
❑ greater opportunity for value-added.

Years before the US Treasury issued TIPS (Treasury Inflation-Protected Securities), we utilised non-US I/I bonds in client portfolios to capture these benefits. The advent of the TIPS market has improved, but not replaced, the global portfolio as the best way to achieve the strategic benefits of a global I/I bond portfolio.

MAINTAINING THE BENEFITS:
DOMESTIC INFLATION HEDGE

Probably the most frequent question we hear when discussing a global I/I bond portfolio is "Would a global I/I bond portfolio be a good hedge for my domestic inflation?" The answer is an emphatic "yes", and we think it is important to address this question first before discussing some of the other benefits of a global portfolio.

In managing global I/I bond portfolios since 1994, one of the things we have seen demonstrated very clearly is that a global portfolio of currency-hedged, I/I bonds maintains almost the same correlation to domestic inflation as a domestic portfolio. Before going into why this is the case, we'd like to show some of the evidence. Table 1 shows the correlation of returns of a TIPS-only portfolio to US Consumer Price Index (CPI) inflation over various time frames. The table also shows the correlation of returns of a global I/I bond portfolio (including TIPS), currency hedged to US dollars. It is important to note that in the table a global I/I bond portfolio, when currency hedged, is as correlated (and sometimes even more highly correlated) to US inflation as the TIPS portfolio, and that neither portfolio is perfectly correlated to inflation.

Table 1

Correlation to US inflation (Jan. 1970–April 2005)					
Period	1 Month	3 Months	12 Months	3 Years	5 Years
US I/I bond portfolio	0.13	0.20	0.31	0.41	0.52
Global I/I bond portfolio	0.11	0.20	0.37	0.59	0.71

Source: Bridgewater analysis. The global I/I portfolio consists of Australia (10%), Canada (10%), Euroland (30%), UK (15%), and US (35%) 10 year duration bonds, hedged to the relevant local currency. Historical returns from 1970–2005 are based on actual real data when available and Bridgewater estimated data for periods before the I/I bonds existed

It sounds counterintuitive that a US TIPS portfolio is not more highly correlated to inflation than a global portfolio, but the reasons become clear when we analyse the returns. While a holder of TIPS receives US inflation as part of the return, returns of TIPS are very sensitive to changes in real yields. The duration of the TIPS index is currently about 10 years, meaning that every 1% rise in real yields will cause a 10% decline in return. This was very clearly demonstrated in 2002 and 2003. TIPS produced a 17% total return in 2002, a year in which inflation fell substantially, and an 8.5% return in 2003 when inflation remained low. The same trends were evident in 2004, when TIPS produced a 9.7% total return while inflation was at around 2.5%. These high returns were driven by changes in real yields, and had very little to do with the level of inflation. This is why the correlation between US TIPS and US inflation is not 100%. This also points out one of the benefits of a global portfolio that we discuss in more detail in a later section: a global portfolio is less sensitive to changes in real yields due to its inherent diversification.

Table 2 shows that this is not just a US phenomenon. The table presents the correlation of domestic I/I bonds to local inflation versus a portfolio of global I/I bonds (including domestic) to local inflation. In most cases, correlations are similar.

Table 2

Correlation of	Correlation to domestic CPI inflation over				
	1 Month	3 Months	12 Months	3 Years	5 Years
Australia					
Domestic I/I portfolio	0.05	0.25	0.40	0.58	0.69
Global I/I portfolio	0.08	0.32	0.52	0.71	0.80
Canada					
Domestic I/I portfolio	0.20	0.23	0.31	0.46	0.61
Global I/I portfolio	0.13	0.23	0.44	0.64	0.75
Euroland (France)					
Domestic I/I portfolio	0.22	0.31	0.50	0.76	0.87
Global I/I portfolio	0.16	0.27	0.50	0.72	0.82
UK					
Domestic I/I portfolio	0.17	0.32	0.68	0.82	0.91
Global I/I portfolio	0.15	0.29	0.60	0.83	0.90
US					
Domestic I/I portfolio	0.13	0.20	0.31	0.41	0.52
Global I/I portfolio	0.11	0.20	0.37	0.59	0.71
Average					
Domestic I/I portfolio	**0.15**	**0.26**	**0.44**	**0.61**	**0.72**
Global I/I portfolio	**0.13**	**0.26**	**0.49**	**0.70**	**0.80**

Source: Bridgewater analysis. The global I/I portfolio consists of Australia (10%), Canada (10%), Euroland (30%), UK (15%), and US (35%) 10 year duration bonds, hedged to the relevant local currency. Historical returns from 1970–2005 are based on actual real data when available and Bridgewater estimated data for periods before the I/I bonds existed

There are three main reasons that a portfolio of currency-hedged global I/I bonds maintains high correlation to domestic inflation:

1. inflation is a global phenomenon – particularly among major developed countries;
2. currency hedging tends to compensate for any differences in local inflation rates;
3. diversification of real yields means lower real yield volatility, which is a primary cause of divergence between domestic I/I bond returns and domestic inflation.

INFLATION IS A GLOBAL PHENOMENON
Inflation rates are highly correlated across developed countries. As shown in Table 3, the correlation of inflation rates across major

I/I bond issuers has been very high. This makes sense given the high integration of economic growth, monetary policy and the fact that all major countries are reliant on the same underlying commodities.

Table 3 January 1960 to April 2005

	Australia	Canada	Euroland	Japan	Sweden	UK	US
Australia	1.00	0.84	0.81	0.77	0.72	0.81	0.72
Canada	–	1.00	0.88	0.69	0.79	0.79	0.87
Euroland	–	–	1.00	0.78	0.84	0.84	0.81
Japan	–	–	–	1.00	0.63	0.80	0.68
Sweden	–	–	–	–	1.00	0.76	0.71
UK	–	–	–	–	–	1.00	0.80
US	–	–	–	–	–	–	1.00
Average	**0.78**	**0.81**	**0.83**	**0.73**	**0.74**	**0.80**	**0.78**

Source: Bridgewater analysis

In challenging the concept that inflation is correlated across developed countries, some people will point to Japan where deflation has been the norm for the past five years. But it is important to focus on the relationship of changes in inflation rates, not on the absolute levels. The correlation between the inflation rates in the US and Japan is 0.68 over the past 30 years. Figure 1 displays year-on-year inflation in the US and Japan since 1970 and, while we do not want to suggest that they are identical, there is a high correlation between the two.

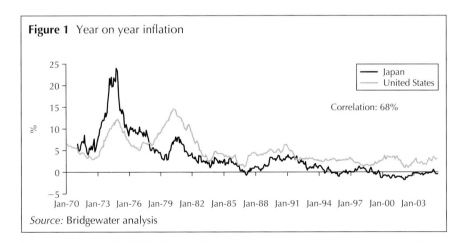

Figure 1 Year on year inflation

Source: Bridgewater analysis

The major developed economies all use similar commodities and this is one of the reasons that inflation rates of major developed countries are so highly correlated. For example, food and energy prices have a large impact on inflation in all of these markets. The absolute impact a rise in food and energy prices will have on the CPI in the US and the Harmonised Index of Consumer Prices (HICP) in Europe will differ, but all else being equal, if food and/or energy prices rise, then inflation in all of the major developed countries will rise.

Energy prices are particularly interesting because not only are they very global in nature but their impact can be substantially greater than what is represented by their direct weight in the CPI. This is true for two reasons: (1) energy prices are implicit in the prices of many other goods in an economy (eg, airfares or manufactured goods); and (2) energy prices are much more volatile than other components of CPI. The combination of these two factors means that energy prices can have a large impact on inflation. In order to quantify the broader impact of energy on overall inflation, we looked to see how well changes in the price of energy can help in predicting the change in the overall level of inflation. As shown in Table 4, changes in energy prices have significant explanatory powers in several of the major I/I bond markets. This underscores how a global inflation pressure (energy prices) can affect inflation similarly in many different countries.

Table 4 Energy's impact on inflation

Country	Impact of energy on domestic CPI (%)	Weight of energy in domestic CPI (%)
Canada	15.5	8.8
Euroland	39.0	8.5
Japan	50.2	6.5
UK	50.6	5.5
USA	39.0	8.0

Note: Coefficient of determination of the regression of 1-yr changes in energy prices to 1-yr changes in CPI.
Source: Bridgewater analysis

As a result of the similarity in the makeup of different countries' CPI indices, we expect inflation to be highly correlated across countries in the future. This correlation is one of the reasons why a portfolio of global I/I bonds hedged to the domestic currency can be a good proxy for domestic inflation.

CURRENCY HEDGING MITIGATES DIFFERENCES IN INFLATION

The global relationship among inflation rates is important directionally, but the next issue is getting the levels of inflation, not just the correlations, to come into line. Fortunately, currency hedging tends to do exactly that. As you may know, currency hedging returns incorporate the spot currency return plus the short-term interest rate differential. Embedded in the short-term interest rate differential, typically, is the inflation differential. Thus, when we hedge the currency risk of a foreign I/I bond, we adjust the inflation characteristics of that bond. This is most easily explained through a further example.

Short-term interest rate differentials are embedded in forward currency pricing. Said another way, the return of a currency hedge is equal to the movement of the spot currency plus the difference in short-term interest rates between the currency being hedged from and the currency being hedged to. So when hedging the currency risk from one currency to another, the spot currency risk is cancelled but the residual return is equal to the difference in short-term interest rates of the two countries. Because, over the long term, differences in short-term interest rates are highly correlated to differences in inflation rates, the impact of currency hedging actually compensates for differences in inflation that may arise between the two countries.

This effect can significantly change the profile of I/I bonds in foreign markets. As an example, consider Japan in the 1990s. Since Japan was going through deflation for much of the decade, at first blush one might think that, even if Japan had issued I/I bonds during that period, the low level of inflation compensation would have been unattractive to a US investor interested in hedging against the higher inflation rate of the United States. What is missing from this analysis, however, is that even though the inflation differential on its own would have severely under-compensated the US investor relative to US inflation levels, this would have been cleanly offset by the interest rate differential embedded in the currency hedge. This is illustrated in Figure 2. As the inflation levels of the two nations diverged, their interest rates also diverged in such a way as to largely (though not completely) cancel out each other: the net level of inflation for which the US investor was compensated (when both the I/I bond's inflation compensation and the currency hedging's effect are considered) would have been much closer to US inflation levels.

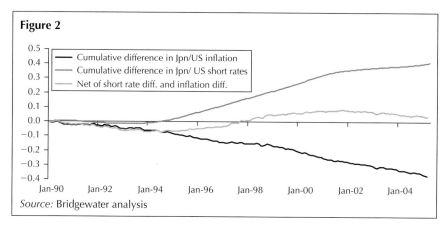

Figure 2

Legend:
— Cumulative difference in Jpn/US inflation
— Cumulative difference in Jpn/ US short rates
— Net of short rate diff. and inflation diff.

Source: Bridgewater analysis

As a second example, consider a Canadian investor who created a portfolio of global I/I bonds. Figure 3 shows the total return of investing in the Barclays' Canadian Inflation-Linked Bond Index and the total return of investing in the portfolio of global I/I bonds hedged to the Canadian dollar. Note that not only are the two return streams well correlated but also the level of the total returns is quite similar (with the global portfolio's returns being less risky).

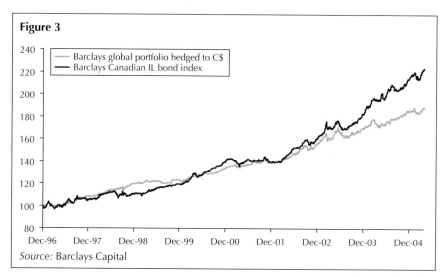

Figure 3

Legend:
— Barclays global portfolio hedged to C$
— Barclays Canadian IL bond index

Source: Barclays Capital

We do not want to suggest that there is a precise relationship between interest rate differentials and inflation differentials, since they do not always match. However, over time, they tend to correlate with each other fairly well. We think it is intuitive that this would be the case, because central banks tend to set short-term interest rates with reference to inflation rates.

REAL YIELD DIVERSIFICATION IMPROVES THE INFLATION IMPACT

The returns from I/I bonds are affected by two basic sources: changes in inflation and changes in real interest rates. Thus volatility in either of these will translate to volatility in the overall return. The important factor for an investor interested in hedging against domestic inflation is that volatility in the real yield will add noise to the inflation hedge. A portfolio of global I/I bonds will have the advantage of diversifying away some of the noise that comes from real yield volatility, and the returns will be more closely related to inflation.

As discussed earlier, over the very short term, I/I bonds (domestic and global) have a relatively low correlation to inflation. This comes as a surprise to many people because they assume the bond's return is based solely on changes in the domestic inflation rate and therefore that the bond's return should be highly correlated with inflation. As shown previously in Table 2, this is not the case over short time periods. In fact, it is the changes in real rates that drive the returns on I/I bonds over the short term.

Historically, the volatility of real yields has had a significant impact on the return profile of I/I bonds. Figure 4 shows the returns of the various I/I markets in 2004 and the year-on-year inflation rate for each of those markets. The returns far outweighed the level of inflation. The reason for the stellar performance was the fall in real yields.

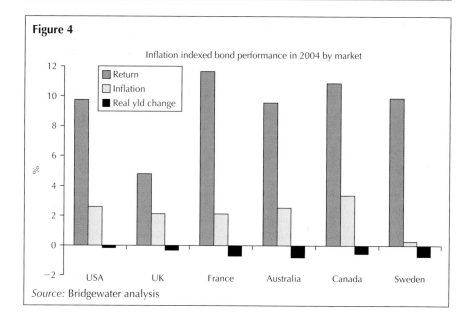

Figure 4

Inflation indexed bond performance in 2004 by market

Legend:
- Return
- Inflation
- Real yld change

Source: Bridgewater analysis

It takes a longer time horizon for the impact of inflation to outweigh that of changes in real yields. Table 2 illustrates that this has been the case for all of the major I/I-bond issuing countries. Interestingly, in Australia the global portfolio of I/I bonds hedged back to Australian Dollars had a much higher correlation to domestic inflation than did the domestic portfolio. This is due to the high volatility in real yields in Australia (see Figure 5).

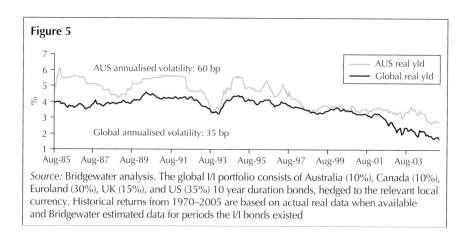

Figure 5

AUS annualised volatility: 60 bp

Global annualised volatility: 35 bp

Legend:
- AUS real yld
- Global real yld

Source: Bridgewater analysis. The global I/I portfolio consists of Australia (10%), Canada (10%), Euroland (30%), UK (15%), and US (35%) 10 year duration bonds, hedged to the relevant local currency. Historical returns from 1970–2005 are based on actual real data when available and Bridgewater estimated data for periods the I/I bonds existed

By constructing a diversified portfolio of I/I bonds it is possible to dampen volatility caused by changes in real yields and thereby produce a higher correlation to domestic inflation. As mentioned earlier, changes in real yields can have a major impact on the return profile of the I/I securities and thereby impact to the issues' ability to track inflation.

THE WHOLE PICTURE
As we noted above, the separate influences of globally correlated inflation pressures, currency hedging and diversifying away real yield volatility complement each other quite well and in combination result in a hedged portfolio of global I/I bonds providing an excellent hedge for domestic inflation.

In addition to preserving the inflation hedging characteristics of a domestic I/I bond, as we noted, a portfolio of global I/I bonds has several key benefits:

❑ lower risk;
❑ better diversification;
❑ improved liquidity;
❑ greater opportunity for value-added.

We will explain these individually.

Lower risk
By diversifying away some of the real yield volatility, global I/I bonds carry less risk than domestic-only portfolios. We think this is intuitively clear, and Table 5 shows the historic volatility of a currency-hedged global portfolio compared to individual domestic portfolios.

Table 5 Annual volatility (since inception of each country's I/I bond market)

Country	Domestic I/I portfolio (%)	Global I/I portfolio hedged (%)
Australia	6.47	3.70
Canada	4.77	3.72
Euroland (France)	4.60	4.01
UK	6.46	3.64
US	5.55	3.81
Average	**5.57**	**3.78**

Source: Bridgewater analysis. The global I/I portfolio consists of Australia (10%), Canada (10%), Euroland (30%), UK (15%), and US (35%) 10 year duration bonds, hedged to the relevant local currency. Historical returns from 1970–2005 are based on actual real data when available and Bridgewater estimated data for periods before the I/I bonds existed

Figure 6 presents the extent to which domestic real yields have been more volatile as compared to a basket of global real yields since the inception of the I/I bond market in each of the issuing countries. On average, the annualised volatility of domestic real yields has been about 45% greater than the annualised volatility of global real yields.

Figure 6

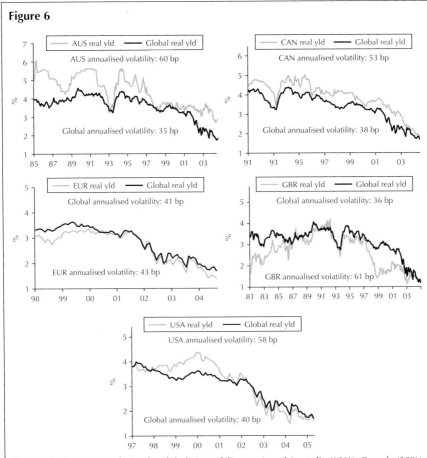

Source: Bridgewater analysis. The global I/I portfolio consists of Australia (10%), Canada (10%), Euroland (30%), UK (15%), and US (35%) 10 year duration bonds, hedged to the relevant local currency. Historical returns from 1970–2005 are based on actual real data when available and Bridgewater estimated data for periods the I/I bonds existed

Better diversification

One of the features of I/I bonds that attract investors to the asset class is that they tend to have a low correlation to other asset classes. Put another way, I/I bonds tend to be good diversifiers versus existing portfolios of equities and nominal bonds. This is just as true for global portfolios of I/I bonds. In fact, global portfolios of I/I bonds can be expected to be less correlated to domestic bonds than domestic I/I bonds and equally lowly correlated to equities. Furthermore, it is important to point out that most investors are carrying global inflation risk in their portfolios, by way of their investments in global equities and bonds. A global I/I bond portfolio helps to diversify this risk. Table 6 shows the correlations of domestic versus global I/I bond portfolios to a variety of asset classes held in a typical portfolio.

Table 6 Correlations of global & domestic I/I bonds (January 1973 to April 2005)

	Domestic government bond index		MSCI domestic equity index		International equities unhedged	
	Domestic I/I bonds	Global I/I bonds	Domestic I/I bonds	Global I/I bonds	Domestic I/I bonds	Global I/I bonds
1-Month	0.57	0.51	0.14	0.12	0.08	0.09
3-Month	0.59	0.52	0.11	0.06	0.07	0.05
1-Year	0.48	0.41	0.00	−0.04	0.00	−0.03
3-Year	0.15	0.07	−0.21	−0.18	−0.01	−0.01
5-Year	0.00	−0.08	−0.27	−0.24	−0.05	−0.15
Average	**0.36**	**0.29**	**−0.05**	**−0.06**	**0.02**	**−0.03**

Source: Bridgewater analysis. The global I/I portfolio consists of Australia (10%), Canada (10%), Euroland (30%), UK (15%), and US (35%) 10 year duration bonds, hedged to the relevant local currency. Historical returns from 1970–2005 are based on actual real data when available and Bridgewater estimated data for periods before the I/I bonds existed

Better liquidity
The current market for I/I bonds of major issuers is presented in Figure 7. Note that the total market is over US$760 billion, and that is significantly larger than any of the individual domestic markets. Even for TIPS, where the market cap is over US$300 billion, the inclusion of global supply into the equation means an increase in the investable market size of almost 140%.

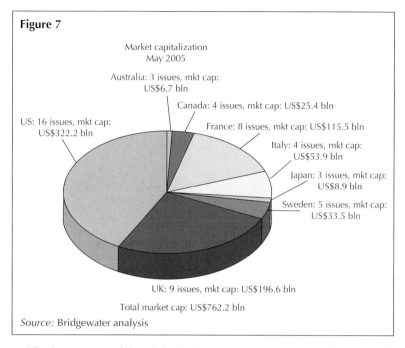

Figure 7

Market capitalization
May 2005

Australia: 3 issues, mkt cap: US$6.7 bln

Canada: 4 issues, mkt cap: US$25.4 bln

US: 16 issues, mkt cap: US$322.2 bln

France: 8 issues, mkt cap: US$115.5 bln

Italy: 4 issues, mkt cap: US$53.9 bln

Japan: 3 issues, mkt cap: US$8.9 bln

Sweden: 5 issues, mkt cap: US$33.5 bln

UK: 9 issues, mkt cap: US$196.6 bln

Total market cap: US$762.2 bln

Source: Bridgewater analysis

The larger size of the global I/I bond market has manifested itself in higher rates of liquidity and turnover. Figure 8 shows the average monthly turnover of the US I/I bond market (the largest single country market) versus the global market. Note that liquidity is higher in the global market and is climbing at a more rapid rate.

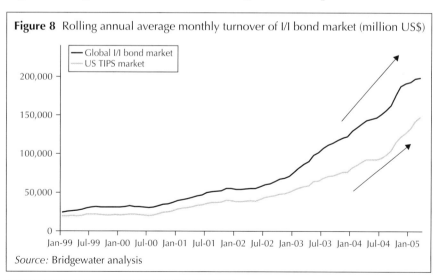

Figure 8 Rolling annual average monthly turnover of I/I bond market (million US$)

Global I/I bond market
US TIPS market

200,000

150,000

100,000

50,000

0

Jan-99 Jul-99 Jan-00 Jul-00 Jan-01 Jul-01 Jan-02 Jul-02 Jan-03 Jul-03 Jan-04 Jul-04 Jan-05

Source: Bridgewater analysis

This will continue for some time as many countries are increasing supply in 2006. Figure 9 shows how we estimate the market will look by the end of 2006.

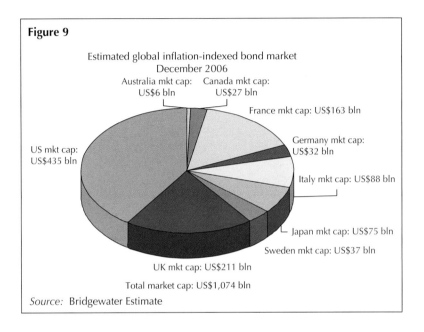

Figure 9

Estimated global inflation-indexed bond market
December 2006

Australia mkt cap: US$6 bln

Canada mkt cap: US$27 bln

France mkt cap: US$163 bln

Germany mkt cap: US$32 bln

US mkt cap: US$435 bln

Italy mkt cap: US$88 bln

Japan mkt cap: US$75 bln

Sweden mkt cap: US$37 bln

UK mkt cap: US$211 bln

Total market cap: US$1,074 bln

Source: Bridgewater Estimate

The bottom line for institutional investors is that global portfolios mean that more money can be invested at a lower transaction cost, and for very large investors it can mean that a significantly larger portfolio can be held than would be possible if limited to the domestic market. Greater liquidity also translates to a better ability to actively manage portfolios to produce value-added.

Greater opportunity for value-added

Global I/I bond portfolios offer significantly more opportunity to add value. As noted earlier, they are more liquid and therefore allow more flexible management. Probably even more importantly, by looking across the global I/I bond markets, we are able to identify pricing inefficiencies. In particular, most investors in I/I bond markets are domestically oriented and do not look at or evaluate pricing discrepancies that may exist across countries in terms of real yield differences or differences in break-even inflation rates. We believe that a well-developed approach can uncover these opportunities.

It is worth noting that comparisons across markets are complicated by a number of factors: differences in inflation calculation, lag period, seasonality, deflation protection and differences in real yields due to fundamental factors such as a country's need to attract foreign capital. One needs to take account of the many differences before one can normalise prices in a way that allows them to be compared. However, after doing so, we often see wide discrepancies in pricing that represent significant value-added opportunities.

Table 7

	Global	Domestic
Outright country decisions	9	1
Relative country decisions	36	0
Break-even inflation decisions	9	1
Security selection	53	1–16
Currency decisions	21	0
Total decisions	**128**	**3–16**

Source: Bridgewater analysis

We believe that more opportunities to add value result not only in a potentially higher return, but also in greater consistency and a higher information ratio. This is a result of the ability of any manager to better diversify the sources of alpha in a global portfolio and better diversification almost always results in higher consistency.

CONCLUDING REMARKS

Investors have recognised the strategic benefits of including I/I bonds in their portfolios. The attractive risk/return profile, high correlation to inflation and diversification benefits improve the overall performance of the portfolio. The inclusion of I/I bonds in a traditional portfolio, as shown in Figure 10, has a positive impact on the return profile of the portfolio. This profile is further improved when the allocation is made to the global I/I bonds.

As we have discussed, a portfolio of global I/I bonds hedged to the domestic currency preserves all of the benefits of a domestic portfolio and more. Relative to the domestic mandate, the global portfolio reduces risk, enhances diversification, improves liquidity and increases the opportunities to add value. When all of these benefits are taken into consideration, it is clear that portfolios should have an allocation to I/I bonds and that a global portfolio is the superior approach.

Figure 10

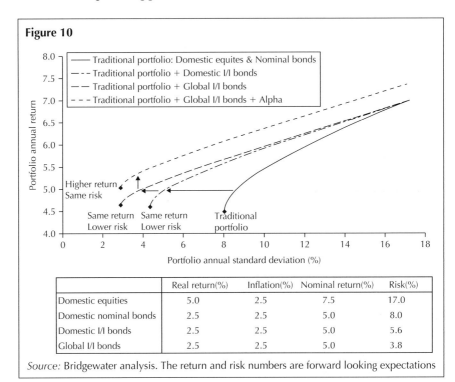

	Real return(%)	Inflation(%)	Nominal return(%)	Risk(%)
Domestic equities	5.0	2.5	7.5	17.0
Domestic nominal bonds	2.5	2.5	5.0	8.0
Domestic I/I bonds	2.5	2.5	5.0	5.6
Global I/I bonds	2.5	2.5	5.0	3.8

Source: Bridgewater analysis. The return and risk numbers are forward looking expectations

3

Inflation Flows and Investment Strategies

Valdimar Armann and Brice Benaben; Bruno Lambert

ABN AMRO;
CIAL

INTRODUCTION

Financial media, conferences and investment banks have publicised the rapid growth and globalisation of the inflation market. In parallel, numerous investment bank and academic research papers have dealt with inflation-linked products, their mechanisms and their correlation with other assets. However, we perceive that few papers analyse inflation-linked products in connection with the evolution of inflation flows. This is, however, an aspect that any investors involved in the inflation-linked market must carefully consider. First, the demand for inflation-linked bonds (or linkers) has not been gradual and has sometimes triggered large price distortions. Second, the market has evolved into a richer and more intricate market. It has been characterised by new products, a transformation of the flows between players and, in parallel, the entrance of new players, who have sometimes been encouraged by specific factors such as regulations (see our section "Understanding the inflation flows").

These changes in flows have a direct impact on investment strategies. Although the analysis of inflation-linked products has similarities with nominal bonds, important differences exist, such as the limited liquidity of short-term instruments and its consequence on forward prices (see our section "Forward strategies"). Moreover, the asymmetrical development of different market

The views expressed in this chapter are those of the authors and do not necessarily reflect those of ABN AMRO or of banque CIAL.

segments has created peculiarities such as price differentials between inflation swaps and linkers. This has direct consequences for the emergence and pricing of the corporate linkers market (see our section "Swap and credit spread strategies"). Another interesting trend in the inflation flows is the development of products linked to non-conventional indices (see our section "Alternative cross-index strategies").

All these aspects, which we have experienced over years of trading and structuring, will be analysed in this chaper, including the implementation issues via detailed examples. We will also explore the areas in which we see new investment opportunities derived from our expectations about the evolution of inflation flows.

UNDERSTANDING THE INFLATION FLOWS

In order to understand the evolution of inflation strategies, it is essential to understand the evolution of inflation flows. This section details how the inflation market has been moving from a simple linkers market (see our section on "Early flows") into a richer and more global market (see "Recent flows"). It also gives our expectations on the development of future flows development ("Emerging flows"). In particular, it deals with important issues for investors such as potential demand shocks, new products and new derivatives' flows.

Early flows
A bond market
In the 1980s and 90s, the inflation product market was predominantly a pool of domestic markets where sovereign issuers (for example, the governments in the UK, Canada, Australia and Sweden) sold bonds to local "buy and hold" investors (pension funds and insurance companies). In general, the liquidity in the secondary and "repurchase agreement" markets was poor. The linkers market widened with the launch of the US Treasury Inflation Protected Securities (TIPS) program in 1997 and of the French inflation-linked Obligation Assimilable du Trésor (OATi) one year later.

Limited investment strategies
Due to limited liquidity and the small number of bond issues, the main investment strategy was to "buy and hold" a linker in a nominal government bonds portfolio. Selling a nominal bond with

a similar maturity and creditworthiness generally financed the purchase of a linker. This resulted in a spread position. This spread embeds a so-called bond Break Even Inflation[1] (BEI), which is reduced by a premium caused by the lower liquidity of linkers compared to nominal bonds. This spread on early linkers generally widened until 2000, benefiting investors. Both the reduction of the "illiquidity" premium and the widening of the BEI explain the benefit. An exception is the UK linkers, which were issued in the high inflation environment of the 1980s. We would say that the government "bet" against the market regarding its ability to lower and control inflation. Since inflation duly fell, so did the BEI.

Recent flows

The recent period has been characterised by:

❏ a sharp rise in linker liquidity;
❏ the completion of the real-yield curve into five-year maturity and;
❏ the addition of new dimensions in the inflation market; this includes inflation swaps and bonds linked to new inflation indices.

Of the large number of new developments and innovations, we have selected three due to their importance in allowing new investment strategies.

Birth of the EMU HICP linkers market

The launch of an OAT linked to the EMU Harmonized Index of Consumer Prices (HICP) ex Tobacco or OATei in 2001 gave rise to a new market. A measure of the OATei's success is the broadening of the investor base, particularly outside of France. This helped convince Greece and Italy to issue bonds linked to the same index in 2003. As a result, EMU HICP became a major benchmark for inflation-linked products.

Importantly, however, it did not drain liquidity from the existing French inflation market. On the contrary, French companies such as the social security funding vehicle CADES became new issuers in the French inflation market (1999, 2002).

The growth of this market has been impressive and net issuance exceeded the US TIPS issuance in 2003. While it was again overtaken in 2004, it remains the second largest market by issuance, followed by the UK Retail Price Index market.

Completion of the real-yield curve

For several years, linkers supply eschewed shorter maturities. This was more the case in the Euro area, as the US Treasury issued a five-year TIPS in 1997 and the UK Debt Management Office issued a six-year linker in 1982.

When the Italian Treasury issued a five-year EMU inflation bond benchmark (2003), it was more than a successful one-off event, as it created a sustainable liquidity for this segment of the real-yield curve. Indeed, it revealed a new range of investors. Substantial demand came from the investment banks to hedge specific inflation-linked products sold for large amounts in the retail market (in Switzerland and particularly in Italy). In addition, it has opened the door to more speculative investors, in particular "carry players"; an important driver of short-maturity linker prices being the change in the carry, as we will see in "Forward strategies".

Infancy of the derivatives market

The derivatives markets originated from banks' demands for hedging structured notes or swaps and developed around the existing linkers market.

The first major source of demand for inflation derivatives was related to inflation products for retail banking (see Figure 1). These products were generally structured notes paying coupon in the form of a spread plus the annual inflation (the so-called additive structure) or combining the return of equity indices and inflation.[2] The structuring teams who built these first notes hedged them with linkers; therefore they "recycled" the inflation from linkers into structured notes via inflation swaps. No new "supply" was created as such.

A second source of demand came from pension funds with inflation-linked liabilities. This has been important in the UK, where pension liabilities are explicitly linked to the Retail Price Index (RPI) or Limited Price Index (LPI).[3] In general, pension liabilities have an annuity structure,[4] which cannot be exactly replicated with linkers. Therefore, investment banks have provided annuity swaps or notes and partially hedged them with linkers, taking on some mismatch risk.

A common issue for most inflation derivatives markets has been the lack of inflation payers. This has resulted in the inflation paid via derivatives having a higher price than via bonds. The inflation

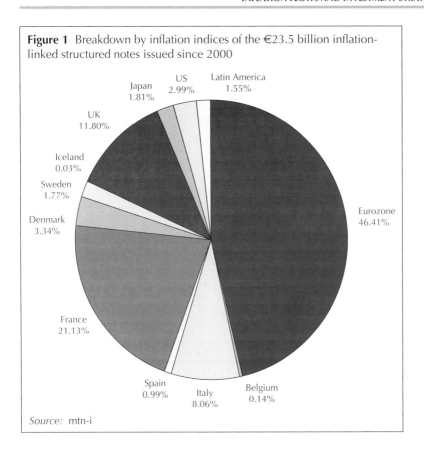

Figure 1 Breakdown by inflation indices of the €23.5 billion inflation-linked structured notes issued since 2000

Source: mtn-i

swap markets have more recently begun to develop at a faster pace. To a large extent the pace is proportional to the growth of new inflation payers. In the UK, where the derivatives market started in the mid-1990s, the Private Finance Initiative (PFI) market[5] has been providing large inflation swap payer flows. Conversely, the newer US Consumer Price Index (US CPI) derivatives market still suffers from a lack of inflation payers. The EUR inflation derivatives market is one of the most liquid and is becoming a two-way market.

Sophistication of investment strategies
A more complete real-yield curve and improved linkers liquidity have helped new types of investment strategies flourish. Some of them mirror classic nominal-yields strategies. Examples include playing the slope or the concavity of either the real-yield curve or

the break-even curve (box trades between nominal bonds and linkers). These strategies have led to more analysis of the term structure of the real-yield curve (see, eg, Roll 2004), usually in relation to the nominal-yield curves. For example, some strategies are based on the so-called "beta" (see Chapter 1 of this book), a simple but incomplete change measure of nominal yield relative to real yield.

An important driver of short-term real yield and BEI curves is the carry of linkers. This is specific to linkers and thus not captured by the "beta". In a nutshell, the volatility of the recent month-on-month inflation is transmitted into the yield of short-maturity linkers. Our section on "Forward strategies" gives examples of such strategies. In parallel, the infancy and growth of the inflation derivatives market has offered many interesting opportunities.

A first set of strategies stems from the difference of structures traded in the swap market (annuity, additive and zero-coupon swap) and in the linkers market (multiplicative). Inflation derivatives' cashflows are usually more equally spread by maturity; they require a full BEI curve, particularly in the 2–5 year segment, which may not be observable from existing linkers. The linker's inflation cashflows are concentrated in the final redemption payment.

A second set stems from the imbalance between inflation receiving and inflation paying. The lack of inflation payers made the swap contract paying inflation "expensive". Better said, swaps BEI levels are higher than BEI levels implied by comparable bonds. This is in turn reflected by asset swap spreads. A combination of factors, the main one being the lack of swap inflation payers, makes asset swapped linkers "cheaper" than nominal bonds. In our section on "Swap and Credit Spread Strategies", we will explore these strategies based on these discrepancies.

Emerging flows

The multiplying number of players in the inflation market makes flows more and more intricate. However, we can identify the following trends.

On the demand side:

❏ some "shocks" which are generally related to regulatory changes, have created new demand for inflation-linked products, particularly in Europe;

❏ the increasing sophistication/specialisation of investors in inflation-linked products has shifted demand towards derivatives and structured notes.

On the supply side:

❏ the near absence of corporate issuance of (unswapped) IL bonds could end;
❏ new inflation paying has been booming through derivatives and structured notes.

New products:

❏ products linked to new inflation indices that are not present in the sovereign linkers market;
❏ products with non-linear or correlation pay-off.

Demand side
Shocks in the demand for linkers. Over recent years the growth of linker net supply has accelerated but not quickly enough to absorb shocks in the demand for linkers.

The UK market experienced rapid demand growth from pension funds and life insurers, which led to significant decreases in real yields. This followed the introduction of new regulations such as the Minimum Funding Requirement as part of the 1995 Pension Act or, more recently, the Financial Reporting Standard 17. These regulations have encouraged pension funds to match their indexed-linked liabilities more closely, particularly following the drop of equity prices in the early part of the last decade. The recent surge in UK RPI swap volumes is also partly a consequence of these regulatory changes (see the next section of this book, which details these pension funds' regulatory aspects).

In France, demand shocks have boosted linkers' prices. For example, the modification of article R. 332–19 of the "Code des assurances" allowed French insurers to allocate part of their fixed income assets into linkers. This again created a surge in the demand for linkers at the beginning of 2003.

From August 2003, the return on French regulated savings accounts was linked to the French inflation rate and short-term nominal-interest rates, following the recommendations of the "Rapport sur l'équilibre des Fonds d'épargne" (Nasse and Noyer

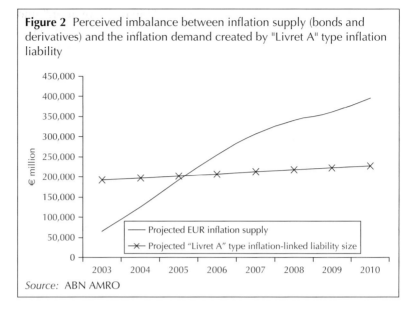

Figure 2 Perceived imbalance between inflation supply (bonds and derivatives) and the inflation demand created by "Livret A" type inflation liability

Source: ABN AMRO

2003). In the summer of 2003, European linkers significantly out-performed nominal bonds. Part of the out-performance was due to anticipations of a potential shortage of linkers necessary for the banks to hedge the inflation exposure of savings products linked to such a formula. At that time we estimated that hedging this new liability pool would have required €185 billion of linkers, whereas the European linkers market amounted to €65 billion at the time (see Figure 2). To some extent, the expected lack of supply may have been overstated as it underestimated the less visible supply coming from the derivatives market.

Are future regulatory shocks still likely to impact linker prices? The current regulatory trend is towards lifting the remaining barriers, which still prevent some investors from entering the linker market. Therefore, the pool of demand for linkers is much more likely to increase than to shrink. An AMTE[6] working group has listed and analysed these barriers (AMTE 2005). Listed below are the barriers that we believe to be of interest, since they should be lifted soon and could move the market.

❏ French life insurers cannot invest in corporate linkers; a removal of this obstacle could push up prices of (rare) existing corporate linkers and, more importantly, could encourage corporate issuing.

❑ In Germany, linkers are classified as a "Finanzinnovation" and all capital accretion over the bond life is subject to capital gains tax;[7] a tax re-classification combined with the FinanzAgentur issuance of a linker would certainly "wake up" the large remaining potential German demand, which would gradually enter the market.

❑ In Spain, mutual funds cannot invest in some inflation-linked products as the CNMV,[8] the Spanish regulator for mutual funds, does not see inflation as an acceptable underlying "reference" for financial assets. We expect a gradual entrance of new investors.

Could "demand shocks" occur in connection with pension reforms similar to that in the UK?[9] In the UK, the hedging of large existing inflation-linked liabilities should remain a feature over the coming years. Outside the UK, a much smaller liabilities pool is explicitly linked to inflation. Here are some examples;

❑ In the Netherlands, pension funds can choose to adopt an inflation-linked liability mechanism but they must specify it to the regulatory body; it seems that some major pension funds will not choose such a route.

❑ In the United States, some public funds give a "Cost of Living Allowances" promise, but it is difficult to say whether such benefits would extend into the private-sector pension schemes.

❑ In Italy, some employees are entitled to a "Trattamento di Fine Rapporto" (severance pay) financed by a salary levy. The money set aside appreciates at a fixed real rate (1.5%) plus Italian inflation. This certainly creates a potential demand for Italian inflation-linked products.

❑ In France and Spain some specific corporate plans provide complementary inflation-linked pensions. The regulatory trend encouraging the matching between asset and liability should add demand for some inflation-linked hedging instruments.

However, most of these liabilities are linked to specific indices (eg, Italian CPI or Spanish CPI), which may have a poor correlation with the "liquid" indices (EMU HICP, US CPI, French CPI, UK RPI). Therefore, we do not expect a wave of demand from hedging this explicit linkage. Rather, such flows could contribute to developing markets for their specific indices as analysed further in our section on " 'Alternative' cross-index strategies".

A large portion of inflation exposure is also in defined-benefit pension scheme obligations, which are linked to final salary. This has only an implicit inflation component, but it justifies investing some assets into linkers. Some pension funds have "tested" the linker market but mainly to benefit from diversification effects and reasonable liquidity, leading to linkers being treated as a separate asset class, rather than a hedge.

Whatever the reasons to invest are, the demand potential is huge compared to existing supply (see Table 1). Reallocation could occur from classic asset classes (such as shares and government nominal bonds) into linkers, directly or through specialised mutual funds. Asset allocation discussions are particularly topical, given the current regulatory changes. However, so far, investment in linkers by pension funds has been roughly in line with the growth of linkers' liquidity. Therefore, while regulatory shocks are possible, we expect more structural, gradual demand growth so that supply will be able to keep pace.

Sophistication of the demand. Figure 3 illustrates how 2004 was characterised by a sharp increase in the number of funds that specialised in inflation-linked products. However, this change in investors' breakdown does not mean a change in the actual final investors, who are mainly pension funds, compensation funds and insurance. Rather, they have been outsourcing part of the management of their inflation-linked assets to specialised asset managers. This is a consequence of:

❏ the growing outstanding amount of linkers and their recognition as a new asset class;
❏ the development of new linkers indices (for example, the EMTXi[10]) and the stabilisation of the average maturity of these indices (Figure 4).

Therefore, it does not really directly raise the pool of demand; however, it could add incentives for greater marketing efforts and could increase the awareness of the inflation risk. A more direct impact is that sophisticated demand has broadened the range of inflation-linked strategies and products substantially, as we will see later.

Table 1 Size of pension funds and breakdown of their investment as of 2003

	Size of pension funds: total investment (USD Bn) in 2003	Cash & deposits	Bills & Bonds issued by public entities	Corporate bonds	Land & Buildings	Mutual funds (CIS)	Others (shares, insurance contracts …)
United States	7,228	513	354	347	58	1,540	4,416
UK	1,179	31	171	55	51	134	737
Netherlands	545	12	139	75	27	–	292
Japan	561						
Canada	446	22	83	24	16	164	137
Australia	296						
France	95						
Germany	85	2	31	–	5	7	40
Denmark	59	0	15	24	2	5	14
Spain	55	2	11	19	0	4	19
Italy	37	3	12	0	4	2	16

Source: OECD

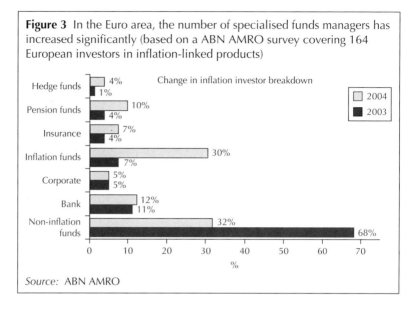

Figure 3 In the Euro area, the number of specialised funds managers has increased significantly (based on a ABN AMRO survey covering 164 European investors in inflation-linked products)

Source: ABN AMRO

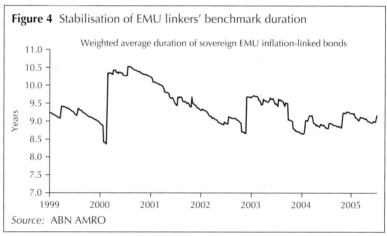

Figure 4 Stabilisation of EMU linkers' benchmark duration

Source: ABN AMRO

Supply side

New inflation paying flows are developing around three axes:

❑ the development of new markets driven, in a traditional way, by new sovereign issuers, for example in Japan, Poland and eventually Germany;

❑ the development of structured notes and derivatives driven by new non-sovereign inflation payers;

❑ the development of the long-awaited corporate linkers market.

New sovereign issuers. Interestingly, the growth of major inflation markets has created a sophisticated demand for new products, in particular new sovereign linkers. Most of the recent Polish linkers were bought by specialised inflation-indexed funds positioning for BEI convergence between Poland and the European Monetary Union (EMU). It is a recent development that a linker market is driven more by external demand rather than the "classic" domestic demand coming from pension funds or long-term investors. Such an example could give incentives for sovereign issuers to step in to the market. More generally, it is well admitted that linkers' issuance allow issuers to broaden demand.

Corporate issuers: myth or reality? A missing player with large potential to pay inflation is the corporate sector. The corporate linkers market is very small compared to the sovereign linkers market. It has been mainly present in the UK (water, electricity and gas bills are explicitly linked to inflation) and to a lesser extent to US municipal issues (see Figure 5).

There are plenty of arguments to support corporates adding an inflation dimension to their financing and risk-management

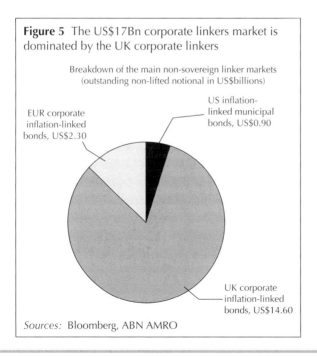

Figure 5 The US$17Bn corporate linkers market is dominated by the UK corporate linkers

Breakdown of the main non-sovereign linker markets
(outstanding non-lifted notional in US$billions)

US inflation-linked municipal bonds, US$0.90

EUR corporate inflation-linked bonds, US$2.30

UK corporate inflation-linked bonds, US$14.60

Sources: Bloomberg, ABN AMRO

strategy (this is developed in the next section of this book). This can mitigate net earnings volatility, reduce interest cost volatility and lower the expected cost of funding. Banks are making a major marketing effort to convince corporates, but it has yet to pay off.

Based on that economic rationale, an important group of issuers are utilities in Europe and in the United States. As utility prices shift from being politically determined to being set on the basis of clear inflation formulas, corresponding cost indexing to inflation makes more sense, as in the UK. However, some obstacles prevent the market from developing.

Obstacles in the supply side. An important obstacle is that treasurers' attention is currently more firmly focused on new accounting regulations and that the accounting treatment for inflation products needs some clarification. Once those issues have been more thoroughly digested, inflation products may get a more careful hearing.

Under US GAAP (FAS 133) there is a requirement for all embedded derivatives (including inflation) to be identified and "bifurcated". This usually creates profit and loss volatility. However, there is an exemption for inflation-linked debt if the inflation index used is local to the corporate. The exemption considers the interest rate and the rate of inflation in the economic environment for the currency in which a debt instrument is denominated to be clearly and closely related.

According to IAS 39, paragraph AG 33f, the inflation-indexed derivative would not be bifurcated from the debt host contract when the inflation index relates to inflation in the entity's economic environment. As a result, a corporate operating in an EMU country issuing in their local inflation is allowed to hedge accounts. From that standpoint, the use of inflation swaps to create synthetic inflation-linked debt is far from clear and becomes a complex issue.

For Libor issuers, the "Libor equivalent" funding cost of linkers appears not to be as attractive due to inflation swap BEIs being higher than implied linkers BEI.

Obstacles in the demand side. Another reason for the scarcity of corporate linkers has been a perceived lack of demand for such bonds. In the UK, demand has significantly decreased partly due to sector and name concentrations conflicting with credit diversification rules. In the rest of Europe, investors have been perceived as

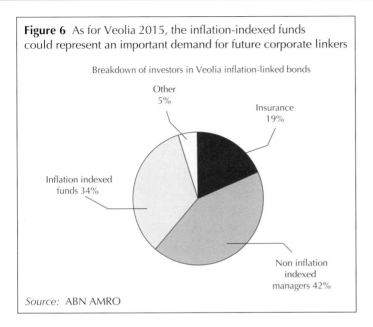

Figure 6 As for Veolia 2015, the inflation-indexed funds could represent an important demand for future corporate linkers

Breakdown of investors in Veolia inflation-linked bonds

Other
5%

Insurance
19%

Inflation indexed
funds 34%

Non inflation
indexed
managers 42%

Source: ABN AMRO

not keen or not allowed to mix inflation and credit risks. It is true that some large investors in linkers are not allowed to invest in corporate linkers. For example, the Insurance Regulation in France (code R.332–19) limits investments in linkers to certain sovereign or quasi-sovereign issuers, even though such a barrier does not exist for nominal bonds. However, demand has been growing, as the recent issuance by Veolia has shown (see Figure 6). This could help other corporate issuers step into the linker market.

Non-sovereign payers via derivatives. Some investors have, for some time, considered inflation products expensive. This was rooted in a perception of excess demand and lack of inflation payers. However, inflation end-paying flows are often underestimated, as a growing proportion of these flows are in the less visible derivatives market. Examples include hedging infrastructure project finance flows, local authority tax revenues or real estate rents.

For example, many real estate holders in the United States, France, Belgium, Italy or the Netherlands have inflation-linked revenues from their rental agreements (either by law or specific agreements), but fixed or floating rate debt payments. This creates

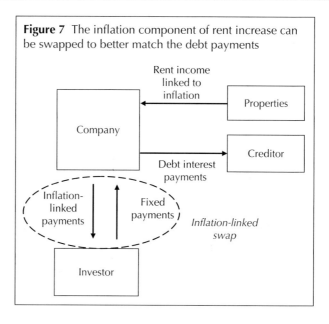

Figure 7 The inflation component of rent increase can be swapped to better match the debt payments

Rent income linked to inflation

Properties

Company

Creditor

Debt interest payments

Inflation-linked payments

Fixed payments

Inflation-linked swap

Investor

an exposure to low inflation and high nominal rates. An inflation swap can hedge this risk (see Figure 7).

Interestingly, many of these new payers are exposed to local inflation in the form of Italian, Spanish, Dutch and Belgian inflation. As a result, the number of indices traded in the derivatives market has started to broaden (for example the Spanish and the Italian CPI) and some banks have started to increase risk limits in their inflation indices correlation books. However, the EMU HICP swap market remains the benchmark and has constantly increased in liquidity with bid/ask spreads shrinking. We estimate that between €8 billion and €12 billion of new flows paying European inflation indices are created via the derivatives market every year. This is equivalent to adding a new large linkers' issuer.

New products
Products linked to new indices. The direct consequence of new inflation payers has been the growing number of products linked to new indices. They are new sovereign linkers (Japan, Poland) adopting the standard structure of sovereign linkers. Such products are also inflation-linked structured notes. In 2004, Infrastrutture issued a 15-year note linked to Italian CPI; it amounts to €775 million. The same year,

Great Belt, a Danish bridge and road operator in Denmark issued a structured note linked to Danish CPI; its outstanding notional is €665 million. It can be said that the market is developing due to the crystallisation of both demand and supply. This is detailed in our section on "'Alternative' cross-index strategies".

Short maturity instruments in the established market. So far, the available short-term inflation instruments have been old off-the-run linkers. Their liquidity is generally poor. The Chicago Mercantile Exchange tried to launch US CPI futures but its liquidity remains poor, partly due to unpopular structure. A similar CPI futures contract on the EMU HICP has been launched this year with a different design; it is a monthly contract using the year-on-year inflation instead of quarter-on-quarter inflation. However, it is difficult to expect a liquid short-term inflation curve to develop without an inflation-linked money market. Indeed, the experience in nominal interest rates show that speculative players are necessary for the liquidity of short-term markets, where an important strategy is the so-called "cash and carry" trade, which requires a parallel development of the cash and futures market. Unless a sovereign issuer commits to issuing short-term inflation-linked instruments, we do not expect a development of the very front end of the real yield in the United States, the EMU or the UK.

Products with non-linear or correlation pay-off. The most common option is the embedded floor on year-on-year inflation and, specifically for the UK, the LPI. The year-on-year inflation floors are embedded in structured notes paying a coupon equal to year-on-year inflation plus a fixed rate. The floor prevents the coupon from being negative. An important development of the option market is related to the trend towards shifting pension-fund investment risk from institutions to individuals. A broad re-think of pension funds risk allocation has fostered interest in inflation hybrid products. In particular, the concept of protection is shifting from nominal to "real" capital protection (ie, protecting the purchasing power). As a result we should see more and more inflation-protected notes with an active or passive participation in other risk classes (credit, equity, hedge funds index, etc). The main drawback of inflation protection is that the inflation component consumes a large part of the participation. Conversely, option-based structures that pay the highest return between inflation and equities (but not both) allow for greater exposure to the equity return.

New investment strategies – exploring the borders of the inflation markets

An important advance for inflation indexed investors is the perception that the market is now better able to absorb new, potential regulatory "shocks". Information about such events is generally asymmetric and therefore is considered by investors as adding more risk and making the market less efficient. As these risks have receded, liquid linkers have been driven less by supply/demand "shocks" expectations but more by analysis of the carry or of the connection between BEI and oil price, currency rates, and short-term rates. This helps the entry of new inflation-indexed managers, which has important repercussions on the investment strategies. It has created:

❏ periodic demand due to the benchmark replications (usually monthly);
❏ needs for "alternative strategies" aimed at outperforming the benchmark.

This is exacerbated by the sharp competition to win mandates. The larger and more stable size of some inflation linked portfolios has allowed their managers to explore less liquid inflation products, usually offering a good carry. A first example is the structured note linked to less generic inflation indices (such as Spanish, Italian or Danish CPI) or corporate linkers. Another example is the more frequent use of inflation swaps by such specialised managers to play BEI strategies or cross-index strategies more accurately and more cost effectively or to exploit basis spreads between linkers and derivatives.

Summary chart

Figure 8 summarises the inflation flows' changes. It splits the flows between bonds and derivatives and differentiates between inflation payers and receivers:

❏ inflation payers, for example a sovereign issuer "paying" inflation by issuing a cash bond or a real-estate company paying inflation and receiving fixed cashflows in a swap to hedge inflation-linked rent revenues;

Figure 8 Evolution of the flows and products in the inflation market

	Inflation payers	Inflation receivers	Products
Early flows	State debt management UK, France, US, etc.	**Pension funds/life insurance** Long-term liabilities **Asset managers** Risk diversification	**Bonds** EMU HICP, FR CPI, US CPI, UK RPI
Recent flows	**Non-sovereign issuers** CADES, RFF, etc. **State debt mgt** Italy, Greece	**Pension funds/life insurance** **To hedge inflation liabilities** **Bank ALM** **Hedging inflation swaps book** **Leveraged Investors** Carry & relative value strategies	**Swaps** EMU HICP FR CPI UK RPI
Emerging flows	**State debt mgt** Japan, [Germany expected] **Project finance** Infrastructure, Private finance initiative **Regions/municipalities** Tax revenues **Real-estate asset holders** Commercial rent **Bank ALM** Mortgage houses **Active debt managers** Reduce cost of funding volatility **Corporate** ALM	**Regional banks** Italian and swiss retail Structured notes **Inflation-linked funds** Benchmark replication Alternative inflation strategies Relative value/overlay **Bank ALM** Hedging "Livret A" type accounts	**MTN** **Swaps** IT, SP, US CPI **Futures** US CPI CME **Swap** Other indices **Options** Non-linear and correlation payoff **Futures** EMU HICP

Bond market

Derivatives market

❏ inflation receivers, such as an investor buying inflation bonds or a pension fund receiving inflation and paying fixed to hedge inflation-linked liability in a swap.

FORWARD STRATEGIES

Fundamental information for a strategy that is taking a "view" on a financial variable (BEI, real yield or spread) is its forward value. In the risk-neutral world, if the variable moves gradually to meet the forward value, then a strategy would neither make nor lose money. The forward values are pretty much measurable for any forward dates in the nominal-yield world but this is not the case in the real-yield world. A main reason is the absence of short-term inflation instruments. In the derivatives market, the forward inflation can be extracted for forward maturity for longer than two years. In the cash market the carry, the difference between the forward real yield and the spot real yield, is known over a horizon of between two weeks and one and a half months.

The carry of a linker is particularly volatile as it absorbs the fluctuation of the change in the latest CPI figures (realised or expected). As a result it explains part of the short-term changes in BEI and real yield, both the levels and the curve shapes. In the early flows, we did not observe that the carry drove the real-yield or BEI curves. This was understandable as the early investors were long-term investors purchasing linkers in the primary market with a focus on long-term return rather than on short-term fluctuations and the carry volatility tends to fade in the long run. Moreover, distortions between linkers demand and supply had more dramatic impact than the carry.

As shown in "Understanding inflation flows", the inflation market has changed dramatically in recent years and this has changed price drivers and the fundamentals of the instruments. With a growing liquidity of linkers and with more sophisticated investors, the carry now plays an important role as a driver of the BEI and real-yield curves. Moreover, derivatives strategies based on forward BEI rates are becoming popular as the liquidity of inflation swaps is increasing.

Forward from the derivatives

In the derivatives market, the zero-coupon swaps are forward contracts on the CPI. At the initiations date of the contract, t_0, the two counterparts agree a contract maturity, t, and a "Break Even Inflation" rate, $z_{t_0,t}$, running between the initiation date and the maturity date. At contract maturity two flows are exchanged:

❏ $\frac{CPI_t}{CPI_{t_0}} - 1$, known only at the maturity date;[11]
❏ $(1 + z_{t_0,t})^{t-t_0} - 1$, a quantity fixed at the initiation date.

Therefore, it is possible to extract forward CPI curves but only for maturity points longer than two years. The simplicity of this instrument, its low counterpart risk and its increasing liquidity has attracted investors wishing to take "pure" BEI views. The quick narrowing of bid/ask spread has smoothed forward curves (Figure 9) but has also raised the importance of some "secondary" effects, detailed in Chapters 5 and 6 of this book. Let us mention two.

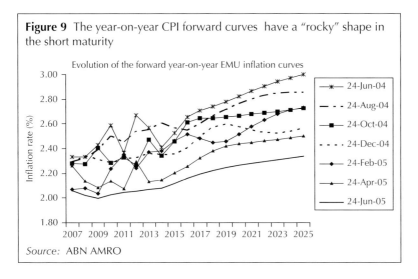

Figure 9 The year-on-year CPI forward curves have a "rocky" shape in the short maturity

Source: ABN AMRO

❑ Seasonal adjustment, particularly in the interpolation of intermediary maturity points.

❑ Convexity factor for forward inflation calculations; for example a forward on inflation running between dates t and $t + 1$, is given by $E(CPI_t/CPI_{t-1}) - 1$.[12] This is different to $[E(CPI_t)/E(CPI_{t-1})] - 1$ and therefore cannot be extracted simply from the forward CPI curve. In other words, the ratio of mean is not the mean of the ratio, which makes the situation more complex. This convexity may be worth several bps for long maturity but there is no standard definition and valuation of the convexity as there is not (yet) a standard inflation model in finance.

The different methods used to calculate convexity adjustments have caused differences in forward pricing. However, playing these discrepancies was difficult because the quite large bid/ask spread was larger than the differences. Moreover, even if the bid/ask spread has been narrowing; it has been coupled with more accurate adjustments as the inflation modelling improved. It is important to account for these factors while taking a view on forward inflation rates based on derivatives.

Forward for the linkers: carry mechanisms
Perhaps one of the first "forward" strategies was based on the carry[13] of linkers. This carry mechanism is detailed in Chapter 1 of this book. Here are our main conclusions.

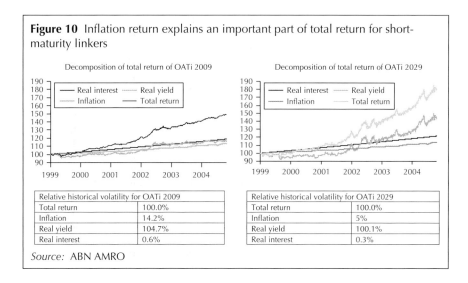

Figure 10 Inflation return explains an important part of total return for short-maturity linkers

Decomposition of total return of OATi 2009

Legend: Real interest, Real yield, Inflation, Total return

Relative historical volatility for OATi 2009	
Total return	100.0%
Inflation	14.2%
Real yield	104.7%
Real interest	0.6%

Decomposition of total return of OATi 2029

Legend: Real interest, Real yield, Inflation, Total return

Relative historical volatility for OATi 2029	
Total return	100.0%
Inflation	5%
Real yield	100.1%
Real interest	0.3%

Source: ABN AMRO

Table 2 Oil price change in € explains a large portion of the month-on-month CPI changes

	French CPI ex Tobacco	EMU HICP ex Tobacco
Volatility of (seasonality adjusted) month-on-month inflation	0.26%	0.23%
Volatility due to change in oil price (Brent) expressed in €	0.07%	0.10%

Sources: ABN AMRO, Insee, Eurostat

Over a short horizon, inflation return explains a large part of the total return levels and volatilities for short-maturity bonds but is overshadowed by the real return volatility for long maturity linkers (see Figure 10). In addition, short-term changes in latest inflation rates can actually drive the carry between −20 bps and +20 bps for short maturity bonds and between −4 bps and +4 bps for longer maturities and therefore impact also the real yield return. Over a long horizon the inflation return seems smooth and the carry fluctuations tend to fade as they are driven by month-on-month inflation jumps.

The fluctuations of the inflation (and by extension of the carry) are partly explained by a seasonal pattern, fluctuation of oil prices (see Table 2), exchange rates, fiscal policy, and change in the CPI structure (see Table 3). Most of these factors have a good degree of

Table 3 Examples of change in the CPI structure

Dutch health care cost reform	2006 Dutch year-on-year HICP could be abruptly lowered from 1.4% (October 2004 forecast) to −3.0%. This would translate into roughly a 0.2% negative impact on 2006 EMU-wide HICP. This would result from health insurance system reform in the Netherlands, which aims at putting in place a universal, mandatory, basic system for all. Health care would become effectively "free" or there would virtually be no longer a "retail" market for health care. This would lead to a "one off" reduction of health care component in the HICP.
French health care reform	2005 Health care reform in France had an economic impact on consumer prices (reduction in the medical reimbursement, potential de-listing of drugs from reimbursable formulary…). Because of different methodology in the calculation of the CPI and HICP, this led to add divergence pressure between the EMU HICP and French CPI.
Change in the housing costs in HICP	Current housing costs incurred by households that own the property they inhabit (owner-occupied housing) was excluded from the original methodology of Eurostat calculation. Eurostat is considering the addition of these costs. This could have an upward impact on measured HICP.
Change in EMU HICP weights due to EU countries joining EMU	The EMU HICP is a weighted average of EMU countries domestic HICP. If new accession EU countries join the EMU, it would increase slightly the EMU year-on-year HICP. If the UK joins the EMU, it would reduce the EMU year-on-year HICP.

predictability; the seasonal effect is deterministic, taxation and change in CPI structure are known before the index publication, and oil price changes are usually transmitted into the CPI with a lag of a couple of months. Good econometric models incorporating these factors generally have a good prediction power of the next CPI release (ABN AMRO 2004). The expected fluctuations of the month-on-month inflation (such as seasonal pattern) should be embedded in the forward real-yield path. The unexpected ones (such as oil price shocks) would transmit via the carry to the spot and forward real yields (see Figure 11) and could create large swings in spot real yields for the following reason.

Due to the linker indexing lag (between two and three months) and the lag between CPI date and its publication date (about two

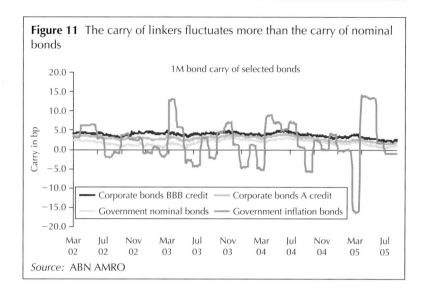

Figure 11 The carry of linkers fluctuates more than the carry of nominal bonds

1M bond carry of selected bonds

- Corporate bonds BBB credit
- Corporate bonds A credit
- Government nominal bonds
- Government inflation bonds

Source: ABN AMRO

weeks), the carry is known only over a horizon varying between two weeks and one and a half months. In the absence of short-term inflation forward instruments,[14] it is not possible to trade a forward price of a linker for a period longer than this horizon. This creates an additional difficulty in implementing views on future prices.

The carry also explains part of the change in the shape of the real-yield curve. An increase in the carry usually lowers the real yield of short maturity linkers and steepens the real-yield curve independently from the nominal-yield curve. This implies a flattening of the BEI curve as the BEI is widening on the short end (see Figure 12).

Case studies

An example of "carry effect" on a French IL bond, the CADESi 2006
Here is an example of opportunities occurring in a price discovery period or when most investors take long-term views focusing less on the factors that impact short-term fluctuations.

The CADESi 2006 is the linker in euros with the shortest maturity. It has been priced as follows:

❑ calculating the real yield of a theoretical OATi 2006 by assuming that the "conventionals" (nominal) spread between the OAT 2006 and OAT 2009 is the same as the linkers spread between the theoretical OATi 2006 and the OATi 2009;

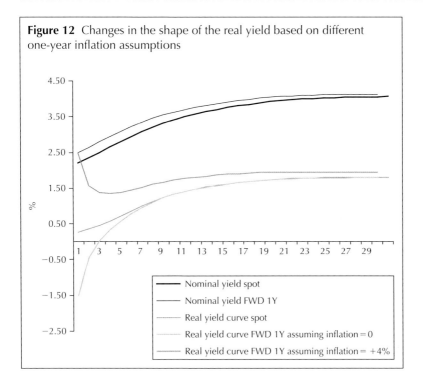

Figure 12 Changes in the shape of the real yield based on different one-year inflation assumptions

- Nominal yield spot
- Nominal yield FWD 1Y
- Real yield curve spot
- Real yield curve FWD 1Y assuming inflation = 0
- Real yield curve FWD 1Y assuming inflation = +4%

❑ adding the credit spread between the CADES and OAT bonds to the theoretical OATi 2006 real yield.

As a result, the spread between the real yields of the CADESi 2006 and the OATi 2009 was stable in spite of the carry fluctuations.

In 2000, the annualised inflation over the second half of the year was at around 2.20%, which is higher than the year-on-year inflation of 1.80%. This increase in the realised inflation should have caused a mechanical 1.5 bps monthly increase of the real-yield spread of the CADESi 2006 relative to the OATi 2009. However, the spread remained stable at ~5 bps. Consequently, a position long €50 million CADESi 2006 and a position short €50 million OATi 2009 made approximately €50,000 per month because the spread did not incorporate the spot inflation fluctuations.

Example of a "surprise" CPI release impact on a French linker, the OATi 2009
As of the 13th April 2005 at 8:44 pm, the last French CPI ex Tobacco published was the February index (110.2), which started accruing

in the OATi 2009 as of the 1st May due to the indexation lag. The March index was about to be released and the economist consensus called for a 0.5% month-on-month rise of the French CPI ex Tobacco (implied March index 110.8).

In an efficient market where all players know consensus prices, spot prices and forward prices should be in equilibrium. In the absence of a forward CPI price we use the economist consensus as a "proxy" measure. Then assuming a position long of OATi 2009 with a clean price of 110 and financed at a collateralised borrowing rate of 2.05%, the price implied by the consensus CPI at the future date of 1st June is 109.05 (positive carry).

As of the 13th April 2005 at 8:45 pm, the March French CPI ex Tobacco index was released at 110.9 with a month-on-month inflation at 0.6%, a higher level than the consensus level. It is very unlikely that this release would have changed the views about future inflation and the forward inflation over the bond life within a minute. Therefore, the release "surprise" should have corrected (1) the spot bond price (keeping the 1st June forward price fixed) or (2) the forward price (keeping the spot price fixed). We observe that the spot price generally absorbs most of the "surprise" effect rather than the forward. In the authors' view, the spot price adjustment is partly justified by the absence of measurable and tradable forward. This was the case as the new spot price went up to 110.15.

If an investor has a view about the level of the next inflation release, how can he benefit from such a carry mechanism?

The OATi 2011 carry is less sensitive to change or a surprise in the latest CPI values than the OATi 2009 carry. Therefore, a position long the OATi 2009 and a position short the OATi 2011 would have benefited from the above scenario. The same idea can also be applied to a BEI position as the carry of a nominal bond is not impacted by CPI release, or to a position *versus* EMU HICP linked bond.

Index calculation methods and carry: "Interpolation"
versus "straight"
In any carry calculation, it is important to take into account the indexation methods. EMU HICP linkers' notional rates are indexed to the Daily Inflation Reference, which is an interpolation between two successive CPIs. Some inflation swaps, such as EMU HICP zero-coupon swaps, use a straight indexation. That means that the index level is

Table 4 Discrepancy in bond and swap BEI levels should occur due to different base convention ("interpolation" *versus* "straight")

	Index at different trading dates		Assumed BEI levels at trading dates	Forward Index at maturity dates		
	3/5/05	31/5/05		3/5/08	31/5/08	15/9/08
Zero coupon Swap 1	115.50		2.09	122.89		
Zero coupon Swap 2		115.50	2.09		122.89	
Linker	115.558		2.16			124.19
		116.37	2.16			124.86

updated on the 1st day of the month and remains unchanged during the month. Table 4 shows the following example as of May 2005. At this time, the published EMU HICO ex Tobacco indices were the February index (115.5) and the March index (116.4).

On May 3rd, the BEI of the BTPSei 2008 was 2.16% and the current three-year zero-coupon swap (swap 1) BEI was 2.09%. From the index (115.5 for the swap 1 and 115.558 for the bond) one could calculate the forward CPI at maturity (122.89 for the swap 1 and 122.89 for the bond).

On May 31st, the index of the new three-year swap (swap 2) is the same as the swap 1 index due to the straight calculation. However, the bond index had accrued linearly for 28 days from 115.56 to 116.37 due to the interpolation. If we assume that the level of the bond BEI has not changed, the forward bond CPI must change to 124.86. If we now assume that the forward bond CPI has not changed then the bond BEI must change to 1.995%. In practice, the bond BEI tends to correct the accrued inflation. Therefore a strategy consisting of a long position of bond BEI and a short position of swap BEI would have captured this differential of accruing inflation. Therefore, the bond BEI should decrease (to 1.995%) to avoid any possible arbitrage.

A similar inflation accruing effect also exists between FR CPI ex Tobacco swaps (interpolation indexation) *versus* EMU HICP ex Tobacco swaps (straight indexation). The BEI spread must correct the difference, even if other factors impact the BEI spreads.

SWAP AND CREDIT SPREAD STRATEGIES

Linkers and inflation swaps have developed in an asymmetrical way. Linkers' issuers, who provided inflation "supply", created the linkers market. The inflation swaps have been driven by a "demand" to receive inflation for hedging purposes (see "Infancy of the derivatives market") as inflation swaps were structured to match a string of liability inflation risks that linkers could not. The lack of inflation payers on the swap market led the swap providers to "recycle" the inflation from linkers into swaps taking the mismatch risk. This contributed to making the price to receive inflation via swap (swap BEI) higher than via bond (bond BEI). New inflation payers in Europe (see "Supply side") have partly helped to remove this distortion in the euro inflation market. Chapter 5 of this book deals with the analysis of these distortions or "paradigm" as the authors call it.

These asymmetries between bonds and swaps do not offer risk free arbitrage opportunities as swap collateral, funding cost or liquidity issues explain some frictions. Consequently, more views about the development of the inflation swap liquidity (see "Supply side") must motivate strategies playing a reduction in distortions between bonds and swaps. This will be detailed in "Asset swap differentials between sovereign inflation-linked and 'conventional' bonds".

An interesting development, particularly in Europe, is the increasing diversity of linkers' issuers. After Greece and Italy, the new corporate issuer, Veolia has moved the linkers into lower credit ratings. The credit linker market is only emerging but it is expected to grow (see "Supply side"). Adding the credit dimension in the calculation of the asset swap spreads requires some analysis. This is the subject of "Asset swapping of credit linkers".

As for many strategies "testing" the border of a new market, an important consideration is their implementation. This is the subject of the case studies.

Asset swap differentials between sovereign inflation-linked and "conventional" bonds

With the growing liquidity of the inflation swaps, linkers' asset swap levels have "commoditised". In general, a linker asset swap level looks as if it is cheaper, ie, higher, than the asset swap level of

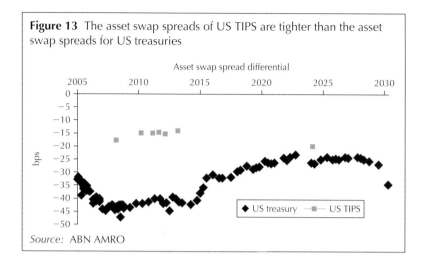

Figure 13 The asset swap spreads of US TIPS are tighter than the asset swap spreads for US treasuries

Asset swap spread differential

Source: ABN AMRO

a similar nominal bond (see Figure 13). This is related to the higher swap BEI compared to the (implied) linker BEI; the present value of a linker's cashflows, which were fixed via an inflation swap, is higher than the price of a comparable nominal bond.

A first reason for this discrepancy is the lack of inflation payers in the derivatives market. To simplify, most of the banks pay inflation in swaps and hedge the risk by receiving inflation from linkers matching the BEI sensitivity. The hedge consists of a long position in a linker (borrowed at the rate, Ri) and a short position in nominal bond (lent at the rate, Rn).

As the inflation swap market is a one-way system, the banks are accumulating these bond positions, being exposed to the higher Ri fluctuations than Rn. This adds costs and limits to the hedge and swap BEI becomes more expensive.

A second reason is that linkers' asset swaps require more collateral. A conventional bond matures at par (100) and, in the nominal interest rate swap, the final notional payment of the fixed leg (mirroring the bond cashflows) is equal to the floating leg; both are worth 100. A linker matures at an inflated notional. If inflation is 2% on average over ten years, a ten-year linker will mature with notional 121.89. This results in a notional mismatch at maturity (the bank receives 121.89 and pays 100). If the swap counterpart defaults before the swap maturity, the bank has a larger exposure for the linker's asset swap than for the nominal bond's asset swap (see Figure 14).

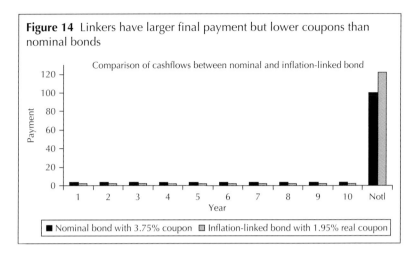

Figure 14 Linkers have larger final payment but lower coupons than nominal bonds

Comparison of cashflows between nominal and inflation-linked bond

Nominal bond with 3.75% coupon   Inflation-linked bond with 1.95% real coupon

Such a risk is usually managed by credit line or collateral agreement. A counterpart, who buys a linker's asset swap, has to place much more collateral, and therefore consume more of its economic capital, to guarantee this notional mismatch. This has been an important obstacle for leveraged funds entering into an asset swapped linkers position.

A third reason is the bid/ask spread on the inflation swap. Swapping the cashflows of a linker requires two swaps:

❑ Inflation Swap (IS) fixing the future inflation cashflows;
❑ Nominal Interest Rates Swap (IRS) where fixed cashflows are swapped into a classic Euribor/Libor floating leg.

Unwinding the global swap requires the payment of the bid/ask spread of the two swaps. As an IS is less liquid than an IRS, the unwinding is more expensive and the linker's asset swap incurs an additional cost (between 2 and 5 bps) compared to unwinding a conventional asset swap. This should decrease as the bid/ask spread of inflation swaps narrows.

Asset swapping of credit linkers

Highly rated sovereign issuers have dominated the linkers' market so far. Therefore, the credit spread of a linker was not really an issue. However, the entrance of new European linker issuers has raised the question. Indeed, there are significant credit differences between some sovereign linkers issuers such as France (Moody's: Aaa,

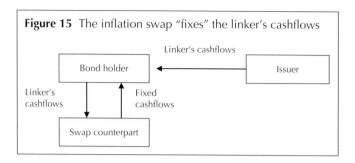

Figure 15 The inflation swap "fixes" the linker's cashflows

S&P: AAA), Italy (Aa2, AA-) and Greece (A1, A). Although they are all sovereign, the subject is now becoming even more important after Veolia (A3, BBB) issued its first linker and other corporate issuers could follow.

Let us take two credit bonds from the same issuer: a conventional bond and a linker. We assume that the two bonds have the same liquidity. Is the credit spread of the linker higher, lower or equal to the conventional bond credit spread?

Even if part of the answer is intuitive, the modelling of linker credit spread can be a complex topic.[15] Here, we do not deal with these modelling issues but give some insight into risk and pricing. An example is given later in "Veolia pricing".

The inflation cashflows are fixed with inflation swaps, so the analysis consists of comparing two fixed-coupon bonds with different cashflows (see Figure 15). This is only possible under certain assumptions:

❑ no correlation between the BEI curve and the credit curve, which is not always observed,[16]
❑ a corporate default risk much higher than the swap counterpart default risk, which is usually the case due to swap collateral agreement.

The previous analysis (see "Asset swap differentials between sovereign inflation-linked and 'conventional' bonds") dealing with "risk-free" linkers is also valid for credit linkers. As the inflation cashflows are fixed with inflation swaps, the inflation-linked and conventional bonds have the same asset swap discrepancy as the "risk-free" bonds.[17] Therefore, in addition to this discrepancy is there a difference of credit risk in the inflation-linked and conventional credit bonds?

Intuitively, the exposure to the issuer default is larger for a linker than for a "conventional" bond; the linker carries a larger final payment and in the case of default the loss would be larger. Therefore, the credit spread should be wider for the linker than for the conventional bond. This will be exacerbated if the default or downgrade risk increases with the maturity (steep credit curve). Moving into the quantification, the choice of the measure of the credit risk is important before drawing any conclusions, as we will see.

A first measure is the z-spread; the cashflows discounted on the zero-coupon swap curve plus this z-spread is equal to the bond dirty price. An approximation for the z-spread when the bond is priced at par is

$$z\text{-}spread = [PV^{SWAP} - PV^{CREDIT}]/[D_{MOD}^{SWAP} \times PV^{SWAP}] \qquad (1)$$

where PV^{SWAP} (respectively, PV^{CREDIT}) is the present value of the bond cashflows discounted by the swap yields (respectively, by the credit yields), and D_{MOD}^{SWAP} is the modified duration, namely the time-weighted average of the cashflows discounted by the swap yields.

A second measure is the "par–par" Asset Swap Spread (ASW); the bond cashflows are swapped into Euribor plus the ASW, an upfront payment corrects the deviation of the bond price from par. From Equation (1) it is possible to derive a similar relationship between the z-spread and the asset swap spread:

$$ASW = [PV^{SWAP} - PV^{CREDIT}]/[N \times sum(DF^{SWAP})], \text{ which is equal to}$$
$$ASW = [z\text{-}spread \times D_{MOD}^{SWAP} \times PV^{SWAP}]/[N \times sum(DF^{SWAP})] \qquad (2)$$

where N is the bond and swap notional, and $sum(DF^{SWAP})$ is the sum of the discount factors derived from the swap curve.

If there is no credit risk, then $[PV^{SWAP} - PV^{CREDIT}] = 0$ and $z\text{-}spread = ASW = 0$ for both the nominal bond and the linker.

To gain an insight into these relationships it is useful to investigate how asset swaps and z-spreads change (ΔASW and ΔZ) for a given move in credit, swap or BEI curves (respectively ΔC, ΔS and ΔBEI). An approximation of the change in the bond cashflows present value due to change in swap and credit curves is:

$$\Delta PV = -(\Delta S + \Delta C) \times D_{MOD}^{CRED} + 0.5 \times (\Delta S + \Delta C)^2 \times Convexity \qquad (3)$$

Using these relationships together with the knowledge that both duration and convexity are greater for linkers (because of the low coupons and large final payment) we analyse shocks on the credit curve, BEI curve, and nominal curves.

Change in the credit curve
Let us analyse the bond price change due to a move in the credit curve only ($\Delta S = \Delta BEI = 0$). Differentiating Equation (1) for ΔC and using Equation (3) places a duration term in both the denominator and the numerator of the change in z-spread (ΔZ). This would cancel out for a parallel shift; z-spread changes for the nominal bond and the linker would nearly be the same.

If the curve steepens, the convexity adjustment would not be offset; this would result in a second-order increase in z-spreads relative to a nominal bond.

The situation changes for asset swaps. The duration term is no longer cancelled out and this will result in a higher increase in the linker's ASW compared to the nominal bond's ASW, ie, a larger discrepancy due to the increase in duration.

Change in BEI curve
A positive move in the BEI curve only ($\Delta S = \Delta C = 0$) increases the duration of a credit linker (as future cashflows will be higher with higher BEI). However, this increase in duration is again mostly offset by other duration terms, therefore the z-spread is again fairly insensitive to changes in parallel shift. However, the asset swap differential is dramatic; as BEI increases, both the duration and the present value increase for the credit linker, creating a large discrepancy between nominal bonds and linkers.

Change in swap curve
As in the change in the credit curve, the z-spreads are fairly insensitive to changes in the swap curve ($\Delta C = \Delta BEI = 0$) due to duration elements offsetting each other. However, under this scenario, the asset swaps differential is also small; an increase in swap yield decreases the duration and price of both linkers and nominal bonds, and this move is offset by the swap discount factors in the denominator (see Table 5).

Table 5 How shifts in level/slope of the credit, inflation and swap curves impact the z-spreads and ASW levels. " − −"means an important decrease, "−" a decrease, "=" no change, "+" an increase, "++" a high increase, ↑ is a positive parallel shift and ↗ is a positive tilt of the yield curves

Difference of linker v. nominal	CREDIT		INFLATION[1]		SWAP[2]	
	↑	↗	↑	↗	↑	↗
PV^{SWAP}	=	=	+	++	−	−
PV^{CREDIT}	−	−	+	++	−	−
D_{MOD}^{SWAP}	=	=	+	++	++	++
$sum(DF^{SWAP})$	=	=	=	=	−	−
z-spread	=	+	=	=	=	+
ASW	+	++	++	++	−	−

[1]A shift on the break even inflation curve does not change the swap curve
[2]A shift in the swap curves maintains the current credit spread

To summarise, with a positively sloped credit or BEI curve, linkers will have higher asset swap spread than a nominal bond with the same maturity. Intuitively this is logical as the heavy weight of the inflation accumulation at the maturity date results in a longer duration of the linker.

CASE STUDIES
Playing the swap BEI versus the BEI implied by the US linker, TIPS 2013
At the beginning of the inflation derivatives market, the linkers' asset swap could not be directly traded. A proxy for the asset swap was: (1) to purchase a linker; (2) pay fixed coupons in a plain vanilla interest rate swap; and (3) hedge only the final linker inflation payment with a plain vanilla zero-coupon inflation swap.

Which transactions could be carried out?

❑ Buy TIPS 1.875% July 2013 at a clean price of 101–8+ or a real yield of 1.706%; the purchase amounts to 107.797.
❑ Finance the purchase of the TIPS with a collateralised loan at Libor −12 bps.
❑ Pay plain vanilla swap of 4.431% and receive Libor flat (same maturity as TIPS).

❑ Pay inflation in zero-coupon BEI swap *versus* receiving fixed of 2.61% (same maturity as TIPS).

How to measure the "richness" or "cheapness" of the TIPS? The idea is to compare the yield differences (yield/yield), z-spread and asset swap spread (ASW) of the TIPS *versus* a similar conventional Treasury Note. The first step is to "fix" the inflation cashflows at the forward CPI levels (implied by the zero-coupon swap). The second step is to calculate the z-spread and ASW as for conventional fixed-coupon bonds.

In Table 6, the sub-table "BOND" (columns 1–5) shows the TIPS cashflows. First the seasonally adjusted forward CPI index is extracted from the term structure of the inflation zero-coupon swap at each coupon date (column 2 "Ref index"). Then the expected coupons and redemption price of the bond can be calculated (column 4 "CF with inflation"). The nominal yield of the TIPS (now fixed) cashflows can be compared to the nominal IRS yield. The implied nominal yield of the TIPS fixed cashflows is 4.32%; the "yield/yield" becomes −0.111%.

We also compute the "z-spread" of the bond by calculating the Net Present Value (NPV) of the inflation cashflows (column 4) using the swap discount factors (columns 12 "DF" and 13 "Bond flows x DF"). The implied yield is 4.297% implying a z-spread of −0.134%.

The asset swap spread is calculated as the margin below the Libor forward yields that makes the bond cashflow NPV and the Libor NPV equal. The asset swap spread was close to the z-spread.

Note that the intermediate cashflows are capitalised at the swap rate (column 5 "funding of CF"). The "Notional gap" (column 8) is the difference between the all-in price of the bond (the bond price minus its funding cost) and the IRS nominal; this gap is also funded at the swap rate (column 9 "Funding of the gap").

The yield/yield spread, z-spread and ASW indicated that bonds are "cheap" compared to the conventional Treasury notes with similar maturity.

How to implement the position? A first issue is how to hedge the future inflation path. In theory we could hedge all the cashflows with as many swaps as there are coupon dates. In practice, the zero-coupon swaps may not be tradable for all cashflows dates (in particular, for the short maturity). Moreover, the main inflation risk

Table 6 Cashflows of the position (1) long TIPS 1.875% July 2013 (the "BOND" section); (2) payer fixed coupons in a plain vanilla swap ("NOMINAL SWAP" section); and (3) payer of inflation and receiver of the fixed in a zero-coupon inflation swap ("BEI SWAP" section)

Date	BOND					NOMINAL SWAP				BEI SWAP		DF	Bond flows x DF
	Real Cash flows	Ref index	Index ratio	CF with inflation	Funding of CF	IRS flows	Funding of CF	Notional gap	Funding of the gap	Fixed leg IL swap	Floating leg IL swap		
	1	2	3	4	5	6	7	8	9	10	11	12	13
15/07/2005	0.9375	193.90	1.056	0.990	0.398	−0.110	−0.044	0.008	0.003			0.999	0.989
15/01/2006	0.9375	196.42	1.069	1.003	0.373	−2.252	−0.936	0.190	0.071			0.980	0.983
15/07/2006	0.9375	198.96	1.083	1.016	0.349	−2.512	−0.864	0.187	0.064			0.961	0.976
15/01/2007	0.9375	201.54	1.097	1.029	0.325	−2.512	−0.793	0.190	0.060			0.941	0.968
15/07/2007	0.9375	204.16	1.112	1.042	0.301	−2.512	−0.725	0.187	0.054			0.921	0.959
15/01/2008	0.9375	206.80	1.126	1.056	0.276	−2.512	−0.657	0.190	0.050			0.901	0.951
15/07/2008	0.9375	209.49	1.141	1.069	0.251	−2.512	−0.591	0.188	0.044			0.882	0.943
15/01/2009	0.9375	212.20	1.155	1.083	0.226	−2.512	−0.525	0.190	0.040			0.863	0.934
15/07/2009	0.9375	214.95	1.170	1.097	0.202	−2.512	−0.462	0.187	0.034			0.844	0.926
15/01/2010	0.9375	217.74	1.186	1.111	0.177	−2.512	−0.400	0.190	0.030			0.825	0.917
15/07/2010	0.9375	220.56	1.201	1.126	0.152	−2.512	−0.339	0.187	0.025			0.807	0.909
15/01/2011	0.9375	223.42	1.216	1.140	0.127	−2.512	−0.279	0.190	0.021			0.789	0.899
15/07/2011	0.9375	226.32	1.232	1.155	0.102	−2.512	−0.222	0.187	0.017			0.771	0.890
15/01/2012	0.9375	229.25	1.248	1.170	0.076	−2.512	−0.164	0.190	0.012			0.753	0.881
15/07/2012	0.9375	232.23	1.264	1.185	0.051	−2.512	−0.108	0.188	0.008			0.736	0.872
15/01/2013	0.9375	235.24	1.281	1.201	0.025	−2.512	−0.053	0.190	0.004			0.719	0.863
15/07/2013	100.9375	238.29	1.297	130.958	0.000	−2.512	0.000	0.187	0.000	27.1198	−27.1198	0.702	91.895

Source: CIAL

is concentrated in the last cashflow. Therefore, it seems intuitive that one zero-coupon inflation swap corresponding to the last cash-flow date would accurately hedge the inflation risk.

What should the notional size of the IRS be? The position is based on a quantity of 100 of the TIPS. Having fixed the TIPS cashflows it is possible to calculate the duration or better the dollar value of a deviation by 1 basis point of the discount nominal-yield curve (DV01). Therefore, the swap notional is calculated to immunise the position against any parallel shift of the nominal-swap yield curve (duration neutral). In the example, the nominal-swap notional is 116.52.

What should the notional size for the zero-coupon inflation swap be? The inflation exposures are in the TIPS BEI position (TIPS and nomi-nal swap) and in the swap BEI (zero-coupon inflation swap). As we focus only on the final inflation cashflow of the bond, which is floored at 0%, the TIPS "final" BEI profile is not linear (see Figure 16).

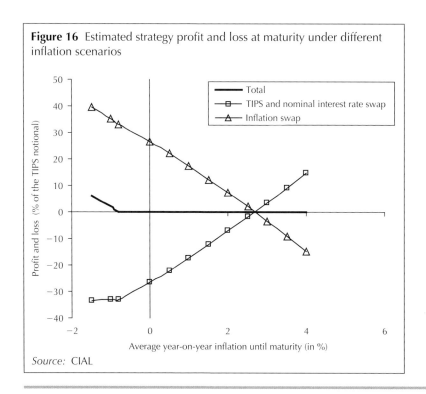

Figure 16 Estimated strategy profit and loss at maturity under different inflation scenarios

Source: CIAL

If the year-on-year inflation is lower than -0.8% on average over the bond life, the floor is in the money. Therefore, the zero-coupon notional is seized to match the TIPS "final" BEI profile. In particular, as long as the year-on-year inflation is above the TIPS floor level, then the zero-coupon inflation swap profit (or loss) offsets the TIPS BEI loss (or profit). In the example the inflation swap notional is 118.

"Carry" revenues of the strategy. An important consideration for such a strategy with limited liquidity is the revenues or losses if the strategy is held to maturity. Under the above assumptions (in particular a 2.61% average year-on-year inflation over the period), the position would have a yearly carry of 0.15%. This is the sum of the net carry of each instrument plus the difference between the redemption price of the bond and the dirty price. Here are the details calculated from Table 6:

❏ the bond's carry is $+20.89$ basis points, which is calculated from the sum of column 4 and 5 from 15th July 2005 until 15th January 2013;
❏ the nominal swap's carry is -43.90 bps, which is calculated from 15th July 2005 until 15th July 2013;
❏ IL swap's carry is 0.00 bps, which is calculated from the sum of column 10 and 11 from Table 6;
❏ notional exchanges $+23.16$ calculated from the repayment of loan 107.797 and receiving 130.958 at maturity.

Other risks. The strategy is mainly hedged against parallel shifts of the BEI and swap curves. However, non-parallel shifts of the curves would impact the return positions. This risk is acceptable for the nominal swap curves, as the main moves are parallel shifts. The inflation risk may be similar but the lack of historical data makes BEI curve change analysis techniques (eg, Principal Component Analysis[18]) not robust.

An important risk is also the spread between the treasury yield and the nominal IRS yield. The under-performance of Treasury notes relative to swaps would reduce the strategy mark-to-market. An alternative to the IRS would be to "short" a Treasury note, preferably an old "off-the run" note to avoid too large a discrepancy between the TIPS and Treasury note repo rates.

Veolia pricing

Veolia Environnement, a French utility company, issued a ten-year corporate linker in June 2005. The bond is linked to the EMU HICP ex Tobacco and has the standard multiplicative structure of the sovereign linkers. At the time of issuance the market had to derive a fair value for this bond. We illustrate an approach for the preliminary analysis for the bond pricing based on the results of our section on "Asset swapping of credit linkers". To simplify, we did not deal with "liquidity premium" due to the potential lower liquidity of the linker compared to the nominal bonds or "innovation premium".

The first step is to build a credit curve. Veolia has several nominal bonds in the market (2008, 2012, 2013 and 2018) making it possible to bootstrap a credit curve from the asset swap levels.[19] Looking at Figure 17, the bootstrapped credit spread is gently widening as maturity increases – this is as expected, the market prices larger annualised default/downgrading probabilities with growing maturity due to the additional risk that the investor takes.

Given the bootstrapped credit curve, swap curve and BEI curve it is possible to calculate a fair pricing for a credit linker.

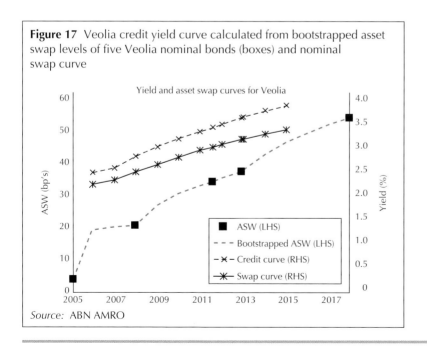

Figure 17 Veolia credit yield curve calculated from bootstrapped asset swap levels of five Veolia nominal bonds (boxes) and nominal swap curve

Source: ABN AMRO

From the bootstrapped credit curve we calculate that a nominal 2015 would asset swap at 43 bps, which is in line with the 2013 and 2018 nominal bond (asset swaps are at 36 and 52 bps respectively). From the analysis in our section on "Asset swapping of credit linkers", the asset swap spread difference between the nominal bond and the linker comes mainly from their duration difference. Linker duration is around 9% higher which will increase the asset swap to 48 bps. Table 7 provides the sensitivity analysis explained in our section on asset swapping of credit linkers.

Importantly, the above calculations assume no correlation between inflation and default probabilities. If there is a negative correlation then an investor is more exposed in a low-inflation environment, which adds a convexity adjustment to the BEIs.[20] In this case, simple bond pricing no longer works for calculating the real coupons and swap spreads. If an investor buys the corporate linker hedged with an inflation swap (pay inflation and receive fixed), the consequence due to the convexity is that the investor needs to dynamically hedge this position. With low inflation and BEI levels, the return of the inflation swap will be positive but the default probability has also increased. Therefore, the convexity adjustment is in favour of this position.

Note that such convexity adjustments are classic in interest rate modelling and are derived directly from the choice of model. As no standard model exists for inflation, the adjustment would differ (see Chapters 5 and 6 of this book).

"ALTERNATIVE" CROSS-INDEX STRATEGIES

Cross-index strategies refer to strategies playing the difference of return between two inflation products linked to different indices. Several factors can explain these differences such as different seasonal patterns, different sensitivity to shocks, currency effects and different macro-economic factors. Chapter 1 of this book deals with such strategies.

In this section we would like to focus on products linked to "non-conventional indices", meaning indices that are not available in the sovereign liquid linkers market. European country inflation indices offer a panel of such indices. As previously mentioned,

Table 7 Coupon (CPN), z-spread and asset swap spread (ASW) of theoretical 2015 nominal and inflation-linked bonds calculated from credit and BEI market curves (spot curves) and from these curves shocked (parallel shift and rotation). Note that the z-spread is only sensitive to credit curve rotation whereas the asset swap spread is sensitive to moves in credit or BEI curves

	NOMINAL (1)			INFLATION (2)			(1)–(2)		
	CPN (%)	z-spread (%)	ASW (%)	CPN (%)	z-spread (%)	ASW (%)	CPN (%)	z-spread (%)	ASW (%)
spot curves	3.74	0.44	0.43	1.71	0.45	0.48	2.03	−0.01	−0.05
+100bp credit shift	4.74	1.46	1.43	2.69	1.47	1.58	2.05	−0.01	−0.15
+100bp credit tilt	4.74	1.43	1.46	2.73	1.51	1.62	2.01	−0.08	−0.16
+100bp BEI shift	3.74	0.44	0.43	0.74	0.46	0.51	3.00	−0.02	−0.08

Infrastrutture issued a €775 million 15-year note linked to Italian CPI and Great Belt issued a €665 million 15-year note linked to Danish CPI.

These products can offer some investment opportunities or risks in the sense that there is (currently) no pricing convention, their liquidity is generally improving and they are a way for a bank's structuring book to offload their risk, which has a price. Therefore, investing in such products requires an understanding of the flows behind these products and the need to have a view about the development of the flows behind these products (see " 'Non-conventional' inflation index flows") and their pricing (see "Considerations for pricing forward country indices"). Some case studies are also presented.

"Non-conventional" inflation index flows
Interestingly, we observe an increase in the range of inflation indices that can be traded. The derivatives and the structured note markets offer a much wider range of indices than the benchmark bonds. Some structured notes have been linked to Italian, Danish or Spanish inflation indices. The trend for more index diversification and for a growth of these markets should remain for the following reasons.

Regular inflation payers with incentives to pay domestic inflation
Most of the non-sovereign inflation payers have revenues explicitly or implicitly linked to domestic inflation, coming through project finance, tax revenues or real estate rents, making them exposed to a unique domestic index they want to hedge. This is driven by new accounting rules or rating agency guidelines, which encourage direct matching (see "Supply side").

Growing demand from Asset-Liability Managers (ALM) and sophisticated investors
The demand has been from the retail market in Italy and Switzerland, where banks have issued retail notes linked to the domestic inflation. This is a volatile demand and alone is insufficient to drive a market. However, a more stable demand comes from: (1) asset and liability management driven investors exposed to specific inflation index variation; and (2) sophisticated investors (see "Demand side").

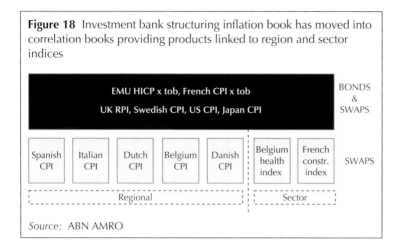

Figure 18 Investment bank structuring inflation book has moved into correlation books providing products linked to region and sector indices

Source: ABN AMRO

Improved risk management providing flexibility to manage correlation risk

The investment banks have increasingly been dealing with domestic inflation. In the structuring books that initially integrated bonds and swaps for "liquid" indices, a segment of "non-conventional" indices have usually been added (see Figure 18). Part of the risk of "non-conventional" indices cashflows can be hedged with "liquid" indices products or other financial products. However, the remaining risk cannot be hedged unless it is offloaded. In order to absorb the irregular flows linked to these indices and their increasing variety, this remaining risk is usually managed globally as a correlation book (eg, using a Value at Risk framework). As a way of managing this risk, investment banks have been offering some products linked to domestic indices to the specialised investors (see "Growing demand from asset-liability managers and sophisticated investors").

Considerations for pricing forward country indices

Pricing inflation products requires a forward index curve. In the case of "non-conventional" indices these curves are very fragmented or even do not exist. However, the connection between "non-conventional" to "liquid" indices, historical inflation analysis and certain macro-economic theories help to take a view on pricing these curves.

To complete the analysis, it is important to analyse specific issues or risks for example:

❑ do macro-economic factors or shocks (such as oil price shock) affect all domestic inflations equally?
❑ how can single domestic shock (such as VAT change) be handled?
❑ how do new accession countries affect the pricing?

This section will describe an approach (among many available) to build an EMU country CPI curve. The purpose is more to give an intuitive approach rather than discussing the mathematical coherence of the model (see Chapter 6 of this book).

The convergence assumptions of EMU countries future inflation levels

As seen in the previous sections, products linked to EMU country indices have a strong potential to develop further. Some country inflations are already quoted[21] and the EMU HICP curve is liquid. Moreover, the EMU HICP is a weighted average of EMU countries HICPs. Historical country CPI data and macro-economic theory about the inflation evolution also gives information. This provides guidance to shape the "non-quoted" EMU country HICP curves.

A possible approach could be based on the idea of inflation convergence within the EMU countries. As the countries within the EMU are open and closely related to each other, it is reasonable to assume that the prices in each country, and eventually inflation, will converge with time. They may not converge exactly (in fact this is highly unlikely), but dispersion of long-term average inflation rates should converge. Indeed, there is no reason to assume that a single country should experience a long and sustained divergence.[22] The "productivity hypothesis" of Balassa (1964) and Samuelson (1964) confirms these assumptions; it suggests that increasing productivity in the tradable sector creates inflationary pressure through the non-traded or service sector. However, open and closely related economies will create convergence in productivity (due to open markets of goods, services and employees) that will drive inflation convergence in the long run.[23]

This convergence assumption can also be argued. Firstly, the productivity theory of Balassa and Samuelson might fit better to very wide inflation differentials than to countries that have already converged to some extent. Secondly, the structural rigidities in the European economies dampen the convergence. Thirdly, as all EMU

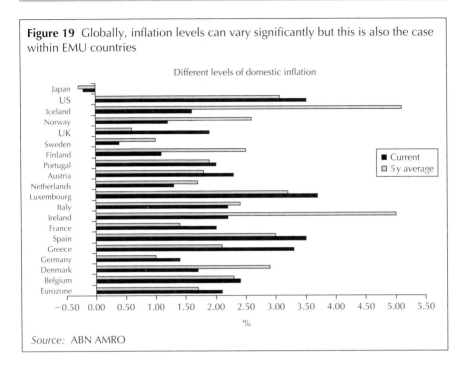

Figure 19 Globally, inflation levels can vary significantly but this is also the case within EMU countries

Source: ABN AMRO

countries have the same nominal interest rate, they do not have the same real interest rate due to the inflation differentials (Figure 19). This results in a monetary policy that is too loose for high inflation countries and too tight for low inflation countries.

Modelling the inflation levels convergence

As the EMU HICP curve is liquid, it is intuitive to model the inflation spread between an EMU domestic inflation and the EMU average inflation. Existing forward inflation spreads present a certain mean-reverse pattern (in particular, French CPI *versus* the EMU HICP). For example, the spreads could be modeled as a stochastic process: $ds = sadt + \sigma(s)dW$ where s is the spread differential, $\sigma(s)$ the volatilities and correlations of the spreads, dW a Brownian and a the convergence speed. The whole domestic inflation curve can be built as illustrated in Figure 20.

Without any market data for domestic inflation and therefore for the spread, the model could be calibrated with historical inflation spreads or to the productivity differential to remain within the

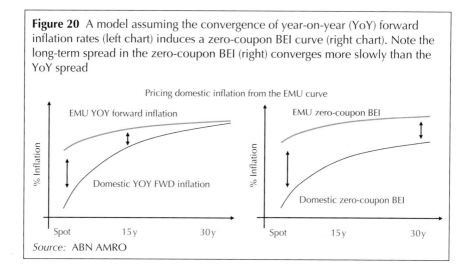

Figure 20 A model assuming the convergence of year-on-year (YoY) forward inflation rates (left chart) induces a zero-coupon BEI curve (right chart). Note the long-term spread in the zero-coupon BEI (right) converges more slowly than the YoY spread

Pricing domestic inflation from the EMU curve

EMU YOY forward inflation

Domestic YOY FWD inflation

% Inflation

Spot   15y   30y

EMU zero-coupon BEI

Domestic zero-coupon BEI

% Inflation

Spot   15y   30y

Source: ABN AMRO

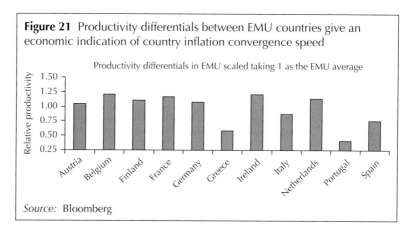

Figure 21 Productivity differentials between EMU countries give an economic indication of country inflation convergence speed

Productivity differentials in EMU scaled taking 1 as the EMU average

Relative productivity

1.50
1.25
1.00
0.75
0.50
0.25

Austria Belgium Finland France Germany Greece Ireland Italy Netherlands Portugal Spain

Source: Bloomberg

Balassa–Samuelson approach. In the authors' experience, historical calibration creates high convergence speed and does not fit to the available market data for existing curves (particularly French and EMU inflation spread). When calibrating to the productivity differential one needs to relate it to the convergence speed. The productivity differential is measured as the ratio between the GDP volume and number of employed persons. This ratio is very different between countries as Figure 21 shows, where a Relative Productivity above one has a higher productivity than the EMU average and should have a higher convergence speed, ie, higher a.

Furthermore, an additional constraint exists that the EMU infla-tion index is a weighted average of the domestic inflation rates. Using this constraint with the assumption that the weights are constant, it is possible to fit forward CPI curve for all the domestic EMU inflations.

Of course, taking the convergence view and incorporating historical information is one approach. This, however, makes many arguable assumptions. For example, the weights of domestic inflation in the EMU inflation are assumed constant with time. The single biggest risk here is the UK, as it would proportionally reduce the other countries' weights significantly and impact the EMU inflation negatively compared to the Central and Eastern European countries that will affect it positively.

Other issues to be considered

The previous approach can help to define a view on forward "non-quoted" CPI, which is coherent with market and historical infor-mation. Investing in products linked to such indices would also require other analysis as described below.

Global economic shocks. Global inflation shock affects domestic inflation to different degrees. Countries have different consump-tion behaviour and have different sensitivities to global activities. Probably the most important global shock is through commodities and currency, especially oil price expressed in Euros. Pass through effects for countries depend on their imports; for example, Belgium, Ireland and the Netherlands are more open outside the Euro zone than other countries, as Figure 22 shows. The effect of global inflation shock can be split into two factors:

❏ The first effect is simply the transmission of the price increase into the CPI and is a one-off effect.
❏ The secondary effects are more complicated as the first effect can feed into other parts of the CPI.[24] It is likely that, in the long run, global inflation shocks should not have a major impact on the convergence level and convergence speed but rather add some volatility on the inflation spreads. This opens the possibility for the linker fund manager to target inflation products from countries with different sensitivity to commodities or currencies. For

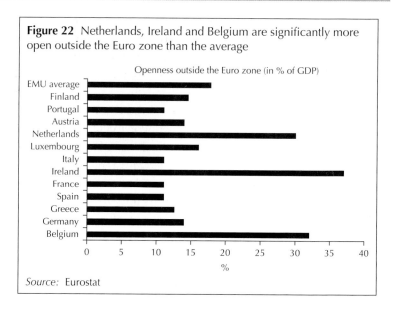

Figure 22 Netherlands, Ireland and Belgium are significantly more open outside the Euro zone than the average

Openness outside the Euro zone (in % of GDP)

Source: Eurostat

example, to buy linkers from oil price sensitive countries when the oil price is rising and reverse when the oil price is decreasing.[25]

Fiscal policy. Each country has its own fiscal policy. Examples include the reduction of alcohol tax in Finland and Denmark in 2003, the scrapping of TV licensing in Belgium in 2002 and tax increases in the Netherlands in 2001. This obviously disconnects the domestic inflation from the EMU inflation and creates some risk. However, importantly these are one-off effects and unlikely to be sustained in one country for a long time in the same direction.

Case studies
Example of high inflation analysis
Some recently issued structured notes were linked to inflation higher than the EMU inflation (eg, Spanish inflation). We have in the previous sections discussed how to split and assess real yield, credit and inflation components of linkers. Here we will focus on comparing two bonds from the same issuer but linked to different inflations.

A ten-year EMU inflation-linked bond is priced at 2.1% BEI and 1.45% real yield implying a nominal yield of 3.55%. The second ten-year bond from the same issuer is linked to Spanish inflation with a real yield of 0.75%. It is not intuitive to compare the two real yields. As the nominal yield is the same for any EMU countries it is possible to calculate the Spanish BEI, which for the Spanish bond is 3.55% − 0.75% = 2.80% BEI. In this case, Spanish inflation should run at 2.80% or 0.70% higher than the EMU inflation until the maturity of the bond to make the total return of the two bonds equal.

This simple approach summarises the investment decision in the view of forward Spanish inflation *versus* EMU inflation. For example, the following view would provide incentives to invest in the Spanish inflation-linked bond; from an historical angle Spain has had persistently high levels of inflation well above 3% and its low relative productivity would suggest this is likely to continue. Obviously, additional parameters such as liquidity and carry etc must also be considered.

Analysing Danish inflation price spread

Recently, Danish inflation-linked products have attracted some specialised investors. The way to analyse their price has been similar to the previous example, even though Denmark is not part of the EMU. This is due to the close integration of the Danish economy to the EMU (due to a pegged monetary policy and controlled currency rate).

Figure 23 shows the frequency of the historical spread. Comparing the Danish and the EMU BEIs' spread *versus* historical inflation spread helps the investment decision. However, the

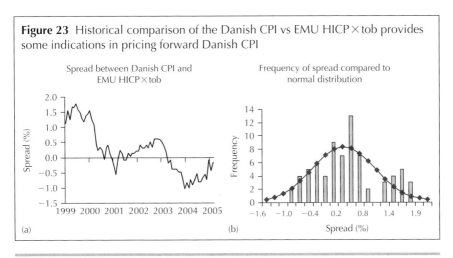

Figure 23 Historical comparison of the Danish CPI vs EMU HICP × tob provides some indications in pricing forward Danish CPI

spread must be further analysed as some one-off tax shocks have occurred in recent years.

CONCLUDING REMARKS

Historically, the inflation market has moved from a limited collection of domestic linkers markets into a richer and global market. An important result is the improving market efficiency, meaning that regulatory or supply/demand shocks are less likely to drive the prices of liquid linkers. Information about such events is generally asymmetric and therefore investors have perceived such shocks as adding risks. As a consequence, strategies based on the growing universe of liquid linkers have developed from "classic" fixed income strategies into more complex strategies. Some involve other asset classes such as commodity instruments or cross-index strategies. Others are based on "carry" analysis, which is particularly important because of the absence of measurable short-term forward inflation.

Around the "benchmark" linkers are also developing new market segments, which are generally prompted by the need to hedge specific inflation-linked assets or liabilities. Investment banks have structured hedging instruments, but the banks themselves can only hedge them partially. The accumulation of the resulting residual positions has created specific price "distortions" attracting the interest of hedge funds and sophisticated inflation investors. An example is the development of the inflation swaps market, which has been driven by the demand to receive inflation for hedging pension funds' inflation-linked liabilities. The lack of derivatives inflation payers compared to the comparatively large number of payers in the cash market created a differential of forward inflation index implied by linkers and swaps. Other similar particularities are also emerging in the developing segments that are related to the credit linkers and to products referenced to "non-conventional" indices. Trading strategies try to benefit from such anomalies and bet on the flows in these segments, eventually becoming more balanced.

A last word is how inflation strategies interact within a portfolio. In general they add significant diversification benefits when mixed with other fixed income or equity asset classes. We also experienced that the combination of different "inflation" investment strategies are also fairly de-correlated. Diverse inflation investment strategies generally improve more the portfolio risk-adjusted return than diverse products. A linker asset strategy (view on derivatives flow) a carry strategy (view on short-term inflation), and a cross-index trade with non-conventional index (view on pricing and on development of asset/liability driven demand) have, in general, a low return correlation to each other.

ACKNOWLEDGEMENTS

We would like to thank David Bieber, Hervé Cros, Teddy Dewitte, Benédicte Guerin-Cribier, Luca Jellinek and Tarik Senhaji and all anonymous reviewers for their input or precious comments, which have allowed us to improve this chapter.

1 The nominal yield can be viewed as a combination of: (1) a real yield; (2) an "illiquidity" premium; and (3) a break-even inflation (BEI). The BEI is usually split into inflation expectations and a risk premium (see Chapter 1 of this book).

2 The Italian Post issued a note linked to equity and inflation in 2001.

3 The LPI is a RPI where yearly variations are floored at 0% and capped at 5% or 2.5%.

4 An annuity structure would pay every year $N \times CPI_t/CPI_0$, where N is a fixed amount, CPI_t is the CPI value at the payment date and CPI_0 is the CPI value as of the starting date.

5 PFIs are a way for government to finance the constructions of public sector facilities. See, for example, HM Treasury (2003).

6 Association des Marchés de Taux en Euro or the Euro Debt Market Association.

7 Capital gains taxes have a higher rate than taxes on coupon or interest rates.

8 Comisión Nacional del Mercado de Valores.

9 A full analysis of the inflation risk for pension funds is out of the scope of this chapter but is covered in the next chapter of this book.

10 The EuroMTS Inflation-linked Index.

11 To simplify matters, we did not specify any lag; for more details see Chapters 5 and 6. Therefore, we would note that CPI_t is the latest CPI known at date t.

12 $E(\cdot)$ is the expected value under the risk-neutral probability.

13 When a bond is financed by a collateralised loan, the carry is the difference between the income of the bond (coupon and inflation) and the cost of the loan. If the carry is positive, the bond price should decrease to offset the excess income in order to avoid arbitrage opportunities. That is why the carry is often expressed in term of the difference between the forward yield (at the maturity of the loan) and the current yield.

14 The inflation swap market maturity starts at two years and has limited liquidity for short maturity. Futures exist for US CPI and EMU HICP but liquidity is currently poor.

15 The authors are not aware of any public research papers dealing with the subject, but some proprietary model exits. An interesting approach is based on the similarity with the "vanishing swaps" that are swaps cancellable in case of specific credit events.

16 An important implication is that the inflation risk must be dynamically hedged as, for example, the risk of higher default (wider credit spread) may occur while BEI levels are wider in case of positive correlation. This is detailed in Chapter 5 of this book.

17 One of the reasons for this discrepancy is the difference in credit risk in the inflation swap legs. Even if the credit risk analysis is similar, the swap credit risk and the bonds credit risk are two dissociated risks.

18 We suspect that the rotation of the BEI curve may explain a larger part of the curve variation than for the nominal curve due to the carry effect detailed in our section on *"Forward Strategies"*.

19 As Credit Default Swap (CDS) trade on the Veolia name, it could have been possible to use a CDS curve and CDS to hedge the credit risk. However, the "basis" between the CDS levels and the asset swap levels is positive and large. This makes the CDS expensive and a Veolia position with which the credit risk is hedged with CDS, expensive to carry.

20 A simple economic interpretation is that in low-inflation environments the economy is not performing too well resulting in companies having lower revenues but fixed costs place more stress onto the balance sheet.

21 ZC BEI swap curves are quoted for Italy, Spain and France.

22 For more information on inflation differentials in the EMU area see paper by European Central Bank (2003).

23 This can be referred to as the "catch-up" effects or "theory of convergence", which states that poorer economies tend to grow faster than richer economies. This results in a country with low prices having price adjustments to match prices in the rest of the EMU but that means a higher inflation in the meantime.

24 It is not the intention here to go into economist modelling of the inflation, but a simple version is that as prices increase and inflation expectations pick up then workers ask for wage increases that corporates will need to transmit into their pricing, ending in a vicious circle.

25 A good example here is lower dependence of France on oil prices than rest of the EMU countries.

REFERENCES

ABN AMRO, April 2004, "Mastering Inflation Products".

AMTE, 2005, "Inflation-Linked Products in the Euro Area: An AMTE Working Group to Standardise, Develop and Promote the Asset Class".

Balassa, B., 1964, "The Purchasing Power Parity Doctrine: A Reappraisal", *Journal of Political Economy*, **72**, December, pp 584–596.

European Central Bank, 2003, "Inflation Differentials in the Euro Area: Potential Causes and Policy Implications".

HM Treasury, July 2003, "PFI: Meeting the Investment Challenge".

Nasse, P. and C. Noyer, 2003, "Rapport sur L'équilibre des Fonds D'épargne".

Roll, R., 2004, "Empirical TIPS", *Financial Analysts Journal*, **60(1)**.

Samuelson, P., 1964, "Theoretical Notes on Trade Problems", *Review of Economics and Statistics*, **46**, pp 145–154.

4

Special Aspects of Japanese Inflation-Linked Bonds

Hidesaka Taki

BNPP

INTRODUCTION

Japan began issuing inflation-linked government bonds (JGBis) in March of 2004, in part because of the major success since 2000 of inflation-linked bonds (ILBs) globally, particularly in France and the United States. By June 2005, Japan's Ministry of Finance (MoF) had issued four JGBis totalling ¥1.4 trillion. The share of the JGBis in the world ILB market reached approximately 2.0%. We estimate that its share will rise to 7.5% by 2008, if issuance proceeds smoothly. Japan will soon be one of the largest sovereign issuers, not only of nominal bonds, but also of ILBs.

ILBs will be attractive tools for Japanese investors who have strong needs to hedge their huge nominal bond portfolio against higher interest rates. Their main concern is the potential risk of decline of their bond portfolio, after an inevitable end to the Bank of Japan's (BoJ's) monetary easing. ILBs add diversity to a portfolio composed of traditional asset classes. In the future, ILBs will meet huge demand from an asset liability management point of view.

The change in taxation rules made the purchase of JGBis feasible by overseas tax-exempt entities from April 2005. Foreign investor interest is also rising because the JGBi was added to the global ILB index in May 2005. For foreign investors, Japanese ILBs offer various trading opportunities. Relative value to TIPS (US inflation-linked government bonds) or EUR linkers will be the key.

The basic product design of a JGBi is the same as that of the ILBs first introduced in Europe and the United States, but JGBis also possess their own unique characteristics that derive from Japan's different economic situation and issuing customs. One of the unique characteristics is the MoF's issuance policy. Redemptions of JGBis occur in March, June, September and December, resulting in clear differences of valuation between issues, something that rarely occurs for ILBs in Europe and the United States (redemptions of EUR sovereign ILBs are only permitted in July or September). Increases in the core consumer price index (CPI) due to consumption tax hikes will also be key to understanding Japanese inflation-linked products. Impact against the core CPI from a tax hike can be greater than the impact from base inflation in Japan. This has greater significance in Japan than in Europe or the United States as Japanese interest and inflation rates are comparatively low.

The market level has shifted frequently due to the imbalance of supply and demand and several factors peculiar to Japan; consequently, we can say that the market is still in the "price discovery stage". This chapter focuses on special aspects of Japanese ILBs, which will be the key for both Japanese and foreign investors to find fair value for Japanese ILBs.

THE JAPANESE ILB MARKET

Table 1 presents an outline of the JGBi compared to ILBs elsewhere. While the JGBi has the same basic structure as the OAT(e)i (French inflation-linked government bond) or the TIPS,[1] its principal redemption is not guaranteed. Because inflation rates in Japan have been almost zero or negative, the absence of a guarantee on the principal at redemption would have a major impact on pricing and investor behaviour (see the sixth section and Appendix B). Moreover, as we will discuss in the fifth section, the core CPI, which is used to calculate the reference inflation rate for the JGBi, fluctuates greatly due to special factors, such as tax changes, and is also affected by the base inflation, which follows economic growth. This has a strong impact on JGBi prices and investors need to be aware of this.

By June 2005, Japan's MoF had issued four JGBis. It is quite probable that future issues will be of 10 years maturity and will occur quarterly. Although the MoF refrained from issuing the JGBi in September 2004 and again in March 2005 due to specific circumstances at the

Table 1 The product design of ILBs globally

CPI	EMU	France	US	Japan	UK
	HICP exc. tobacco (unrevised NSA)	CPI exc. tobacco (unrevised NSA)	Aggregate CPI (unrevised NSA)	Core CPI exc. fresh food (unrevised NSA)	Aggregate retail price index (unrevised NSA)
Issuing authority	Eurostat	INSEE	MoL	Statistics bureau, MIC	Office for statistics
Bloomberg	CPTFEMU	FRCPXTOB	CPURNSA	JCPNGENF	UKRPI
Principal	Indexation of principal at maturity				
Redemption	Minimum redemption at par			No guarantee	
Coupon	Fixed real coupon paid on an indexed principal				
Fixing	In arrears				In advance
Lag	Three months				Eight months
Frequency	Annual		Semi-annual		
Reference index	Daily				Monthly

Notes: The UK will move to a Daily Index with a 3-month lag for their next issue to be launched during H2 2005. NSA = Not seasonally adjusted.
Source: BNP Paribas

Table 2 The issuance schedule for JGBis

Issue	Name	Maturity		Size (bln JPY)
2004 Mar	JGBi #1	2014 Mar	(10y ILB)	100
2004 Jun	JGBi #2	2014 Jun	(10y ILB)	300
2004 Sep	–	–	–	–
2004 Dec	JGBi #3	2014 Dec	(10y ILB)	500
2005 Mar	–	–	–	–
2005 Jun	JGBi #4	2015 Jun	(10y ILB)	500
2005 Sep	JGBi #5	2015 Sep	(10y ILB)	500
2005 Dec	JGBi #6	2015 Dec	(10y ILB)	500

Source: BNP Paribas

time,[2] the MoF will quite likely issue regularly each quarter from now on.[3] Redemptions occur quarterly, resulting in clear differences in valuation, which do not occur for issues of almost the same duration for

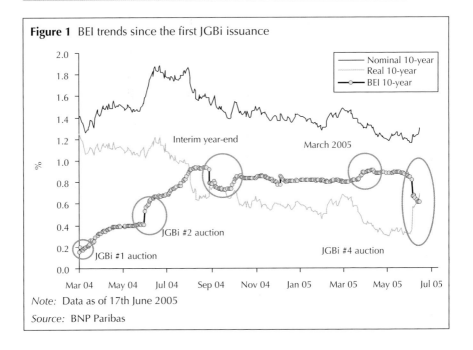

Figure 1 BEI trends since the first JGBi issuance

Legend:
— Nominal 10-year
···· Real 10-year
—○— BEI 10-year

Labels within chart: Interim year-end, March 2005, JGBi #2 auction, JGBi #1 auction, JGBi #4 auction

X-axis: Mar 04, May 04, Jul 04, Sep 04, Nov 04, Jan 05, Mar 05, May 05, Jul 05
Y-axis (%): 0.0, 0.2, 0.4, 0.6, 0.8, 1.0, 1.2, 1.4, 1.6, 1.8, 2.0

Note: Data as of 17th June 2005

Source: BNP Paribas

ILBs in Europe and the United States. As the JGBi market matures, the MoF may well issue ILBs of different maturities such as a 20-year JGBi.

JGBi MARKET TRENDS

Since the first issue, the lack of maturity in the JGBi market has caused levels to shift frequently due to the supply–demand imbalance.

The breakeven inflation (BEI) expanded from 12 bp (0.12%) at the time of the auction of the first JGBi, JGBi #1 (March 2004) to 49 bp at the auction of the second, JGBi #2 (June 2004), and further increased to almost 100 bp in August 2004. After some technical fluctuations in September 2004 associated with the interim year end, the BEI remained at around 80 bp for about six months. The market experienced seasonal fluctuations at the end of March 2005 (see the next section) and then plummeted as supply-demand conditions deteriorated with the JGBi #4 auction (Figure 1).

Out-performance in June–August of 2004 resulted from strong demand. The auction of JGBi #2 took place during this time and the number of market participants increased dramatically due to

Table 3 Relative performance in the first half of 2005

	Factor (month end)			Monthly perform		Relative perform
	Ref CPI	Idx ratio	BEI (%)	JGBi #3 (%)	JB265 (%)	
2005 Feb	97.975	0.998	0.81	−1.26	−1.10	−0.16
2005 Mar	97.329	0.991	0.89	1.61	1.59	0.01
2005 Apr	97.103	0.989	0.89	0.73	0.94	−0.20
2005 May	97.332	0.991	0.86	−0.01	0.13	−0.14

	– Relative perform breakdown –		
	CPI (%)	Carry (%)	Yld Chg
2005 Feb	0.00	−0.06	−0.10
2005 Mar	−0.70	−0.07	0.79
2005 Apr	−0.20	−0.08	0.08
2005 May	0.20	−0.06	−0.28

Notes: Relative perform ≈ CPI effect + Carry effect + Yield effect
CPI effect ≈ d(Index ratio)
Carry effect ≈ d(Yield) · Holding term
Yield effect ≈ d(BEI) · Mod dur ± Dur adj
JB265 is nominal JGB with 1.5% coupon and 20/Dec/14 maturity. JGBi #3 is an inflation-linked JGB with 0.5% coupon and 10/Dec/14 maturity.
Source: BNP Paribas

progress in systems or accounting procedures. Until this time, participation had been limited to large brokers and city banks, but as the investor class expanded to include life insurers, non-life companies and pension funds, the market moved up sharply. Over the next six months, the nominal interest rate inched lower and the BEI remained at approximately 80 bp. As a result, the JGBi #4 auction in June 2005 failed to stimulate investor demand due to concern over the real interest rates, which had fallen to 0.35% on a bond with 9.5 years to maturity.

When considering the fluctuations of the BEI in March 2005, investors must note how the BEI tends to offset the reference index (as we will discuss in the next section, the reference index fluctuates the most in the March–April period due to the seasonal CPI cycle).

Table 3 presents a breakdown of the relative performance of JGBi #3 and its nominal counterpart, the JB265, during the

February–May period of 2005. The reference index dropped 70 bp in March due to seasonal CPI factors. However, the BEI expanded and increased performance by approximately 79 bp, offsetting the reference index drop. In other words, the BEI in March seems to deviate sharply, but actual relative performance is stable.

If investors do not exclude the fluctuations in the reference index caused by seasonal factors they will risk misreading the future expectations about the fundamentals of inflation that are discounted by the market. Alternatively, investors can more accurately comprehend the future inflation discounted by the market by using real interest rates and BEIs that have been corrected for seasonal fluctuations. Looking at real interest rates adjusted for seasonal fluctuations is particularly important in countries like Japan, where interest rates and volatility are low.

THE SEASONAL ADJUSTMENT OF THE JGBi YIELD

The Japanese core CPI has a seasonal cycle, falling in January due to the impact of bargain sales at the start of the year and rising in March and April when sales end and the new school year begins. Because of the 3-month lag in the core CPI used to calculate the daily reference index (DRI) for a JGBi, the DRI declines sharply in the March–April period and then rises in the May–July period (Figure 2). An examination of data over the last five years reveals that this cycle is relatively stable.

As we previously noted, investors can better understand the performance of JGBis by looking at real interest rates and BEIs adjusted for fluctuations from the seasonal cycle of the reference index. Figure 3 proposes a method to adjust real interest rates for seasonality.

By calculating the return of the JGBi over an "imaginary CPI matrix" derived from past data assuming that long-term inflation is zero,[4] we obtain the actual return for an investment made to hedge against long-term inflation.

Of course, when the reference index falls because of the seasonal CPI cycle, the investment utility (the real yield adjusted for this seasonality) should rise. In addition, investors should also adjust for seasonality of a cashflow month. This is because the cashflow pushes up the investment utility in months when seasonality raises the reference index.

Figure 2 Seasonal cycle of the core CPI

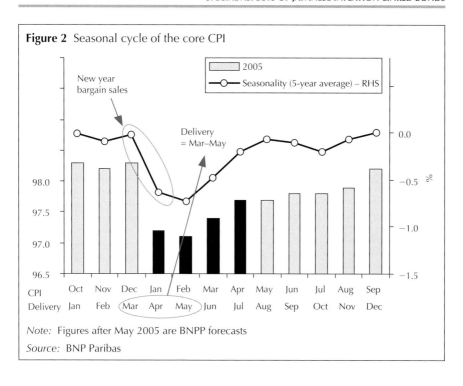

Note: Figures after May 2005 are BNPP forecasts

Source: BNP Paribas

Figure 3 A procedure to calculate seasonally-adjusted real yield

Assuming that long term inflation is 0% and only a seasonal cycle exists

⬇

Calculating "Imaginary CPI Matrix", starting with 100 and ending with 100

⬇

Calculate total return of inflation-linked bonds on imaginary matrix

||

Seasonal cycle adjusted real yield

Source: BNP Paribas

<Sample of imaginary CPI matrix>

	2005	2006	2007	2(
Jan	99.49	99.49	99.49	99.
Feb	99.36	99.36	99.36	99.:
Mar	99.61	99.61	99.61	99.(
Apr	99.89	99.89	99.89	99.
May	100.04	100.04	100.04	100
Jun	99.96	99.96	99.96	99.
Jul	99.79	99.79	99.79	99.:
Aug	99.87	99.87	99.87	99.(
Sep	100.00	100.00	100.00	100.
Oct	99.97	99.97	99.97	99.
Nov	99.97	99.97	99.97	99.!
Dec	100.00	100.00	100.00	100.0

123

Equations (1) and (2) show how to calculate real seasonally-adjusted interest rates[5] after deriving the "imaginary CPI matrix".

<Zero-Coupon Bond Method>

$$\left(1+\frac{Real}{2}\right)^{2T} \times \frac{Reference\ Index_{Maturity}}{Reference\ Index_{SD}} = \left(1+\frac{Real_{adj}}{2}\right)^{2T} \quad (1)$$

<Coupon Bond Method>

$$Price \times Reference\ Index_{SD}$$

$$= \sum_{i=1}^{2T} CF_i \times Reference\ Index_{CF.Month} \times \left(1+\frac{Real_{adj}}{2}\right)^{-i} \quad (2)$$

where

$Real$ = market traded real yield
$Real_{adj}$ = seasonally adjusted real yield
$Reference\ Index(t)$ = Index on imaginary CPI matrix at time t
$CF(t)$ = cashflow of ILB at time t

Figure 4 examines real interest rate trends calculated using this seasonal adjustment procedure. Between the 14th March and 1st April 2005 the real interest rate movement was equivalent to a closing bond price increase of ¥2.4. However, this was reduced by ¥0.5 because of the decline in the reference index from the seasonal CPI cycle. In this case, focusing on seasonally-adjusted yields gives the actual market price trends.

The real interest rate fluctuates by "nominal rate", "inflation view", "supply–demand balance for ILBs" and "seasonal cycle of DRI". This method enables the separation of the fluctuation by "seasonal cycle of DRI" from those by other factors.

The JGBi can also be analysed from another perspective using Equations (1) and (2).

As we previously noted, one special characteristic of the JGBi market is that redemptions are split between March, June, September and December. Issues for which the CPI reference index declines due to seasonality at the time of cash flow (particularly at redemption) are characterised by lower investment efficiency than the neighbouring issues.

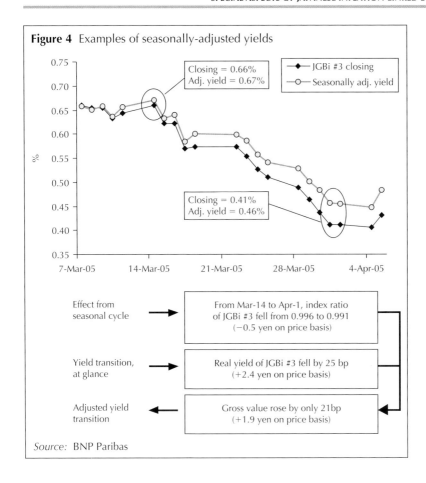

Figure 4 Examples of seasonally-adjusted yields

Source: BNP Paribas

For example, Figure 5 shows that the investment utility of the JGBi #1 and the JGBi #3 should be higher than that of the JGBi #2 and the JGBi #4 that use the March CPI to calculate the notional principal redemption. Figure 6 compares the investment utility of the various JGBis in June 2005 after adjusting yields for seasonality using the methods shown in Figure 3 and from Equations (1) and (2). Over- or under-valuation persists due to insufficient liquidity in the JGBi market and insufficient investor awareness of differences in investment utilities caused by the seasonal cycle.[6]

For example, the DRI rises 28 bp for the JGBi #3 from the time of delivery in the middle of June until its redemption on the 10th December because of the seasonal cycle. Investors should view the investment utility of the JGBi #3 in the second half of June 2005 as

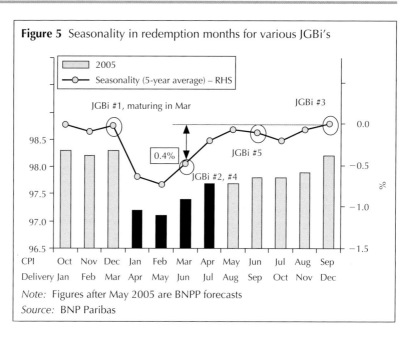

Figure 5 Seasonality in redemption months for various JGBi's

Note: Figures after May 2005 are BNPP forecasts
Source: BNP Paribas

Figure 6 Rich/cheap analysis on the seasonal cycle adjusted rate (SCAR)

Linker			S/A ISMA real yield		Adjustment
	Coupon (%)	Maturity	Closing (%)	SC. adj (%)	spread (%)
JGBi #1	1.20	2014 Mar	0.484	0.519	0.034
JGBi #2	1.10	2014 Jun	0.523	0.514	−0.009
JGBi #3	0.50	2014 Dec	0.603	0.633	0.030
JGBi #4	0.50	2015 Jun	0.677	0.668	−0.008

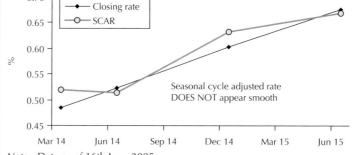

Note: Data as of 16th June 2005
Source: BNP Paribas

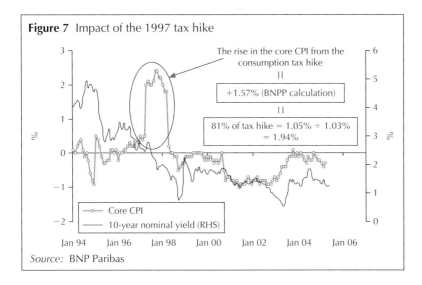

Figure 7 Impact of the 1997 tax hike

The rise in the core CPI from the consumption tax hike

||

+1.57% (BNPP calculation)

||

81% of tax hike = 1.05% ÷ 1.03% = 1.94%

Core CPI
10-year nominal yield (RHS)

Source: BNP Paribas

the sum of the long-term inflation that averages seasonality until 2014–2015, the real yield when the bond is traded (0.60%) and the return from the seasonal cycle (+28 bp ≈ +3 bp/yr).

With real yield low, a 3 bp difference in investment utility from seasonality is significant. Moreover, because maturities are concentrated between 8.5 and 10 years, investors need to consider carefully the differences between issues that arise from seasonal factors when thinking about relative value.[7]

Investors buy ILBs to hedge against long-term inflation, not to hedge against monthly CPI fluctuations that occur because of the seasonal cycle. Investors should understand that fluctuations in the price index cycle that determine returns are greater than the seasonal cycle of the investment cost (the nominal short-term rate to pay).

THE TERM STRUCTURE OF EXPECTED INFLATION

The trend for Japanese CPI is around 0% at present. On the other hand, the expected inflation rate in the 10-year sector in June 2005 was 0.7%, which means that the expected inflation curve is steep. However, it is extremely difficult to estimate the term structure of expected inflation across the entire curve because Japanese issues are concentrated in the 10-year sector.

Increases in the core CPI due to consumption tax hikes constitute another reason why it is difficult to estimate expected inflation rates. Figure 7 shows that the core CPI increased sharply when the

Table 4 Breakdown of inflation

	Nominal DF	CF	<Case 1>			<Case 2>		
			Inflat. fwd CPI (%)	Index ratio	Present value	Inflat. fwd CPI (%)	Index ratio	Present value
0.5	1.0000	0.30	0.05	1.000	0.300	0.03	1.000	0.300
1.0	0.9999	0.30	0.11	1.001	0.300	0.06	1.000	0.300
1.5	0.9997	0.30	0.16	1.002	0.300	0.09	1.001	0.300
2.0	0.9989	0.30	0.21	1.003	0.300	0.12	1.002	0.300
2.5	0.9969	0.30	0.27	1.004	0.300	0.15	1.002	0.300
3.0	0.9943	0.30	0.32	1.006	0.300	0.18	1.003	0.299
3.5	0.9910	0.30	**1.99**	1.016	0.302	**1.83**	1.012	0.301
4.0	0.9867	0.30	**2.04**	1.026	0.304	**1.86**	1.022	0.302
4.5	0.9817	0.30	0.48	1.028	0.303	0.27	1.023	0.301
5.0	0.9758	0.30	0.53	1.031	0.302	0.30	1.025	0.300
5.5	0.9690	0.30	0.58	1.034	0.301	**2.72**	1.039	0.302
6.0	0.9613	0.30	0.64	1.037	0.299	**2.75**	1.053	0.304
6.5	0.9528	0.30	0.69	1.041	0.298	0.39	1.055	0.302
7.0	0.9436	0.30	0.74	1.045	0.296	0.42	1.057	0.299
7.5	0.9337	0.30	0.80	1.049	0.294	0.45	1.060	0.297
8.0	0.9230	0.30	0.85	1.053	0.292	0.48	1.062	0.294
8.5	0.9116	0.30	0.90	1.058	0.289	0.52	1.065	0.291
9.0	0.8997	0.30	0.95	1.063	0.287	0.55	1.068	0.288
9.5	0.8876	0.30	1.01	1.069	0.285	0.58	1.071	0.285
10.0	0.8756	100.30	1.06	1.074	94.349	0.61	1.074	94.334
			PV Total		100.000	PV Total		100.000

Where *Nominal DF* = Discount factor from nominal yield curve, *CF* = Cashflow of 10-year inflation-linked bond, $PV = \Sigma \, CF \cdot Nominal \, DF \cdot Index \, ratio$
Note: Calculations assume that base inflation rises in a linear fashion after June 2005.
Source: BNP Paribas

consumption tax was raised from 3 to 5% in 1997. Over the next 10 years the consumption tax will probably be raised at least once from 5 to 7% or perhaps twice, bringing the rate to 10%.

Table 4 and Figure 8 present a breakdown of the expected inflation rate (0.7% = 1.3%[nominal] − 0.6%[real]) discounted in the price of the 10-year JGBi as of June 2005. The term structure of the expected inflation rate changes depend on whether the consumption tax is raised once (Case 1) or twice (Case 2).[8]

In both Case 1 and Case 2, the final cumulative inflation carry is almost the same (1.074, Table 4). However, the paths followed to reach this are completely different.

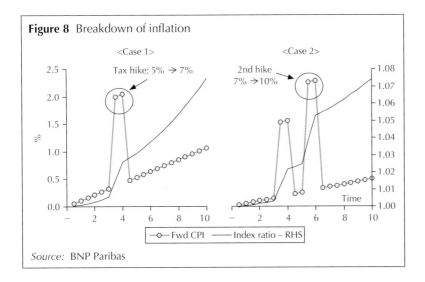

Figure 8 Breakdown of inflation

Source: BNP Paribas

The following equations give approximations for the cumulative CPI that takes into account special factors like a consumption tax hike and the BEI that averages the cumulative CPI.

Cumulative CPI ≈ Average (Base inflation) × Life + Special factors

$$BEI \approx \underbrace{\frac{Cumulative\ CPI}{Life} \approx Average\ (Base\ inflation)}_{(a)} + \underbrace{\frac{Special\ factors}{Life}}_{(b)}$$

As we noted previously, the weight of special factors (term b) on Japan's expected inflation rate is great. The impact of special factors (the numerator of term b) is greater against BEI, when the life of the security is shorter (the denominator of term b). In other words, the fewer years left before a JGBi matures, the more the risk d*(BEI)* will fluctuate in a jump-wise fashion because of special factors d*(Special factors)*.

Consequently, investors should manage the risk of a JGBi by separating it into two components: the shift in the expected base inflation rate [d*(Expected base inflation)* × Dur] and the impact of special factors [d*(Special factors)* × 1] that produces jumps.

Of course, inflation rates in all countries shift with tax system changes. However, this impact is more important in countries like Japan where special factors have a greater effect on inflation.

POINTS TO NOTE ABOUT A ZERO FLOOR OPTION

As Table 1 illustrates, the principal of the Japanese government ILB is not guaranteed at redemption. This is because the product was designed to measure exact inflationary expectations from the pricing of the JGBi.

However, there tend to be limitations on Japanese institutional investors such as banks about holding products that need to be marked to market prices daily due to accounting regulations. Because the principal of the JGBi is not guaranteed, the JGBi cannot be treated as a product for "hold-till-maturity", but instead must be marked to market every day. This lack of principal guarantee is one of the reasons why some Japanese investors have not invested in government ILBs at this stage (see Appendix B, "An example of the accounting treatment of an ILB").

Due to investor demand, most non-government ILBs come with a zero floor (guaranteed principal) when issued. For example, the Euro medium term note (MTN) issued by the European Investment Bank (EIB) came with a zero floor, as did the domestic bond issued by JFM (the Japanese Finance Corporation for Municipal Enterprises). While addition of a zero floor decreases the yield, investors can hold ILBs in the account, which is not subject to daily mark-to-market, on the assumption of "holding-till-maturity."

From another viewpoint, the zero floor is a put option on the cumulative CPI.[9] The underlying asset of this put option is the BEI, which implies the cumulative CPI. As we have noted previously, BEI risk should be divided into two components, special factors that cause a discontinuous jump in inflation and the continuous base inflation rate component. The premium on a zero floor option is thus given by the following equation:

$$\textit{Zero floor premium}$$
$$= \sum_X \text{Prob}\,(\textit{Tax hike impact} = X\%)$$
$$\times \text{Black Scholes}\,(\textit{Undl} = \textit{Base inflation} \times \textit{Life},\ \textit{Strike} = -X\%)$$

The value of the zero floor option will drop sharply when it seems likely that the government will hike the consumption tax. If the government increases the consumption tax from 5 to 7% the core CPI would rise by approximately 1.6% (see Chapter 5) and the

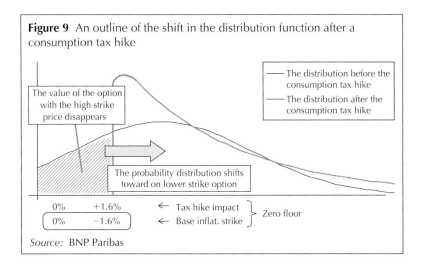

Figure 9 An outline of the shift in the distribution function after a consumption tax hike

The value of the option with the high strike price disappears

The distribution before the consumption tax hike

The distribution after the consumption tax hike

The probability distribution shifts toward on lower strike option

| 0% | +1.6% |
| 0% | −1.6% |

← Tax hike impact
← Base inflat. strike

Zero floor

Source: BNP Paribas

distribution of the strike of the put option on a cumulative base inflation would shift as shown in Figure 9. Hence the option value would plummet.[10]

We expect that the market for non-government ILBs with zero floors will mature in the coming years. Investors need to understand how these option prices will shift because of differing times left to maturity when a consumption tax hike is expected. The underlying asset consists of two components that follow completely different probability paths. One of these traces a probability path of irreversible upward shifts.

THE CONVEXITY VALUE GENERATED AFTER THE TERMINATION OF QUANTITATIVE EASING

Aside from June 2004 and 2005 when the BEI level shifted, the beta of the JGBi market (the relationship between nominal and real rates) has been relatively stable for the short history of this product. However, we expect the level of this beta to shift greatly when the BoJ terminates its quantitative easing policy (zero interest rate policy with quantitative provision of liquidity). We will now consider precisely how this beta will move.

In general, there are limits as to how far real rates rise when nominal rates are increasing. This is because the constraints of population, capital and productivity limit excessive increases in real

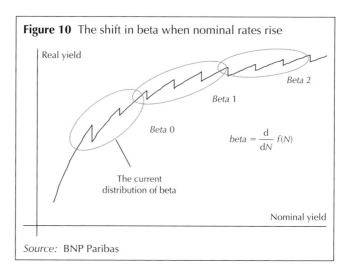

Figure 10 The shift in beta when nominal rates rise

Real yield

Beta 2

Beta 1

Beta 0

$$beta = \frac{d}{dN} f(N)$$

The current
distribution of beta

Nominal yield

Source: BNP Paribas

interest rates. As a result, the beta tends to decline as nominal interest rates increase (Figure 10).

As a result, profits or losses arise when the hedge ratio (beta) shifts in cases where investors have hedged a JGBi with a fixed nominal bond ratio.

The following equations express the convexity value, defining that the profit or loss that is generated when investors use a beta hedge on the ILBs against nominal bond (Figure 11) is given by a quadratic approximation:

$$\Delta R \approx \frac{dR}{dN} \cdot \Delta N + \frac{1}{2} \frac{d^2R}{dN^2} (\Delta N)^2$$

$$\approx beta \cdot \Delta N + \frac{1}{2} \frac{d^2R}{dN^2} (\Delta N)^2$$

$$\Delta ILB\ price \approx \Delta R \cdot Mod\ dur + \frac{1}{2} Cvx \cdot (\Delta R)^2$$

$$\approx beta \cdot \Delta N \cdot Mod\ dur + \frac{1}{2} beta^2 \cdot Cvx \cdot (\Delta N)^2$$

$$+ \frac{1}{2} \frac{d^2R}{dN^2} \cdot Mod\ dur \cdot (\Delta N)^2$$

$$ILB\ convexity\ value = \frac{1}{2} \frac{d^2R}{dN^2} \cdot Mod\ dur \cdot (\Delta N)^2$$

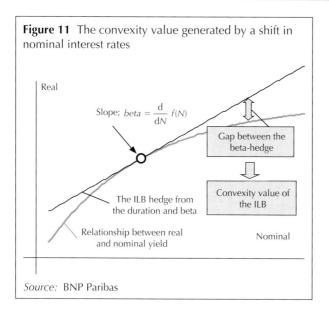

Figure 11 The convexity value generated by a shift in nominal interest rates

Real

Slope; $beta = \dfrac{d}{dN} f(N)$

Gap between the beta-hedge

Convexity value of the ILB

The ILB hedge from the duration and beta

Relationship between real and nominal yield

Nominal

Source: BNP Paribas

where
  Mod dur = modified duration
    Cvx = convexity
      R = real yield of the ILB
      N = nominal yield of nominal bond which has same outstanding term with the ILB

From this perspective, the convexity value peculiar to the ILB can be treated in the same dimension as the convexity of a normal bond.[11]

The convexity risk that is generated when nominal interest rates rise (= gamma speed) can be expressed by the second derivative of $R = f(N)$ or the first derivative of $beta = f'(N)$. It is difficult to estimate the first derivative of beta because of the lack of sufficient historical data for the JGBi, but estimates using data from Europe or the United States may serve as a reference (Figure 12). Of course, estimates will vary depending on the treatment of the second-order approximation for $R = f(N)$ and the beta model used (the estimation period, the use of a normal or log normal distribution, and the degree of the differentiation).

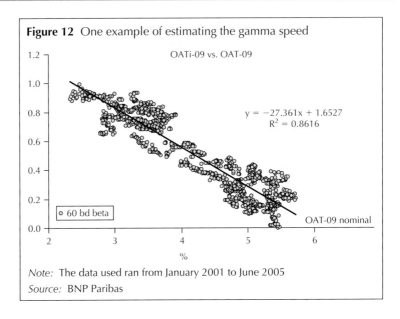

Figure 12 One example of estimating the gamma speed

OATi-09 vs. OAT-09

$$y = -27.361x + 1.6527$$
$$R^2 = 0.8616$$

o 60 bd beta

OAT-09 nominal

%

Note: The data used ran from January 2001 to June 2005

Source: BNP Paribas

Betas in Japan may decline more rapidly than they have in the United States or Europe because investors will need to hedge against rising interest rates when the BoJ terminates its quantitative easing policy. Investors may need to control for gamma speeds in excess of those in Europe and the United States as they manage risk on a nominal basis.

APPENDIX A. FOREIGN INVESTOR PARTICIPATION

The change in taxation rules made feasible the purchase of JGBis by overseas tax-exempt entities from April 2005. Foreign investor interest is also rising because the JGBi was added to the global ILB index in May 2005, which is used as a performance benchmark by foreign pension funds.

With the auction of the JGBi #4 in June of this year, the JGBis share in the world ILB market rose from 1.2 to 2.0% approximately. We estimate that its share will rise to 7.5% by 2008, if issuance proceeds smoothly. This would put Japan second behind Italy, the country that has pioneered ILB issuance.

Investors in the United States and Europe, where ILB markets have matured, may be interested in comparing the ratios of real

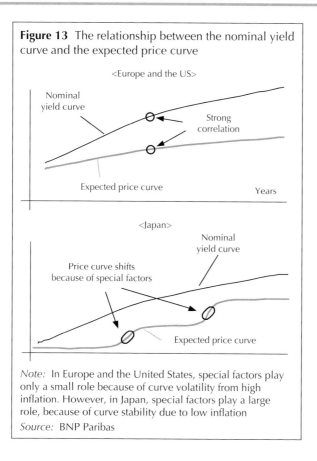

Figure 13 The relationship between the nominal yield curve and the expected price curve

<Europe and the US>

Nominal yield curve

Strong correlation

Expected price curve

Years

<Japan>

Nominal yield curve

Price curve shifts because of special factors

Expected price curve

Note: In Europe and the United States, special factors play only a small role because of curve volatility from high inflation. However, in Japan, special factors play a large role, because of curve stability due to low inflation

Source: BNP Paribas

interest rates to nominal rates or the ratios of BEI to nominal rates, as a means to assess market levels across countries. However, investors should bear in mind that there is only a precarious theoretical justification for the equalisation of real to nominal rate ratios across countries.

Investors need to be particularly careful of special factors that have a major impact on the Japanese inflation curve. In general, the correlation between real and nominal interest rates tends to be high because an increase in inflation leads to a rise in the nominal interest rate. However, it is extremely unlikely that the inflation increase caused by a consumption tax hike would increase nominal interest rates. Hence the correlation between expected inflation and the nominal interest rate in Japan is low. As Figure 13 illustrates, the

5

Inflation-Linked Derivatives:
From Theory to Practice

Sébastien Goldenberg; Dariush Mirfendereski

ABN AMRO;
UBS

INTRODUCTION
Objective
This chapter covers the topic of inflation derivatives from a practical, trading-oriented angle, presenting the relevant concepts and ideas using real-world examples encountered by the authors in the main inflation derivatives markets over recent years. The latest market developments in inflation derivatives are presented within a historical context and with close linkage to the developments and growth in the underlying inflation-indexed bond markets.

The readers should emerge with an essential toolset of ideas that should enable them to better comprehend market behaviour, avoid pitfalls related to the particular features of this market, and confidently use the available traded instruments to achieve their investment and hedging goals.

Why inflation derivatives?
As with other derivatives, inflation derivatives exist to complement the underlying market, meeting needs for issuers (payers) and investors (receivers) that the bonds cannot satisfy on their own. Inflation derivatives allow market participants to transfer risk, access increased liquidity, optimise market timing, meet portfolio hedging requirements, customise cash flows, realise market arbitrage, and create hybrid structures.

The views expressed in this chapter are those of the authors and do not necessarily reflect those of ABN AMRO and UBS.

The development of the inflation derivatives market over the last decade in different countries has been largely demand driven and has highlighted all the above applications. It is anticipated that the available instruments and their further developments will be driven by the need to fulfil additional needs of the market.

Outline

Inflation derivatives have traded for just over a decade and a brief historical outline serves to put the later sections in the correct chronological context. The focus throughout will be on the three main markets: UK, Euro-zone, and US since those represent over 95% of global inflation-indexed markets. However, the themes presented can each be translated to other markets. The main types of inflation-linked swaps (ILSs) are defined and the concepts of seasonality and convexity are explored. The important area of inflation-linked bond (ILB) asset swaps is studied in detail as it can be used as an indicator of the balance of flows in the ILS markets. After a discussion of inflation options, the chapter ends with some insights into the likely near- and long-term future developments in this fast-expanding market.

A BRIEF HISTORY OF INFLATION-INDEXED DERIVATIVES

Many publications have described the evolution and history of the inflation derivatives markets around the world (see references). Rather than provide an exhaustive history, our approach in this section is to briefly outline the historical developments as an introduction and background to the more recent significant developments in the three major markets of the UK, the Euro-zone (French domestic and Euro-zone indices), and the US over 2004 and the first half of 2005. These recent developments have now helped to unify an interpretation of those markets and their behaviour. Additionally, they provide pointers to how each market may further evolve given the parallel developments in the other two.

Four stages of inflation linked swap market development

ILS markets can be broadly divided into four stages of development. This is illustrated in Figure 1.

The stages of development and liquidity are ranked from S_1, the least developed and liquid, to S_4, the most developed and liquid. In S_1 markets, swaps are traded on a back-to-back basis or through taking some basis risk with instruments traded in higher-stage

Figure 1 The four stages of development and liquidity of the ILS market

No tradable underlying instrument	One or more tradable underlying instrument	Many tradable instruments possibility of building a complete "fair value" forward CPI curve	Liquidity comparable to IRS market
eg, Belgian, German, Spanish indices, or even EUR HICP prior to the launch of the OATei 2012 in 2001	eg, Italian inflation-indexed swap market	eg, UK, FR, EU and US CPI swaps	No model dependency, bid/offer tight
			eg, some maturities in the EUR and UK ILS market from time to time
S_1	S_2	S_3	S_4

Increasing liquidity of inflation linked swaps: S_1 to S_4

markets. This, for example, was the case for the Euro-zone inflation swap market in Q2 2001, prior to the issuance of the OATei 2012. S_2 markets have one or more tradable instruments linked to the inflation index (typically bonds) but lack a sufficient number of instruments to cover most maturities of interest and are characterised by low liquidity in the swaps. S_3 markets have a full set of tradable instruments (typically bonds) at most maturities, ie, a full real curve can be built and used to hedge swaps at all maturities. In S_4 the market has reached a level of maturity and liquidity analogous to the interest rate swap (IRS) markets such that "the price is the market clearing price" independently of any models inferring prices based on the underlying real and nominal asset yields.

With the development of a full bond curve in the major markets of UK, Euro-zone, and the US, each of these markets have reached stage S_3 or higher. Although certain gaps exist in the US curve (between 10 to 20 years maturities) and the French domestic bond curve consists of five bonds, the market maker experience in other markets and their capacity to take on risk mean that these are not impediments to maintaining S_3 market status. Italian inflation is an example of an S_2 market while Spanish and Dutch inflation are examples of S_1 markets.

Many maturities in the Euro-zone (5 and 10 years) and UK (20 through 30 years) markets trade more akin to S_4 markets due to the high volumes associated with those maturities. However, due to periods of lower liquidity, even these market segments are prone to reverting back to S_3. It is therefore important to understand the S_3 characteristics for those markets.

UK RPI – the oldest market

The earliest inflation-indexed swaps are believed to have been transacted in the UK market in the early 1990s. Among the G7 economies, the UK was the first to issue inflation-indexed bonds in 1981 and currently has over 25% of its sovereign debt linked to inflation. The structure of the market is such that corporations (mostly utilities) and other issuers[1] routinely issue inflation-indexed bonds while the demand side is closely related to pension regulations that link over £400 billion worth of pension liabilities to the retail price index (RPI). Given the existence of a developed underlying bond market plus two-way counterparty interest, it should be no surprise that the UK RPI swap market developed the earliest.

The use of inflation swaps by corporations and project companies as well as lease/rental securitizations provided the source of inflation streams, while pension liability hedging absorbed those flows directly through swaps and/or through purchase of swapped new issues. The market developed rapidly in the late 1990s and into the 2000–2003 period, encompassing special path-dependent collars on RPI known as Limited Price Index (LPI) swaps. The liquidity in the UK RPI market went through a dramatic increase in 2004 and 2005 where the PV01-weighted volumes often surpassed both the more liquid Euro inflation market as well as the underlying index-linked gilt market for certain months.[2] It is estimated that £1.2 billion in 30y equivalent zero coupon inflation swaps (ZCIS) traded in H2 2004, followed by £2.1 billion in H1 2005 through the broker markets alone.[3] Client deals with notionals between £0.5 and £1 billion now trade periodically in the market and H1 2005 has seen upwards of £2.5 billion in pension business coupled with an estimated £2 billion in corporate/PFI/ securitization deals.

Euro inflation – the most liquid market

Following the UK Debt Management Office (DMO) and the US Treasury, the Agence France Tresor (AFT) officially launched its first inflation-linked bonds (ILBs) in 1998 with the OATi 3% 25-Jul-2009, followed a year later by the 3.4% 25-Jul-2029. With this, the first real rate curve in the Euro-zone was born. In the following years, the AFT created a parallel real curve linked to the Euro-zone Harmonized Index of Consumer Prices (HICP) with the launch of the OATei 3% 25-Jul-2012 and the OATei 3.15% 25-Jul-2032 issues.

Short-dated French inflation-indexed swaps were trading as early as 1999, ie, soon after the AFT issuance of the OATi 2009, however, the non-existence of a "curve" and payers of inflation swaps made this a very limited market. The first officially reported large transaction was by Peugeot on behalf of its pension fund, which entered into a 30-year amortising swap linked to French inflation as a hedge for its pension scheme liabilities. Due to the lack of inflation swap payers, the only available hedge was to buy the existing OATi bonds, specifically, the OATi 2029.

With the Italian Post Office's inflation-protected equity product launched in 2001, some months before the AFT issued the OATei 2012, the inflation swap market linked to the Euro HICP was born. Again, hedging was with the French inflation-indexed bonds and the market was trading at large premiums[4] to French break-even levels until the AFT announcement of the OATei 2012 in October 2001.

Developments in 2003, involving the swapped issuance of approximately €8 billion of MTNs linked to inflation, as well as an expanding curve of ei [5] bonds, especially the 5 year benchmark BTPei08s, all helped to propel the Euro ILS market to an S_3 market, with some maturities exhibiting characteristics of S_4 markets. This trend has continued in 2004 and into 2005 where asset swap trades have now become a liquid feature of the market, complementing the ZCIS activities.

US CPI – a sleeping giant

The inflation-indexed bonds in the US, Treasury inflation indexed securities, more commonly known as TIPS,[6] were first issued in 1997 and since 2000 have been the largest such market. As of mid-year 2005, the market capitalization for TIPS is close to $300 billion, approximately 10% of the total Treasury market. Despite this size advantage, the US CPI derivatives market remains the smallest amongst the major markets, albeit with potential to become the biggest – a sleeping giant.

Although a few limited trades went through in 1998 after the TIPS program had begun,[7] there was no ILS "market" as such. The ILS market started to trade in earnest in 2003, trading approximately $3 billion notional in the broker market and dominated by a handful of banks. The market then expanded rapidly in 2004, trading an approximate $12 billion notional in the broker market,[8] encompassing traditional zero-coupon swaps and also TIPS asset swaps. There was a further estimated $10 billion in customer trades and direct inter-bank trades.[9] A similar pace of growth has been seen in 2005, with more banks participating.

Despite its recent growth, this market remains predominantly one of one-way natural flow,[10] complemented by buyers of cheap TIPS asset swaps. The lack of "supply" from payers of inflation swaps in an economy where no issuer other than the Treasury has kept inflation exposure in its issuance program[11] has held back the level of liquidity in this market. It is only with the development of a "natural" two-way flow market[12] that we will see the US ILS market go through the next stage of expansion and fulfil its potential to be the largest and most liquid amongst the major markets.

INFLATION-INDEXED SWAPS
Defining some basic notation

In this section, some basic notation is defined in order to simplify the explanation of concepts in the sections that follow. A convenient way of illustrating the relationship between Government/sovereign real and nominal yields (G_R, G_N), the real and nominal LIBOR swap rates (L_R, L_N) and the Corporate real and nominal yields (C_R, C_N), is to use two perpendicular axes. The horizontal axis will denote inflation expectations plus risk premium (which is the definition of the breakeven inflation in the Fischer equation), while the vertical axis will denote credit risk (the safest assets being at the bottom of the graph). This framework is illustrated in Figure 2. The breakevens are denoted by G_{BE}, L_{BE} and C_{BE} for Government, LIBOR flat, and Corporate issuers, respectively. Swap spreads in real and nominal space are denoted by R_{SS} and N_{SS} while real and nominal credit spreads are denoted by R_{CS} and N_{CS}.

Leaving out the C_R and C_N, all remaining instruments in LIBOR and Government space trade in the market except for L_R. When G_R, G_N, and L_N all trade liquidly, we are clearly in S_3 markets or above

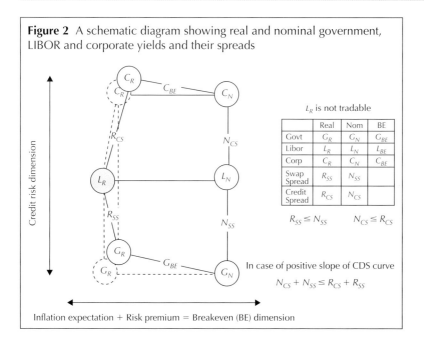

Figure 2 A schematic diagram showing real and nominal government, LIBOR and corporate yields and their spreads

L_R is not tradable

	Real	Nom	BE
Govt	G_R	G_N	G_{BE}
Libor	L_R	L_N	L_{BE}
Corp	C_R	C_N	C_{BE}
Swap Spread	R_{SS}	N_{SS}	
Credit Spread	R_{CS}	N_{CS}	

$$R_{SS} \leq N_{SS} \qquad N_{CS} \leq R_{CS}$$

In case of positive slope of CDS curve

$$N_{CS} + N_{SS} \leq R_{CS} + R_{SS}$$

Credit risk dimension

Inflation expectation + Risk premium = Breakeven (BE) dimension

(defined in previous section). Real LIBOR swap rates, L_R, however, are not liquidly traded market instruments at the current time. Nevertheless they represent a conceptual point of reference for discussing and interpreting market behaviour.

The liquidly traded inflation-indexed swap instruments

The most commonly traded ILS instrument is the zero-coupon inflation swap (ZCIS), followed closely in most markets by ILB asset swaps (ILASW). Many other variations of ILSs, such as year-on-year (YoY) and real rate swaps, do exist. However, they do not qualify as standard traded instruments due to their often bespoke nature and because they do not trade liquidly in the inter-bank and broker markets. Even though up to €20 billion notional of YoY inflation swaps have traded as end user trades in the Euro-zone market alone, YoY inflation swaps typically trade between banks and end users (banks' clients) rather than as a standard market instrument in the inter-bank or broker markets.

Figure 3 illustrates where the two most commonly traded ILS instruments fit within the schematic relationships introduced in

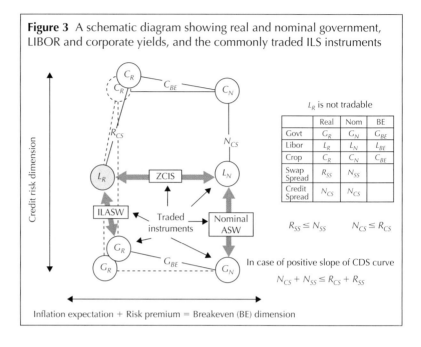

Figure 3 A schematic diagram showing real and nominal government, LIBOR and corporate yields, and the commonly traded ILS instruments

L_R is not tradable

	Real	Nom	BE
Govt	G_R	G_N	G_{BE}
Libor	L_R	L_N	L_{BE}
Crop	C_R	C_N	C_{BE}
Swap Spread	R_{SS}	N_{SS}	
Credit Spread	N_{CS}	N_{CS}	

$$R_{SS} \leq N_{SS} \qquad N_{CS} \leq R_{CS}$$

In case of positive slope of CDS curve

$$N_{CS} + N_{SS} \leq R_{CS} + R_{SS}$$

Inflation expectation + Risk premium = Breakeven (BE) dimension

Figure 2. ZCIS are analogous to L_{BE}, being the zero-coupon analogue of coupon bearing L_{BE}. ZCIS have come to prominence and have maintained their top market share as the instrument of choice within the universe of ILS because of the following three attributes: (i) their simplicity – counterparties in the swap are effectively trading the forward price index;[13] (ii) their analogous nature to G_{BE} – a concept traders are already familiar with, especially in relation to the bond markets where the closest trade in risk terms is the bond breakeven trade, ie, G_{BE}; and finally, (iii) the credit "neutral" nature of the transaction – as opposed to, say, a real rate swap (equivalent to L_R in Figure 2), the ZCIS allows relatively little exposure to build up between the two swap counterparts.

3.3 Hedging inflation-indexed swaps with bonds and IRS

In markets where the underlying ILB (G_R), nominal bonds (G_N), and interest-rate swaps (L_N) trade liquidly and where a full curve exists in each, it is possible to hedge inflation-indexed swaps (L_R) using these three types of instruments. This is typical of an S_3 market in its early stages of development. Although the UK and

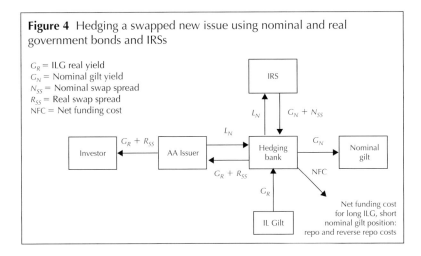

Figure 4 Hedging a swapped new issue using nominal and real government bonds and IRSs

G_R = ILG real yield
G_N = Nominal gilt yield
N_{SS} = Nominal swap spread
R_{SS} = Real swap spread
NFC = Net funding cost

Euro-zone swap markets currently exhibit many features of S_4 markets, in many instances, patchy ZCIS swap liquidity in relation to deal size often results in transactions adopting features more in common with S_3 markets.

Figure 4 shows a possible hedge for a LIBOR flat swapped inflation-indexed issue using G_R, G_N, and L_N. The suggested hedge shown in the figure shows the hedging bank going long G_R, short G_N, and long L_N, thus being left with net receiving nominal swap spreads (N_{SS}) and paying real swap spreads (R_{SS}) plus paying out a net funding cost (NFC) associated with the repo, reverse-repo bid/offer on the long/short bond positions.

Assuming positive forward breakevens, the present value of 1 basis point (PV01) on the N_{SS} leg is, however, smaller than the PV01 on the R_{SS} leg. Therefore one basis point change in N_{SS} translates into a smaller change in R_{SS}. The swap flows are typically valued off a LIBOR flat discount curve therefore as N_{SS} goes up or down, the differential in discounting results in a necessary adjustment to the initial static hedge shown in Figure 4.

Figure 5 shows historical G_{BE} and N_{SS} levels for the long-end of the UK market in 2003 and 2004. In 2003, N_{SS} narrowed by approximately 20 bps while G_{BE} went up by 30 bps – G_{BE} and N_{SS} were *negatively* correlated. In 2004, N_{SS} went up 15 bps in the first half of the year followed by a 10 bps down move in the second half while G_{BE} went up 35 bps then down 20 bps – G_{BE} and N_{SS} were *positively*

Figure 5 Evolution of nominal swap spreads (N_{SS}) and government curve breakevens (G_{BE}) in the UK market, 2003–2004

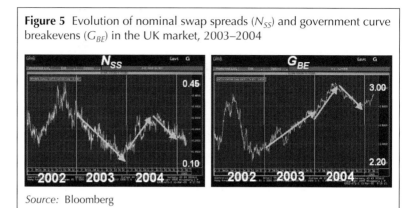

Source: Bloomberg

correlated. In a narrowing N_{SS} market, re-hedging would involve buying more G_{BE}s. This would have resulted in a net loss in 2003 since G_{BE}s went higher with drops in N_{SS}. The converse is seen in 2004 where there was positive correlation between N_{SS} and G_{BE}.

The above example is similar to hedging "quanto" LIBOR swaps in that the assumed correlation between two trading parameters or sets of market instruments results in a net cost or saving in the required dynamic re-hedging. The recent historical data from the UK market suggests that there is no consensus as to whether the correlation is positive or negative and pricing large trades or building up large one-way positions would require a conservative approach, thus making a "quanto" adjustment to the naive price, eg, reducing the level of the real coupon offered on the swapped issue shown in Figure 4. The net result is that R_{SS} would be further reduced, thus pushing L_{BE} higher than the corresponding G_{BE}.

Of course, pricing the reverse swap would incur similar (but opposite) costs if hedged with G_R, G_N, and L_N in a similar conservative fashion to the above. However, if the reverse swap is used to unwind the static hedge in the swapped issue, ie, hedging an ILS with another ILS as shown in Figure 6, the "quanto" charge as well as the NFC would effectively disappear. It is therefore the net supply and demand for ILS flows that determine the net "quanto" adjustment that the market typically prices in. In a balanced market, with equal payers and receivers of inflation swaps, this adjustment should indeed be zero.

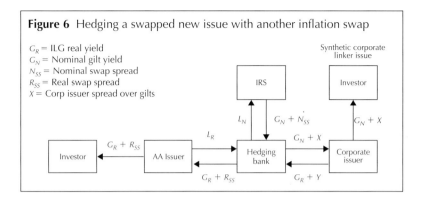

Figure 6 Hedging a swapped new issue with another inflation swap

G_R = ILG real yield
G_N = Nominal gilt yield
N_{SS} = Nominal swap spread
R_{SS} = Real swap spread
X = Corp issuer spread over gilts

Structures based on year-on-year inflation swaps

An IRS exchanges a floating interest rate for a fixed coupon. It is very appealing to extend this floating rate *versus* fixed concept to inflation, whereby the floating coupon becomes the year-on-year (YoY) increase in the inflation index – the annual inflation rate that many central banks now target. Since the inflation rate is such a well-recognized number, eg, for consumers, as it is constantly quoted in the media and by politicians, it is no surprise to find that the most popular payout for retail bonds indexed to inflation involves the YoY inflation rate through Interest Indexed Bonds (IIB). IIBs unlike Capital Indexed Bonds (CIBs), have the drawback of not having a compounded inflation payout.[14] Figure 7 shows example payouts on a 5 year IIB with payout defined by year-on-year inflation + 1% and a CIB with a 1% real coupon, with a combination of low and high, but always positive, annual inflation rates, resulting in an increase in the CPI every year.

IIBs have proven to be more attractive than CIBs for sale to retail investors for three principal reasons: (i) selling a product that pays a coupon equal to the familiar YoY inflation rate (plus an additional return) is much easier than a product with the real coupon payouts and redemption pickup of CIBs; (ii) tax advantage over CIBs – in many jurisdictions, with each rise in the relevant price index, the positive accretion in the redemption payment on the CIB is subject to taxation, even though the investor does not receive this until the bond maturity; and finally, (iii) the higher coupon payouts on IIBs

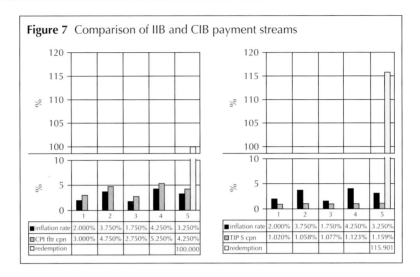

Figure 7 Comparison of IIB and CIB payment streams

typically give retail investors a higher perceived income, albeit at the expense of eroding the inflation-protected capital.

Since, in theory, we can have deflation (or negative inflation) and bonds cannot have negative payouts,[15] IIBs typically have either a 0% floor on the total coupon (as is popular in the US market) or a 0% floor on the YoY inflation rate. So unlike CIBs that either have no floor on the redemption (eg, the UK Inflation-Indexed Gilts) or simply a par guarantee, swapped IIBs necessarily spawn an options market for inflation products related to YoY floors. This is further discussed in the context of inflation option markets in the following sections.

Impact of the seasonality in the pricing of IL derivatives

Inflation, like many other economic measures, exhibits seasonality, ie, largely repeatable patterns of peaks through the calendar year. January and summer sales, and higher energy prices in the winter season for example, result in predictable patterns of month-on-month changes in the consumer price index, eg, prices consistently drop in January even though the annual rate of inflation may still remain positive. This seasonality can have a significant impact on the pricing of inflation derivatives. Therefore understanding and correctly using seasonal adjustments is an essential component of pricing inflation derivatives.

Presenting models for seasonality is beyond the scope of this chapter and interested readers are referred to the current literature for

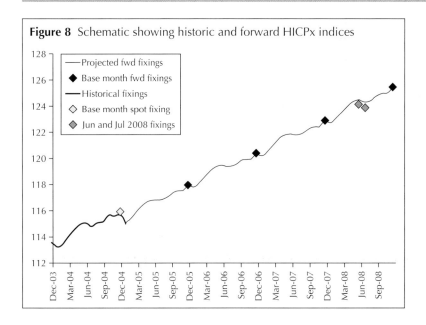

Figure 8 Schematic showing historic and forward HICPx indices

some of the latest developments in this area [eg, Belgrade and Benhamou (2005)]. However, it should be noted that any model for seasonality is no more than a plausible "best guess" for future seasonal variations. The most sophisticated of current models in the literature still only use past observations and are thus *statistical seasonality* models. These models typically cannot concurrently price all liquidly traded instruments in the market correctly (typically a set of ZCIS and ILASWs). This is simply because these models only cover "statistical seasonality" and ignore supply/demand drivers – *flow seasonality*[16] – that can further distort forward price indices (for some shorter-dated ILASWs, the discrepancy can be up to 4 bps). More practical models for seasonality will require an overlay of adjustments that take into account both statistical and flow seasonality.

Figure 8 relates to early March 2005 and shows historical levels of HICP ex-tobacco (HICPx) indices available up to and including the January 2005 print as well as a forward set of possible levels for the price index using a simple statistical seasonality model – in this case taking the average of the past five years of available data. The base month spot fixing for ZCIS at the time was December 2004 and 1-year, 2-year, 3-year, and 4-year ZCIS mid-market levels directly give us the forward December fixings in 2005 through 2008. Points in between, however, do not commonly trade and by using the seasonal assumption, a "best guess" can be made about these indices. The CPI of the month m of the year t can be defined as the linear interpolation between CPI_t and CPI_{t+1}, adjusted by a seasonal correction, with the sum of the corrections between t and $t+1$ equal to 0. One method for applying this correction is detailed in Belgrade and Benhamou (2005).

One important feature of seasonality is the monthly "roll" in ZCIS swap quotes. Moving from December fixings to January fixings changes the base month from December 2004 to January 2005.[17] In Figure 8 the January 2005 HICPx fixing (115.1) is already available and represents a bigger drop (-0.69%) from the prior month's fixing (115.9) than that which the statistical seasonal model is predicting based on historic data (eg, -0.35%). This disparity in actual fixing month change and predicted forward index change results in a jump (or drop) in ZCIS levels when going through a monthly roll. This effect is clearly magnified in shorter maturities, eg, if the $ZC_{2yDec} = 2.05\%$, given the above data, ZC_{2yJan} would likely trade at 2.225%, a 17.25 bp jump from ZC_{2yDec}, as shown in Equation (1):

$$
\begin{aligned}
ZC_{2yJan} &= \left(\frac{CPI(Jan\ 2007)}{CPI(Jan\ 2005)} \right)^{1/2} - 1 = \left(\frac{CPI(Dec\ 2006)*(1-0.35\%)}{CPI(Jan\ 2005)} \right)^{1/2} - 1 \\
&= \left(\frac{CPI(Dec\ 2004)*(1+ZC_{2yDec})^2*(1-0.35\%)}{CPI(Jan\ 2005)} \right)^{1/2} - 1 = 2.225\%
\end{aligned}
$$

(1)

When observing market behaviour, there appears to be some consensus on statistical seasonality among market participants. The convergence to consensus has been made more rapid with the advent of so-called "calendar" trades. Since the end of 2004 and increasingly in 2005, banks have been trading a spread between two ZCIS with the same maturity, but using different lags. Figure 9 illustrates the flows for a calendar trade on a 10-year ZCIS (March 2005 versus Feb 2005 basis).

As flow-related hedging using calendar trades dominate, however, flow seasonality may become more important than statistical

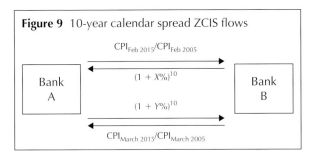

Figure 9 10-year calendar spread ZCIS flows

seasonality. In the next section, hedging of ILSs with ILBs and offsetting with ILASWs will be discussed. In the Euro-zone market, large volumes of BTPei2008s[18] were purchased on asset swap in 2004. This created a "supply" of swaps mainly concentrated in the redemption payment of the bond, using an equal weighting of June and July 2008 HICPx fixings.[19] Just as overwhelming demand in swaps on the back of swapped retail issues raised levels of ZCIS and L_{BE} relative to "fair value" implied by bonds, it is plausible to assume that the overwhelming supply of swap payments concentrated in the June and July 2008 fixings will lower levels for these forward indices to reach or go through "fair value" (the displaced points for June and July 2008 fixings in Figure 8). This implies that the forward fixings for June and July 2008 are unlikely to be equal to that implied by statistical seasonality alone.

On the French index the "Livret A hedging" is another example of flow-related distortion in seasonality. The formula of the interest paid by those French saving accounts is 50% linked to the French inflation using the May and November fixings as shown in Equation (2). Many banks have hedged their liabilities perfectly using swaps that exactly replicate the formula. Therefore, there is a net "shared" position in the market linked to the May and November fixings of the French CPI. As a consequence, the forward index levels for May and November can differ from that implied by statistical seasonality alone. This, once again, underlines the need for the inclusion of flow seasonality adjustments in pricing models.

$$\sum_n \frac{\left[\text{Monthly3MEURIBORaverage} + \left(\dfrac{CPI_N}{CPI_{N-1}} \right) \right]}{2} + 0.25 \text{ bps} \quad (2)$$

The convexity associated with trading forward inflation swaps

When pricing a ZCIS, the market is assuming a fixed base, known at the beginning of the transaction. For example, both 5-year and 10-year ZCIS will be defined using the same basis, ie, March 2005 if traded in June 2005 (using a standard 3 month lag). From both ZC_{10} and ZC_5 one can deduce the forward CPI_5 and CPI_{10} using the formula Equation (3), where CPI_0 is the CPI for January 2005.

$$[1+ZC_t]^t - 1 = \frac{CPI_t}{CPI_0} - 1 \tag{3}$$

When trading IRSs, the forward rate between t and T, $f(t, T)$, is obtained without any possible arbitrage from both IRSs, IRS_T and IRS_t:

$$f(t,T) = \left[\frac{(1+IRS_T)^T}{(1+IRS_t)^t} \right]^{(T-t)} - 1 \tag{4}$$

Using the same methodology, one would be tempted to compute the forward $ZC_{(t, T)}$ with the following formula:

$$ZC_{(t,T)} = \left[\frac{(1+ZC_T)^T}{(1+ZC_t)^t} \right]^{(T-t)} - 1 = \frac{CPI_T}{CPI_t} - 1 \tag{5}$$

These formulas look similar and the result is straightforward. However, CPI_t is unknown at pricing date. Therefore, in the cash flows generated by the hedge using two ZCIS, there will be an intermediate payment during the life of the trade at time t. This cash flow can be positive or negative, depending on the realized inflation at time t. Hence, the total return of the strategy will depend on the interest rates between t and T used to either reinvest (or fund) the positive (negative) flow between t and T. This simple dependency introduces a correlation risk between the evolution of both the forward CPI curve and the interest rate curve. The correlation between CPI_t and CPI_T and the volatility of the forward CPI and LIBOR curves will also impact the final return of the trade. This is illustrated in Figure 10.

If $T-t = 1$, then we are pricing a 1-year forward between t and T. We see immediately that the convexity problem also applies to YoY

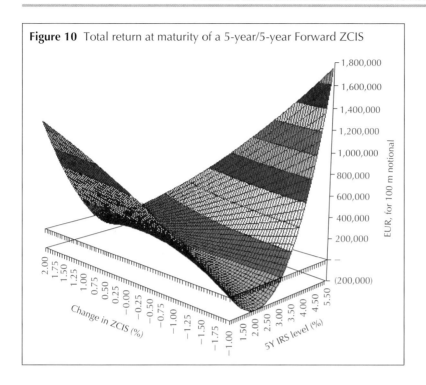

Figure 10 Total return at maturity of a 5-year/5-year Forward ZCIS

swaps (repetition of 1-year forward inflation swaps). The convexity effect will come from the lag between trade date and hedge date, and that is true for each payment.

Another related effect of interest is that of delayed payment ZCISs. In certain transactions such as lease payments linked to CPI, prices are often set for periods of more than a year, for example, leases may increase only once every 5 years. The lease recipient therefore receives CPI-indexed cash flows, but with delayed payments. Once again, the correlation between the forward CPI and forward LIBOR and their volatilities play a role in determining the correct price.

Kazziha (1997), Hughston (1998), Belgrade *et al* (2004), and Mercurio (2005), amongst others, have studied this convexity and some propose analytic solutions to price the convexity adjustment. All of these approaches, however, require careful calibration of volatilities and correlations in a market that does not (yet) provide a rich array of implied volatilities or correlations.

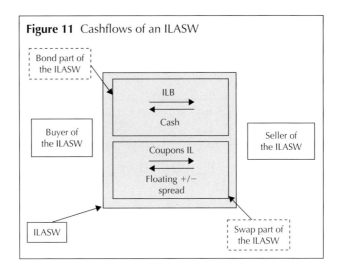

Figure 11 Cashflows of an ILASW

INFLATION-LINKED ASSET SWAPS
Definition

An asset swap is a combination of an interest rate swap and a bond, transforming the cash flow characteristics of a bond into LIBOR-based floating coupons. This transaction is often dealt by selling the bond at 100.00 or par.[20] For nominal bonds, redemption is always at par and the investor only pays out the coupons to the asset swap seller. For ILASWs, the investor additionally pays out the difference between redemption and par at maturity. The cash price for an ILB involves the real price multiplied by the index ratio, resulting in values increasingly away from par as the index ratio grows over time (regardless of the yield/coupon differential). The ILBs that have a dirty price far from 100.00 are usually traded on a "proceeds" basis in order to avoid large cash positions and increasing credit exposure.[21] In these proceeds asset swaps (PRASWs), the bond is traded at the market price at trading time, the notional on the LIBOR leg is the same as this proceeds amount and the difference between redemption amount and initial proceeds is exchanged between the counterparties at the end of the swap. Figure 11 illustrates the cash flows on ILASWs and a sample term sheet is included in Appendix A.

An indicator of the balance of flows in the inflation swap market

The traded ZCIS levels translate into forward inflation index levels and these can be compared to "fair value" levels derived from nominal and real government bonds (G_N and G_R). This bootstrapping of forward CPI is easier in a market with a full curve from the same issuer, eg, in the UK and US markets. In the Euro-zone inflation market, with 9 traded ILBs,[22] four are issued by France, four by Italy, and one by Greece, making the fair value derivation of forward CPIs a somewhat more cumbersome task as different nominal discount curves need to be used for each issuer.

In our GLC paradigm, the richness/cheapness of ZCIS is closely related to the spread between LIBOR curve breakevens and Government curve breakevens, ie, the quantity $L_{BE} - G_{BE}$. This spread which is often positive, is also reflected in the $R_{SS} - N_{SS}$ spread, ie, the differential between the real and nominal swap spreads.[23] Neither the fair level comparison of ZCISs nor the $L_{BE} - G_{BE}$ spread can be directly observed using liquidly traded instruments. However, the $R_{SS} - N_{SS}$ spread can be observed between standard market traded instruments and can thus provide direct insights into the richness/cheapness of ZCIS.

In a market that has "natural" two-way flow, ie, payers and receivers of inflation exist in equal measure, the level of ZCISs and the implied L_{BE} should be very close to the G_{BE} levels implied in the bond market.[24] The level for G_{BE} is determined by the trading activities of bond market investors. So long as the supply/demand dynamics in the inflation swap market are similar to the bond market, we can expect L_{BE} to be similar to G_{BE}. However, this is not always the case. Reasons that lead to a discrepancy between L_{BE} and G_{BE} will now be discussed.

Most ZCIS maturities in the UK RPI market up to 15–20 years trade with L_{BE} very close to G_{BE}. The UK is a market where natural supply has existed mainly through the PFI, corporate (mostly utilities), and real estate securitisation avenues offsetting the demand from pension liability hedging. However, in the longer-dated maturities, the demand tends to somewhat outstrip supply and one does observe a certain "richness" in L_{BE} levels compared to G_{BE} levels.

The US market is at the other extreme. To date, there have been no "natural" payers of inflation flows into the market. Demand exists for inflation-indexed swap flows, mostly for swapped retail issues. Swap houses generally hedge these using TIPS and Treasury positions as well as IRSs. Because these proxy hedges are (a) costly to hold (eg, net funding cost of crossing repo/reverse-repo in TIPS and nominal Treasuries); (b) need dynamic readjustment as G_{BE} and N_{SS} move relative to one another; and (c) are subject to mark-to-market,[25] the market is reluctant to show L_{BE} levels close to G_{BE} and the ZCIS trade at a large premium. What helps bring the market into balance is the sale of ILASWs to relative value players who take advantage of this richness in ZCIS which then translates into "cheapness" of ILASWs. By selling ILASWs, the swap houses get a better hedge for their YoY swaps and can for the most part offset the difficulties introduced by (a), (b), and (c) above. As long as ILASW investors are prepared to buy TIPS ASWs at richer and richer levels, the discrepancy in L_{BE} *versus* G_{BE} will reduce and the richness in ZCISs will come down. Note that this situation used to be similar in both the French and Euro HICPx markets between 2001 and 2003.

ILASW price thresholds and market price corrections

Given the claim in the previous section, can ILASWs trade at any price or are there some limits to where they can trade?

ILASWs will face the following pricing thresholds as they trade more expensively: (i) trading at LIBOR plus, (ii) trading cheaper than the GC-LIBOR spread, and (iii) trading more expensively than nominal bond ASW levels.

Since ILASWs have lower liquidity compared to their nominal counterparts, there is little chance of prices getting to threshold (iii) and this is borne out in the markets. Market evidence further suggests that the bulk of investors are reluctant to trade ILASWs any more expensively than the GC-LIBOR spread.[26] For example, most TIPS ASWs now trade around that threshold of LIBOR – 17. Accounts can lock into these trades knowing they are buying Treasury paper much cheaper than nominal paper and they have a good "carry" position as the interest they receive is higher than the interest they pay to fund their long position in the bonds (they pay the repo rate). Figure 12 illustrates this for the January 2014 TIPS.

Looking at the numbers for January 2014 TIPS asset swap levels and nominal 10-year spreads slightly differently (as shown

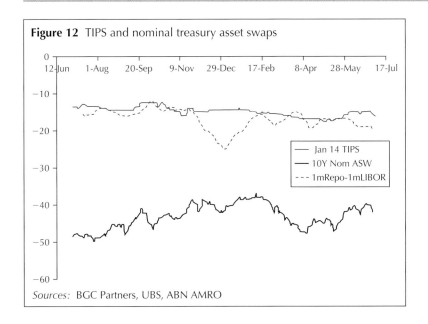

Figure 12 TIPS and nominal treasury asset swaps

Sources: BGC Partners, UBS, ABN AMRO

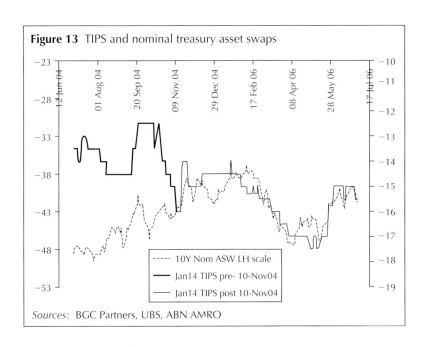

Figure 13 TIPS and nominal treasury asset swaps

Sources: BGC Partners, UBS, ABN AMRO

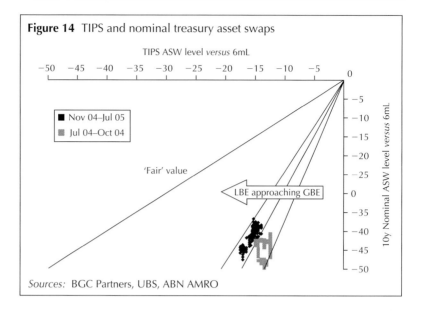

Figure 14 TIPS and nominal treasury asset swaps

Sources: BGC Partners, UBS, ABN AMRO

in Figure 13 where the axes have been shifted) it can be noted that since early November 2004, the two have been highly correlated whereas prior to this date the TIPS asset swap levels appear to have been going through a transition or "price correction" phase.

By further observing the volumes of trades in the broker market and the transition to "cheaper" ZCIS levels (or "richer" TIPS asset swap levels) as demonstrated in Figure 14 we can recognise that the market went through a "correction" phase as buyers of TIPS asset swaps drove prices higher until they approached levels close to threshold (ii) noted above.

Therefore, it appears that the instruments that currently provide the "supply" in the US inflation swap market, ie, TIPS ASWs, trade at a level that implies a *permanent* richness in the L_{BE} levels *versus* G_{BE} levels. At the initial phase of trading, asset swap trades "correct" an overpriced ZCIS curve, but even when the asset swap trades fully offset the demand side in volumes, there could still be a richness in the L_{BE} levels *versus* G_{BE} levels. For example, if nominal Treasury asset swaps are trading at LIBOR − 37 bps and TIPS ASW are trading at $L − 17$, $R_{SS}−N_{SS} = 20$ bps thus implying an approximate 20 bps premium in the ZCIS *versus* "fair value" or G_{BE} implied levels. In other words, the spread between GC-LIBOR and

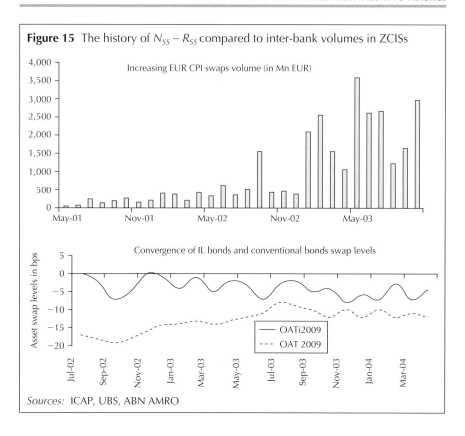

Figure 15 The history of $N_{SS} - R_{SS}$ compared to inter-bank volumes in ZCISs

Sources: ICAP, UBS, ABN AMRO

longer-dated nominal ASW levels, ie, the slope of the term structure of N_{SS} appears to be the main determinant of the "richness" of
the L_{BE} *versus* G_{BE}. Note that the above applies when the "supply"
in the swap market is primarily (or completely) due to asset swap
trades. Due to the "natural" two-way flow in the UK inflation swap
market (which has similarly wide N_{SS}) the disparity between L_{BE}
and G_{BE} is mostly close to zero in maturities up to 15–20 years. It is
only in the longer maturities where supply/demand imbalances
come into play that the richness in ZCIS is observed.

Finally, it is instructive to look at the European market to see
how it fits into the above hypothesis. Natural flow is not quite as
one-way as is in the US since there are supply flows through some
corporate deals as well as rental securitisation, toll-road deals, etc.

Figure 15 points out that the level of the $N_{SS} - R_{SS}$ in the case of
the OATi 2009 is highly correlated to the volumes of ZCISs traded

in the inter-bank market. The European market was at an earlier stage of development, not too dissimilar to where the US market is today, ie, with a strong imbalance between payers and receivers. There was therefore intensive use of ILASWs. The emergence of some new payers in 2003 and 2004 has changed the face of the European market which has gradually tilted towards being a two-way flow market. The rise in inter-bank volumes is simply the consequence of that new situation and the "supply" would gradually result in a reduction of the cheapness of the ILASWs and ultimately, convergence to fair valuation.

Figures 16(a), (b) and 17(a), (b) show price corrections trends for BTPei and OATei bonds in the short- and long-end maturities, respectively.

Collateral

Derivative transactions often use a Credit Support Annex (CSA). The collateral used as credit mitigation is, in most cases, cash or near risk-free sovereign bonds. As the ILBs have a growing redemption, the present value (PV) of the associated swaps are decreasing fast for the buyer of the ILASWs. Figure 18 illustrates this discrepancy over time. Therefore, the holder of the ILASW will be forced to post regular collateral to compensate the negative PV of the ILS embedded in the asset swap. When buying an ILASW, a counterpart will have to post more collateral than for a nominal asset swap of the same maturity and will therefore consume more of its economic capital. This is most likely to affect leveraged accounts such as hedge funds as they would be most averse to posting a large collateral. The counterpoint to this is that the holder of the bond, the ASW investor, is also likely to be funding the position with a rolling Repo agreement, which also results in increasing cash accumulation related to the upward indexation of the bond. The funding discrepancy between this cash amount (interest paid at the Repo rate) *versus* the posting of collateral (interest received at the collateral agreement rate) is also a factor for investors.[27] The arbitrage trade of buying cheap ILASWs to sell more expensive nominal ASWs is typically an area in which hedge funds would be expected to provide a balance to the market. If hedge funds do not play their full role due to objections to posting increasing collateral, the ILASW levels may not converge to the levels of the nominal

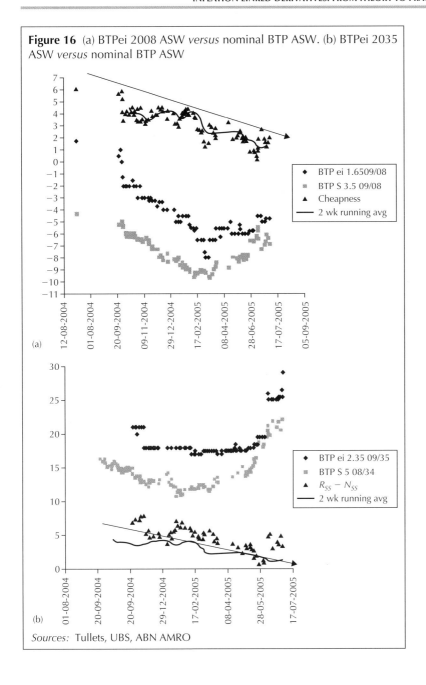

Figure 16 (a) BTPei 2008 ASW *versus* nominal BTP ASW. (b) BTPei 2035 ASW *versus* nominal BTP ASW

Sources: Tullets, UBS, ABN AMRO

Figure 17 (a) OATei 2012 ASW *versus* nominal OAT ASW. (b) OATei 2032 ASW *versus* nominal OAT ASW

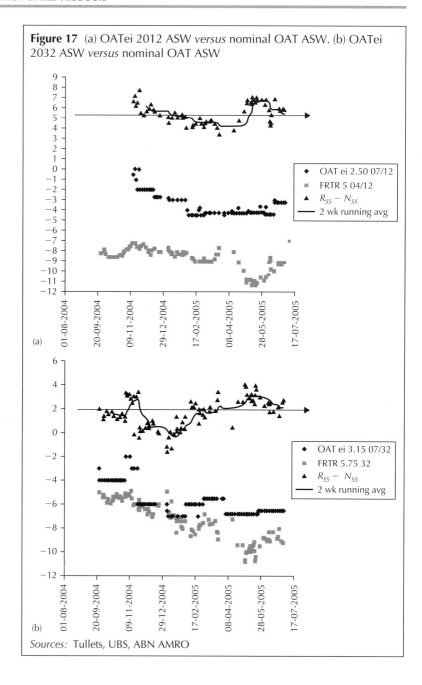

Sources: Tullets, UBS, ABN AMRO

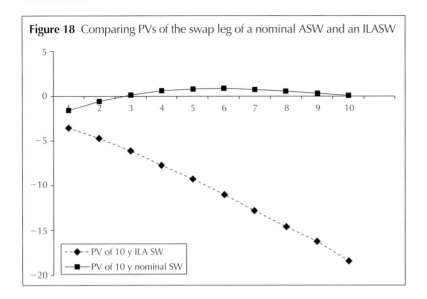

Figure 18 Comparing PVs of the swap leg of a nominal ASW and an ILASW

ASWs as fast as can be otherwise expected. On the other hand, the offsetting cash position from the rolling Repo can negate the above.

Asset swaps and credit exposure

If the ILASWs help to balance the ILS market, the difference between N_{SS} and R_{SS} should no longer exist as soon as the ILS market turns to a balanced state, like many maturities in the UK curve. But does that mean that both OATei and BTPei should have converged towards their nominal ASW levels? If not, how should the difference between N_{SS} and R_{SS} be interpreted? Furthermore, what would be the impact in the case of larger credit spreads such as for corporate ILBs and how can R_{CS} be extracted from N_{CS} (see Figures 2 and 3)?

The answer to the first question is clearly no. Figure 18 in the previous section showing the PV of the swap attached to the ILASW can be used for the underlying bond as well. An investor that would buy a BTPSei 2035 on asset swap at first issuance will invest 100. However, as time goes by, the inflation will have cumulatively increased, thus increasing the redemption amount of the bond. Assuming an average inflation rate of 2% over 30 years, the nominal redemption amount of the bond would be 180 at maturity. In case of a default, the loss will be 180 and not the 100 initially invested. As a consequence, investing in a non-secured bond ILASW implies an increasing credit exposure through time, an increase in the exposure to the potential default of the issuer. The investor should therefore expect a better return than when investing in a nominal BTP of a similar maturity. Therefore, the pick-up provided by the BTPSei 2035 ASWs compared to its nominal reference bond needs to be better than the one embedded in the OATei 2032.

The term structure of credit spreads on the nominal BTP curve is very steep (LIBOR – 8 to LIBOR +20 bps as of early August, 2005). The accreting nature of ILB cash flows compared to bullet nominal bonds, especially the back-ending of payments into the growing redemption, increase the weighted average credit spread on an ILASW for the BTP curve. All things being equal (eg, $L_{BE} = G_{BE}$), this should imply greater (cheaper) spreads in the ILASW than for the nominal BTP ASW. Therefore if BTPei35 ASWs trade at identical spreads to BTP 2034, this would in fact imply that the ILASW is trading at "rich" levels *versus* the nominal ASW. For a flat term structure of credit spreads, as is the case for the OAT curve, the above will not apply in the same way.

The same applies of course for lower rated issuers such as corporates, and the ASW pick up should be a function of the credit risk and the shape of the credit spread curve. As an example, the issuance of Veolia Environnement in 2005 came cheaper by almost 20 bps ($N_{CS} - R_{CS} = 20$ bps) than its nominal bond in term of ASW. Note that R_{CS} pricing can also make use of Credit Default Swap (CDS) levels.

INFLATION-LINKED OPTIONS (ILO)

Inflation-linked options have already traded in large size in the major markets of UK, Euro-zone, and the US, typically of the floored year-on-year coupon variety discussed in the previous section. In the Euro-zone and the US, several billion notional of such trades have dealt between banks and end users since the start of 2003. In the UK market, Limited Price Index collars on RPI known as LPI swaps have traded between banks and investors and issuers since 2001. However, to date in Q3 2005, they have not traded in the broker market.

The state of affairs in each of the major markets is such that it is premature to state that an option "market" exists. The market still trades "by appointment only" and broker market quotes exist from time to time in some of the more popular options such as floors on YoY inflation swaps or LPI. There is one exception which is the option embedded in ILASWs of Euro HICPx and French CPI ILB (redemption floored at par) since ILASW trade and get quoted on a daily basis in the Euro-zone and US markets. These floors are typically worth very little and have a negligible effect on prices of asset swaps.

The concentration of transactions on very specific out of the money strikes (such as 0% or negative strikes in YoY swapped structures) and specific maturities (typically shorter 5 to 10-year retail issues) makes it difficult to price options with longer maturities or with strikes closer to the money. The implied volatility of the traded options is by definition bid-driven and therefore high. Furthermore, these traded options do not yet provide complete information on the volatility term structure or the smile structure, if any, making it difficult to calibrate volatility surfaces at the current time.

Options embedded in retail notes

When considering embedding inflation into retail products, it is often as a tool to protect the purchasing power of a risky asset class such as equities. When protection is added to risky assets, it is typically purchased through a reduction in returns for those assets. The most classical protection is capital protection. It is simply achieved by buying a zero coupon bond and some risky assets for the rest. If the risky asset has a negative return at maturity, the protection is activated and the redemption of the note is 100.00. However, if inflation has been 20% over the same period, the redemption of 100% is only worth 80% of the real investment in term of purchasing power. Therefore, a new class of products was invented: *the purchasing power protected notes*. In that case and using the same example, the nominal redemption of such a note would be 120% and not 100%. The term-sheet shown in Appendix C is an example of a "best of" equity/inflation note.

In case of low performance of the equities combined with high inflation, the payment at maturity will be the face value plus the inflation over the period. Therefore the purchasing power of the investor will be protected.

Although a full hedging strategy for this product is beyond the scope of this chapter, one can easily understand what it may involve: the correlation between inflation and equity indices and use of options in both markets. A part of the hedge will likely involve using a cap on the increase of the inflation over the period, with a strike at 25%. It can be written as follows:

$$\text{Max}\left\{\frac{\text{CPI}_f}{\text{CPI}_i}-125\%,0\right\} \tag{6}$$

It is clearly an option on the zero coupon swap over the period, with a strike at 25% as it can be rewritten as follows:

$$\text{Max}\left\{\left[\frac{\text{CPI}_f}{\text{CPI}_i}-1\right]-\left[(1+2.2565\%)^{10}-1)\right],0\right\} \tag{7}$$

One can recognize that this payout is equal to a cap on the 10 year ZC inflation swap with a strike at 2.2565%.[28]

LPI swaps

A large proportion of the estimated £400 billion in pension liabilities linked to inflation in the UK is actually linked to a variant on RPI, the limited price index (LPI). LPI is defined based on the UK RPI but with an annual floor and collar applied to the index growth. The most common collar strikes are 0% and 5%. LPI(t), ie, LPI at time t is defined in terms of LPI(t−1), ie, LPI a year prior to time t, and RPI(t), and RPI(t−1) as shown in Equations (8) and (9):

$$\text{LPI}(t) = \text{LPI}(t-1) * \text{Min}\left\{1+\text{Cap},\text{Max}\left[1+\text{Floor},\frac{\text{RPI}(t)}{\text{RPI}(t-1)}\right]\right\} \tag{8}$$

$$\text{LPI}(t) = \text{LPI}(t-1) * \text{Min}\left\{1.05,\text{Max}\left[1.00,\frac{\text{RPI}(t)}{\text{RPI}(t-1)}\right]\right\} \tag{9}$$

A few corporate issues linked to LPI do exist, however, most pension liabilities linked to LPI have typically been hedged with RPI-linked assets.

In recent years, LPI swaps in the UK RPI market have developed in response to the pension liability demand. Additionally, banks have been able to "source" LPI flows through swaps with corporates and on the back of rental/lease securitisations and loans.

Looking at Equation (9), LPI is clearly a path dependent index and pricing swaps based on this index requires sophisticated models capable of pricing inflation caps and floors, as well as being able to cope with the path dependence of the payout. However, by generating two-way interest, much of the optional risk can be offset, while having forward inflation well within the floor and strike levels makes it "safer" to price up LPI swaps. The increasing liquidity in the RPI swaps means that delta-hedging LPI swaps is now an available alternative. However, the LPI "market" remains one of banks dealing with clients rather than dealing with one another. Starting in Q2 2005, a steady stream of broker quotes emerged in LPI ZC swaps such that 5 bps wide prices were available on most days and for most maturities from 5- to 30-years.

Nevertheless, and even in the case of the emergence of a second liquid market of LPI swaps next to the RPI ZC swaps, it would be extremely difficult to extract a volatility surface from the combination of both LPI and RPI swaps, due to the complexity of the combination of the past dependency on the one hand, and the addition of two options non equidistant from the money (0% floor and 5% cap) on the other hand. Finally, since the LPI market is driven by the balance of supply and demand (mostly demand), any calibration using this data would only provide a rough guide to ATM volatilities.

CONCLUSIONS AND FUTURE DEVELOPMENTS

The readers should be completing this chapter with a good understanding of the practical aspects of the inflation linked derivatives markets. The main trading instruments have been described and the market drivers behind pricing and trading these instruments and how they relate to the underlying inflation linked bonds have been discussed in detail.

The inflation-linked derivative markets have grown rapidly in response to the practical needs of end users. In most cases, the derivative market has developed after the establishment of an underlying ILB curve and/or is less liquid than the latter. The ILS market therefore often depends heavily on the ILBs for pricing (S_3 markets). As a result, the relative value between ILS instruments and the underlying ILBs will often be driven by the supply and demand in the ILS market as compared to the ILB market. While in some markets the natural supply of ILSs is established through the existence of payers of inflation (who use both issuance and ILSs for hedging purposes), in other markets, the ultimate "supply" is provided by asset swap buyers of ILBs. In the latter case, the dynamics of ILASW pricing will determine the richness/cheapness of the ILS breakevens relative to ILB-implied breakevens.

The further development of the IL derivatives market will depend to a large extent on the development of corporate issuance and associated alternatives to issuance such as the use of swaps. For the ILS market to be on par with IRS markets in terms of size and liquidity in relation to the underlying bond market, the regular use of ILSs by all issuers must become a reality. The precursor to this will be the wider acceptance of unswapped ILB issuance by non-sovereigns, including corporates, as a natural part of their debt management – moving away from a floating/fixed debt mix to add a third type of debt instrument: real rate bonds. This may seem like a natural evolution for the market for those who fully appreciate the appropriateness of real debt, however, it is still limited by various regulations and other practical aspects.

In many markets such as the UK, buyers of corporate ILBs are abundant. However, the growth of the IL derivatives market can also be limited by the ability of the investor community to absorb the new supply. For example, French insurers who are large buyers of ILBs have to abide by the insurance investment regulations (see R332.19 and R332.20). Unlike mutual funds, French insurers are currently unable to buy corporate ILBs. As they represent a large segment of the investor community, any change in that specific regulation would have a very strong impact on the relative value of corporate ILBs in the Euro-zone and on the future development of that market.[29]

Moving beyond ILSs, the options markets have had varying degrees of success and development. Just as in the case of ILSs, inflation option markets have been largely demand driven. The largest types of option trades in the market to date have been floors on year-on-year inflation in the Euro-zone and US markets and LPI swaps (collared RPI swaps) in the UK market. The option market can be expected to expand beyond these areas as demand for more sophisticated products increases and the market makers become more confident about delta-hedging their exposure and as two-way option flows become available.

In the case of swaptions, the absence of public fixings for ZCIS or even better L_R (LIBOR real rates) holds the development of the market. Although some good progress has been made and some ISDA documentation has given a clear framework for ILSs, there is still some work to be done as far as options are concerned. Some trades have been reported but only on a swap settlement basis due to the lack of available fixings.

Associated with the above developments in the options market, one can expect a more unified approach for pricing models. The acceleration in the publication of papers on new model developments is a sure sign that the market is responding to the demand. The next chapter will focus on some of these modelling approaches.

ACKNOWLEDGEMENTS

The authors would like to thank the book review committee for a number of useful comments and suggestions.

Both authors would like to thank the following brokerage houses: ICAP, Collins Stewart Tullet, and BGC. Their help and the data they have provided has been invaluable.

Sébastien Goldenberg would additionally like to thank Nicolas Tabardel, Etienne Broos, Valdimar Armann, Philippe Derimay and other ABN AMRO colleagues for their precious help and advice.

Dariush Mirfendereski would additionally like to thank Paul Canty for useful discussions on the recent developments in the inflation derivatives market and many other UBS colleagues and staff for providing him the opportunity to be involved at the forefront of developments in this exciting market.

TABLE OF ABBREVIATIONS

Abbreviation	Full name
DMO	(UK) Debt Management Office
ILASW	Inflation-Linked Asset Swap
LPI	Limited Price Index (associated with RPI-indexed payments)
AFT	Agence France Tresor
C_{BE}	Corporate Break Even
CIB	Capital Indexed Bond
C_N/C_R	Corporate Nominal/Real Yield
DMO	(UK) Debt Management Office
G_{BE}	Government Break Even
G_N/G_R	Government Nominal/Real Yield
HICP	Harmonized Index of Consumer Prices
HICPx	HICP ex-tobacco
IIB	Interest Indexed Bond
ILASW	Inflation-Linked Asset Swap
ILB	Inflation-Linked Bond
ILO	Inflation-Linked Options
ILS	Inflation-Linked Swap
IRS	Interest Rate Swap
L_{BE}	LIBOR Break Even
$L_N/ZCISL_R$	Zero Coupon Inflation Swap LIBOR Nominal/Real Yield
LPI	Limited Price Index (associated with RPI-indexed payments)
NFC	Net Funding Cost
PFI	Project Finance Initiative
PRASW	Proceeds Asset Swap
PV	Present Value
PV01	Present Value of 1 Basis Point
RPI	Retail Price Index
YoY	Year-on-Year
ZCIS	Zero Coupon Inflation Swap

APPENDIX A: TIPS ASSET SWAP TERM SHEET

Notional:	TBA
Start date:	$T+1$
End date:	Maturity date of bond
Client receives:	3 Month US LIBOR – X bps, Qtr, Act/360 MFol Adjusted Reset Lag 2 days
Holiday calendar:	Payment: NY Fixing: Lon
Client pays:	TIPS coupon:
	Coupon% *{DIR[C]/DIR[base]}, paid Semi-Annually 30/360 MFol Unadjusted full first coupon
	redemption at End Date Max{DIR[end]/DIR[base] – 1, 0}
	With:
	DIR[base] = Base DIR of the bond
	DIR[end] = DIR for enddate of the swap
	with DIR calculated as:
	DIR[C] = CPI[m–3] + (Daysd/Daysm) * (CPI[m–2] – CPI[m–3]) for coupon date C
	Daysd = exact day for coupon date C–1
	Daysm = number days in month corresponding to coupon date C
	CPI[m–3] = CPI for the month that is 3 months prior to coupon date C
	CPI[m–2] = CPI for the month that is 2 months prior to coupon date C
CPI:	The All–Items Consumer Price Index for All Urban Consumers published by the Bureau of Labor Statistics of the US Department of labor on a monthly basis, Bloomberg: CPURNSA <Index>
Holiday calendar:	Payment: NY Fixing: Lon

APPENDIX B: EXAMPLE OF LIVRET A SWAP TERM SHEET

Start date:	01 February 2005
End date:	01 February 2017
Bank A receives:	EUR Euribor 3 Months – X bps, Quarterly, Act/360, MFol Adjusted
Holiday calendar:	Payment: Target Fixing: Target
Bank A pays:	[Monthly 3M Euribor Average + {CPIN/CPIN-1–1}]/2 + 25 bps, paid Semi 30/360 Fol Non Adjusted

No rounding on the calculation (at the closest quarter of a basis point oras a default at the higher quarter of a basis point)

The monthly 3M Euribor average is calculated with daily fixings as follows:
❑ The daily average from (Including) 01/May/N to (Including) 31/May/N is calculated for the coupon period 01/Aug/N to 01/Feb/N+1
❑ The daily average from (including) 01/Nov/N to (Including) 30/Nov/N is calculated for coupon the period 01/Feb/N+1 to 01/Aug/N+1
❑ Non-Weighted average on Target bus days fixings.

and

To Calculate CPIN
❑ Take the CPI for the month May/N to calculate the rate for coupon period 01/Aug/N to 01/Feb/N+1
❑ Take the CPI for the month Nov/N to calculate the rate for coupon period 01/Feb/N+1 to 01/Aug/N+1

To Calculate CPIN-1 take the month CPI 12Months before CPIN

CPI:	CPI is the non revised French Consumer Prices Index Excluding Tobacco published by INSEE National Statistics office on Reuters OATINFLATION01
Holiday calendar:	Payment: Target Fixing: Target

APPENDIX C: EXAMPLE OF A 10 YEAR BEST OF NOTE
The note return is the best of an Equity basket, inflation and a fixed rate

Issuer:	AA rated issuer
Subscription period:	September 2005
Issue size:	EUR 100,000,000
Nominal amount:	EUR 1,000
Indicative issue price:	100% of the Nominal amount
Tenor: Valuation date:	10 years (ex maturity date 15 september 2015) 3 business days prior to the final settlement date
Redemption:	The notes will be redeemed on the maturity date at the Nominal amount plus an additional amount equal to the greater of: (i) 25% * Nominal amount; (ii) 100% * Inflation value; or (iii) 80% * Equity value.
Inflation value:	$$\frac{HICP_f - HICP_i}{HICP_i} \times \text{Nominal amount}$$
Inflation index final ($HICP_f$):	The level of the inflation index for July 2015 (117.20)
Inflation index initial ($HICP_i$):	The level of the inflation index for July 2005.
Inflation index	HICP (ex tobacco) (Bloomberg: CPTFEMU <Index> The inflation index will be fixed at the level indicated in Eurostat's first official publication of the inflation index for the relevant month. No subsequent revisions of the inflation index will be taken into account. index adjustment and replacement provisions apply.
Underlying basket:	Basket consisting of: W_i (Weight) I_i (Index) 35% S&P 500® 35% Dow Jones Euro STOXX 50 30% Nikkei 225
Equity value:	$$\text{Max}\left(0\%; \sum_{i=1}^{4} Wi \times \frac{I_i(average) - I_i(initial)}{I_i(initial)} \right)$$ $\times$ Nominal amount
I_i (initial):	The official closing level of the relevant index on the Pricing Date.
I_i (average):	The arithmetic mean of the official closing levels of the relevant index taken on each Averaging Date. index adjustment and succession provisions apply.
Averaging dates:	Quarterly last 3 years (12 observations) commencing on 15 Sept 2012 up to and including the Valuation Date.
Settlement currency:	EUR.

1 Under the UK's Private Finance Initiative (PFI), hospitals, schools, etc. are typically guaranteed a real income stream over periods up to 30 years.

2 Eg, June 2005 when over £550 millions 30y-equivalent ZCIS traded in the broker market.

3 Tullets, London.

4 40 bps and up.

5 "ei" stands for bonds linked to European inflation (HICPx), as opposed to those issued previously by AFT so called "i".

6 The product was initially referred to as Treasury Inflation Protected Securities with the acronym "TIPS", which is still commonly used even though they are officially called Treasury Inflation Indexed Securities, "TIIS".

7 Mainly 5 year maturity swapped issues using year-on-year inflation coupon payouts.

8 Data from BGC Partners, NY.

9 Consensus estimate, ABN AMRO/UBS.

10 Typically swapped retail issues with maturities out to 10 or 15 years.

11 Corporate issuers who get swapped back to LIBOR or fixed clearly do not bring any new "supply" to the market and are therefore not counted.

12 One in which issuers other than the Treasury participate in issuing inflation-indexed bonds (and keeping the exposure) and also consider using swaps to get similar exposure and/or to convert existing debt.

13 Exchanging $[CPI_t/CPI_0 - 1]$ with $[(1 + X\%)^t - 1]$ means that once we trade at a known level $X\%$, all components except for CPI_t are known. Hence equating the two sides, one can see that $CPI_t = CPI_0 * (1 + X\%)^t$. CPI_0 is usually the CPI fixed 3 months before the trading date. For example, the CPI_0 used for any transaction on the HICPx at any time during the month of July 2005 will be $CPI_{April05}$. In certain markets, the standard ZCISs use the linear interpolation between the CPI 3 months prior to starting date and 2 months prior the starting date as the base, eg, the ZCISs traded on the French domestic index or the US CPI market. In those cases, the base index, CPI_0, would be linearly interpolated between $CPI_{April05}$ and CPI_{May05}.

14 We define here 2 sub cathegories of Inflation Linked Bonds (ILB): (i) those issued by all sovereigns like OAT(e)i/BTPeis structured as CIB and accumulating inflation on a floating nominal; and (ii) the type IIB, in which the inflation is paid yearly and the redemption is fixed at par.

15 Unless some negative cash flows are integrated in total return notes.

16 We make the distinction between "flow seasonality" which is tradable and subject to distortions according to the balance of the market flows, and "statistical seasonality", which is the best estimate price based on historical fixings.

17 Assuming a 3m lag as defined in 3.2.

18 The BTPSei 2008 was the shortest bond linked to the HICPx and became the 5 year benchmark used to hedge short-dated derivatives. The intensive use of that bond and the large volumes traded in asset-swaps are a consequence of its singularity.

19 The 15 September 2008 maturity uses the average of the June and July 2008 HICPx fixings.

20 Noted as PPASW (par/par ASW).

21 For example, in the case where the index ratio is 1.5 and the real clean price is 100, the asset swap seller buys the bond at a proceeds price of 150, and then sells it at par resulting in a large short cash position of 50 on his books – an amount he will receive back at maturity from the asset swap investor.

22 At time of publication, Q3 2005.

23 This comparison must take into account the accreting nature of the instruments and not simply compare LIBOR spreads of par/par or even proceeds asset swaps of ILBs.

24 This will be true for AAA or near risk free sovereign bonds, but will be untrue for bonds with higher credit margin. See the previous sections in this chapter.

25 Some other players may bid up the swaps to get their hedge and cause some concentration risk in the hands of a few banks.

26 During this period, GC-LIBOR spread has averaged at approximately 20 bps, ie, L – 20 would be threshold (ii) for TIPS asset swaps, investors demanding a spread to this level to be enticed into buying the bonds on asset swap.

27 Note that the collateral funding rate is often a higher rate than the Repo rate, resulting in a positive carry position for the ILASW investor.

28 $(1+2.2565\%)^{10}=125\%$.

29 At the time of writing this chapter, the aforementioned regulation is expected to be amended to allow French issuers to purchase and hold certain corporate ILBs.

REFERENCES

Belgrade, N., E. Benhamou, and E. Koehler, 2004, "A Market Model for Inflation," Working Paper (2004 – IXIS CIB).

Belgrade, N. and E. Benhamou, 2005, "Impact of Seasonality in Inflation Derivatives Pricing," *The ICFAI Journal of Derivatives Markets*, January.

Deacon, M., A. Derry, and D. Mirfendereski, 2004, "Inflation-Indexed Securities: Bonds Swaps and Other Derivatives", 2nd Ed. Wiley Finance.

Hughston, L.P. 1998, "Inflation Derivatives," Working Paper, King's College London, May.

Jarrow, R. and Y. Yildirim, 2000, "Pricing Treasury Inflation Protected Securities and Related Derivatives using an HJM Model," *Cornell University mimeo* (August 31, 2000 revised February 19, 2002).

Jarrow, R. and Y. Yildirim, 2003, "Pricing Treasury Inflation Protected Securities and Related Derivatives Using an HJM Model," *Journal of Financial and Quantitative Analysis*, 38(2), pp. 337–58, June.

Kazziha, S. 1997, "Interest Rate Models, Inflation-based Derivatives, Trigger Notes and Cross Currency Swaptions", PhD Thesis, Imperial College of Science, Technology and Medicine, January.

Mastering Inflation Products, ABN AMRO, February 2005.

Mercurio, F. 2005, "Pricing Inflation-Indexed Derivatives", *Quantitative Finance*, 5(3), forthcoming.

6

Modelling Inflation in Finance

Nabyl Belgrade; Eric Benhamou; Etienne Koehler

Université Panthéon – La Sorbonne, IXIX CIB; Pricing Partners;
Université Panthéon – La Sorbonne, Natexis-BP

INTRODUCTION

Nowadays, the world financial market covers a large range of sophisticated derivatives, distributed on several submarkets. Each of these markets, such as the fixed income, the equity, the credit or, more recently, the indexed securities market, satisfies specific demands. Indeed, a security linked to a certain index aims at protecting its owners, investors and issuers from the risk due to the fluctuations and variation of this index. Among the most recent index markets one can find the inflation market.

Inflation (conversely, deflation) is a macroeconomic phenomenon that indicates a generalised rise (conversely, fall) of the price level of consumer goods, which is maintained and durable. It can result from many causes but it depends on the whole mechanism of the economy. In today's language, we often wrongly use the term "inflation" for an unspecified variation of prices. Inflation is measured as the relative variation of the consumer price index (CPI), which is an average of the prices of a standard set of goods and services. It is published monthly by the statistics office of each country but has a maximum delay of three months, which is necessary to allow time for the collection and treatment of the price data. There are other existing measures for inflation such as the global domestic product (GDP) deflator, the retail price index (RPI) or the production price index (PPI), for example.

Inflation, in its strictest sense, therefore represents a risk for an investor: the inflation rate can be seen as a value converter of a financial return, from its "nominal" value (in currency) into its "real" value expressed as a quantity of physical goods. This means that, with the variation of the price level, a monetary credit or a financial asset does not have the same value relative to the physical reference in time. In other words, we use a physical reference as the numeraire. We can therefore also use an exchange rate analogy. The investors and issuers cannot protect themselves from the change in the value of the numeraire (ie, the inflation risk) and so bear this risk. They can only try to forecast the future expected inflation but cannot really hedge it.

The financial market thus offers an alternative and becomes a way to manage the inflation by trading securities indexed to the CPI or to inflation. These options are supposed to protect the borrowers as well as the investors from future price changes in the real economy by guaranteeing that they have a minimal purchasing power.

Motivation

As this is a relatively new market, there is no standard model or reference as there exists for interest rate derivatives. The aim of this chapter is to give the reader a brief description of the inflation market, its participants and its products, and the models used in academic and professional research to price inflation derivatives. The reader should emerge with a better idea of the inflation market and its components, and gain insight into the different inflation market models. However, first we present the characteristics of the inflation market.

Historically, indexing to inflation finds its roots in the 18th century when bonds indexed to the prices of some invaluable goods (eg, gold and silver) were issued. This principle was supported by several economists of the time, such as Sir GS Evelyn (1798) (who was the first to define the CPI), R Musgrave, M Friedman and JM Keyes. After the Second World War, during a period of important and volatile inflation, the bonds indexed to inflation became the reference mark for inflation for several years.

However, in the 1990s a parallel market of inflation derivatives very quickly developed. Its sales turnover reached a significant proportion of that of the indexed bonds. For example, in the middle of 2003, the sales turnover of the European market, the largest swap market of inflation, represented between €3 billion and €5 billion per month. Contrary to what happened in the nominal interest rate market, where the development of the derivatives reduced the development of the bond market, the fast growing inflation-derivative market reinforced the liquidity of the linker market. The rate of increase in volume between 2002 and 2003 increased to €3 billion per month for the inflation swap market.

The inflation swap market is closely connected to the linker market in terms of pricing and flows. One important reason for this is that bonds are hedged with swaps (and *vice versa*) depending on where the liquidity is. However, an important trend is that the inflation is usually recycled from the bond market into the swap market, making inflation more expensive to buy in the swap market than on the bond market. This asymmetrical liquidity between the bond and the swap market is very important and must be taken into account when modelling the market.

As for the derivatives in general, the inflation derivatives appeared so as to satisfy particular requests from entities to manage the risks associated with a fluctuating rate of inflation, which the bond markets could not achieve. For instance, when an investor cannot find an appropriate inflation bond, he can use inflation derivatives to get a tailor made solution in terms of the maturity, index, risk profile and size of the contract.

The inflation derivatives allow their operators to extend investment strategies, transfer risks, hedge asset or liability exposure to inflation, produce hybrid products such as "best of" structures that pay the maximum between an equity return and inflation, and create synthetic credit bonds indexed to inflation. The possibilities are endless. These derivatives give access to more modest inflation market operators than on the indexed bond market. They give the possibility of instigating and increasing the activity and the liquidity of the market. The users of derivatives belong to two categories: the payers and the receivers of inflation flows. They are analogous to investors and borrowers in the indexed bond market. Payers of inflations flows are, for example, a sovereign issuer paying inflation via the bond cashflows or a real-estate company paying

inflation and receiving fixed cashflows in the swap to hedge inflation-linked rent revenues. Receivers of inflation flows are, for
example, investors in inflation bonds or pension funds, receiving
inflation and paying fixed to hedge inflation-linked liabilities.

Description of inflation derivatives
The current inflation market deals mainly with the CPI and the
RPI. It consists of a diversified range of European vanilla derivatives: swaps and options which have a range of structures for risk
management needs. The inflation market covered by these products allows the following features to be guaranteed:

❑ a forward inflation rate computed according to bond convention
   (zero-coupon) and defined as the inflation return between the
   bond issue date and a future date;
❑ a periodical inflation forward rate (usually annual) and defined
   as the inflation return between two future dates;
❑ these two markets are called, respectively, the zero-coupon and
   the year-on-year markets.

The first and the most liquid category of derivatives are the inflation swaps. Let us define $CPI(t)$ as the CPI value at time t; T_i,
$i = 1,...,n$ as the dates of flows of the product; T_0 as the initial time;
N as the nominal; and $N' = (1 + c)N$, where c is a coupon rate, as
the nominal at time T_i.[4]

Classic inflation swaps

❑ A payer zero-coupon swap, maturing at time T, pays the inflation cashflow $CPI(T)/CPI(T_0) - 1$ *versus* a pre-agreed zero-
   coupon rate $(1 + Z_T(T_0))^T - 1$:

$$
\begin{array}{c}
N\left(\dfrac{CPI(T)}{CPI(T_0)} - 1\right) \\
\uparrow \\
T_0 \qquad\qquad T \\
\downarrow \\
N\left[\left(1 + Z_T(T_0)\right)^T - 1\right]
\end{array}
$$

❑ A payer asset swap, maturing at time T_n, pays every year at time T_i a coupon indexed to the CPI, $c \times CPI(T_i)/CPI(T_0)$ *versus* receiving a fixed leg paying $S_n(T_0)$:

$$
\begin{array}{cccc}
N \ c \ \dfrac{CPI(T_1)}{CPI(T_0)} & \cdots N \ c \ \dfrac{CPI(T_i)}{CPI(T_0)} & \cdots N' \left(\dfrac{CPI(T_n)}{CPI(T_0)} - 1 \right) \\
\uparrow & \uparrow & \uparrow \\
\hline
T_0 \quad T_1 & T_i & T_n \\
\downarrow & \downarrow & \downarrow \\
NS_n(T_0) & NS_n(T_0) & N'S_n(T_0)
\end{array}
$$

❑ A payer year-on-year swap maturing at time T_n pays every year at time T_i, $CPI(T_i) / CPI(T_{i-1}) - 1$ *versus* receiving a fixed leg paying $S_n(T_0)$:

$$
\begin{array}{ccc}
N \left(\dfrac{CPI(T_1)}{CPI(T_0)} - 1 \right) & \cdots N \left(\dfrac{CPI(T_i)}{CPI(T_{i-1})} - 1 \right) & \cdots \\
\uparrow & \uparrow \\
\hline
T_0 \quad T_1 & T_i \\
\downarrow & \downarrow \\
NS_n(T_0) & NS_n(T_0)
\end{array}
$$

$$
\begin{array}{c}
N \left(\dfrac{CPI(T_n)}{CPI(T_{n-1})} - 1 \right) \\
\uparrow \\
\hline
T_n \\
\downarrow \\
NS_n(T_0)
\end{array}
$$

The zero-coupon swaps are by far the most liquid products and are the basis of the inflation swap market. There are also some liquid swaps linked to a formula including inflation and the Euribor rate. This formula is used to calculate the return of tax-exempt saving accounts in France ("Livret A", see the section "Incentive to move to other models" later).

Classic inflation-linked options

The inflation options are more diverse and less standardised. One of the most commonly traded is the Floor on year-on-year inflation.

It always guarantees a minimal forward inflation level and exists in the following forms:

❑ A zero-coupon option with a strike of $1 + (1 + k_T)^T$:

$$N\left(\frac{\text{CPI}(T)}{\text{CPI}(T_0)} - 1 - (1+k_T)^T\right)^+$$

T_0 T

❑ A year-on-year option, with a strike of $1 + K$, paying every year at time T_i:

$$N\left(\frac{\text{CPI}(T_1)}{\text{CPI}(T_0)} - 1 - K\right)^+ \quad \cdots \quad N\left(\frac{\text{CPI}(T_i)}{\text{CPI}(T_{i-1})} - 1 - K\right)^+$$

T_0 T_1 T_i

$$\cdots \quad N\left(\frac{\text{CPI}(T_i)}{\text{CPI}(T_{i-1})} - 1 - K\right)^+$$

T_n

❑ An asset swap option, with a strike of K, paying every year at time T_i:

$$N \; c \left(\frac{\text{CPI}(T_1)}{\text{CPI}(T_0)} - K\right)^+ \quad \cdots \quad N \; c \left(\frac{\text{CPI}(T_i)}{\text{CPI}(T_0)} - K\right)^+$$

T_0 T_1 T_i

$$\cdots \quad N' \left(\frac{\text{CPI}(T_n)}{\text{CPI}(T_0)} - 1 - K\right)^+$$

T_n

In the zero-coupon mode, the strike $1 + (1 + k_T)^T)$ is expressed as an inflation actuarial rate comparing the future inflation to a zero-coupon swap level. In the year-on-year mode, the effective strike is $1 + K$. It could be negative covering a range from -2% to 5%. The year-on-year options are the most liquid and the market quotes

volatilities for a strike of 0%. This floor is linked to the development of the inflation-linked structure notes, which pay a year-on-
year inflation rate, floored to avoid negative coupons. However,
the prices of these options are difficult to find and have therefore a
large bid–ask spread.

❑ In the UK, the option market has developed around the limited
price index (LPI) which is a path-dependent product, linked to
the yearly variation of the RPI capped at 5% and floored at 0%:

$$LPI(t) = LPI(t-1) \times \min\left[\max\left(\frac{RPI(t)}{RPI(t-1)}, 1\right), 1.05\right]$$

❑ There are also Asian options on inflation ie, on the cumulative of
future annual inflation:

$$N\left[\frac{1}{n}\sum_{i=1}^{n}\left(\frac{CPI(T_i)}{CPI(T_{i-1})}-1\right)-K\right]^+$$

$T_0 \qquad T_n$

❑ Finally, and more recently, there are swaptions such as the breakeven-inflation (BEI), ie, options on an annual inflation swap of
maturity n years beginning at time $t = T_m$:

$$N\left(S_n(T_m)-K\right)^+$$

$T_0 \qquad T_n$

A VIEW ON INFLATION MODELS
The modelling challenge
Modelling in stochastic calculations applied to finance assumes
that the prices of some liquid products are stochastic functions of
time with a small number of determined, preferably observable,
parameters in the market.[5] The target is then to evaluate the prices
of other non-liquid products that are related to these parameters.

Once this framework is set, the model must satisfy certain
requirements for "reliability" on the market. First, it must have a

reduced number of model parameters, that are though enough to provide consistent prices for liquid products. The necessary numerical procedures (in particular for optimisation) must be stable and make it possible to give more significance and interpretation to the traders. Wherever possible, the model should involve analytical formulas for the new products, in order to have the same stability respective to the parameters and also a sensible computation time. The stability of the so-called "parameter calibration" is important because the hedge stability depends upon it.

Modelling inflation in finance is difficult for many reasons.

❏ First, the specific economic nature of the underlying principles makes it hard to model. The inflation is not a rate quoted in the market, nor a financial credit, nor a traded liquid index. It is defined from a few monthly (not daily like the Euribor fixing time) observations at a fixed schedule following that of the CPI release.

❏ Furthermore, the inflation market presents an additional subtlety, that of the seasonality pattern of the CPI. Indeed, the economic nature of the inflation exhibits secular and permanent movements. The pricing of forward inflation should take these movements into account because the linear evolution between months (that is usually used for interest rates) does not hold. We may say that this has an impact on inflation trend as well as its volatility.

❏ Finally, the current inflation market is not very liquid and gives very little market information or data. As described in the last section, the liquid market prices (which are the inputs of the

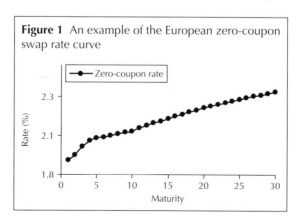

Figure 1 An example of the European zero-coupon swap rate curve

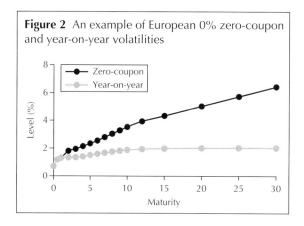

Figure 2 An example of European 0% zero-coupon and year-on-year volatilities

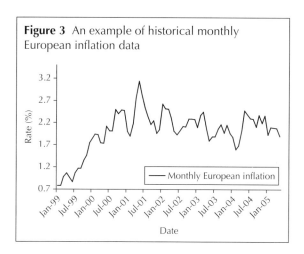

Figure 3 An example of historical monthly European inflation data

modelling) are mostly available for the zero-coupon swaps. They are available for the following indices: the EMU (ex tobacco); French (ex tobacco); the EMU (with tobacco); the UK RPI; and the US CPI. The maturities range between 2 and 30 years. The bid–ask spreads are, however, larger than for the bond market (between 5 and 10 bps) but have been narrowing significantly. Interestingly, other indices like the Spanish and Italian CPI start to be quoted but with currently much larger bid–ask spreads. On the option market, we start to get prices for year-on-year 0% floor, but the liquidity is still limited.

This lack of information also makes the calibration scheme difficult to set up and stabilise. To model this market, we have a choice of two possibilities.

❏ To model the underlying spot value of the derivatives (such as the CPI(t)) and calibrate the parameters from prices of liquid products based on the same underlying (the zero-coupon swap in this example). As we will see in the paragraph "Inflation in Econometrics of Time Series" it could be based on the historical or the economic description of the underlying. This modelling is flexible since we can choose *a priori* any payoff function that could contain non-observable or abstract parameters.

❏ To model the forward values of the underlying with the current values as initial condition for the processes (eg, the forward value of the CPI at T_i). Closer to the market, it assumes a dynamic for the prices of some products through some observable parameters (until the limit of the market liquidity): implied volatilities or implied correlations. As we will see in the Brace, Gatarek and Musiela (BGM) (1997) or market model approaches, a term structure for forward values of the underlying is built to constitute a coherent framework under some conditions.[6]

We will see that some models describe the CPI spot while others tackle the forward CPI inflation rate. Due to the limited liquidity, the first set of models is mainly used. With the improving liquidity of the zero-coupon swaps and (to some extent) of the options, the modelling is gradually moving towards the second framework. These are closer to models used for nominal interest rate products.

Primers on inflation modelling in quantitative economics

A natural starting point for this topic is the macro-economic models developed to "explain" the inflation or CPI. Indeed, there exists a rich literature in quantitative macroeconomics that is devoted to this topic. Typically the models can be differentiated into two classes:

❏ those which only measure and explain inflation; and
❏ those for the purpose of controlling monetary policy and thus long-term inflation.

The first category of models uses explicit macro-economic variables. In these models, inflation is caused by various effects such as

inflation by cost, by the supply or by money but the majority originated through the following three variables:

❑ the first monetary mass (the physical money in circulation);
❑ its speed of circulation; and
❑ the general level of the prices.

Among the reference models for the second category (which
links these three indicators in order to control inflation) is the
money quantitative equation of Fisher (1911), which defines the
money supply created for one period as the total price of the
goods generated during all the transactions. This description
corresponds best to inflation caused by demand which, according to holders of the quantitative (or new quantitative) theory,
eg, Friedman (1956), is explained mainly by an excessive creation
of money.

   A more relevant version of this relationship had been proposed
by Keynes (1923) and Pigou (1932) by expressing the money supply
during a period as the product of the inverse of its circulation
speed, the general level of prices and the GDP:

$$M_t = k_t P_t Y_t \tag{1}$$

where

❑ M_t is the money supply,
❑ k_t is the inverse of the speed of circulation of the money (modified),
❑ P_t is the general level of prices during the period of reference,
❑ Y_t is the GDP.

Importantly, this model embraces long-term inflation dynamics,
defined as the difference between the growth rate of the monetary mass and that of the GDP. The Fisher equation (Fisher 1930)
more famously used this dynamic, describing the long-term target inflation as the difference of the nominal and the real interest
rates,

$$i = r^n - r^r \tag{1a}$$

where we denote n for nominal and r for real. Equation (1a) could
be seen as a direct result of the equation (1), where the nominal

interest rate represents the growth rate of the monetary mass and the real interest rate, the growth rate of the GDP.

These models are not appropriate for mathematical finance, as we do not have non-arbitrage conditions. Furthermore, we cannot calibrate these models to the forward CPI. However, several econometric works inspired by these results have a good explanatory power of forward inflation. They can be used to compensate for the lack of market data, particularly for the short-maturity forward inflation. These models have the additional advantages of stationary properties and seasonality effects. For example, the model seasonality is a direct input of financial models. A third advantage is that these models describe dependent structure and volatility of information, which are not (yet) observable in the market. Therefore, they become calibration inputs for financial modelling. A last important advantage is that they take as their explicit (endogenous) variables of inflation some of the last observations of short-term inflation. This is therefore a first move towards a dynamic modelling as some of these models connect the long- and short-term inflation. This macroeconomic understanding of the inflation dynamic is very important in the choice of the financial modelling of inflation.

Inflation in the econometrics of time series

The usual framework in financial mathematics modelling is in continuous time. One difficulty is to transfer this discrete econometric knowledge into continuous financial modelling. The issue is to first validate a model of a time series (in discrete time) for the underlying CPI and second to define and use its continuous time equivalent model (a stochastic diffusion) to price inflation derivatives.

The important and powerful results of Nelson (1990) showed that GARCH models can be seen as the discrete version of some multi-dimensional stochastic diffusion. There exist some asymptotic conditions to validate this convergence in time. Anecdotally, the first ARCH models proposed by Engle (1982) concerned the modelling of the UK's inflation and its volatility. However, these models would provide diffusions with stochastic volatility and this would be too complex for a "new" and non-liquid inflation market.

As an alternative of the unvaried models, but keeping the same approach, one of the most justifiable starting points would be to make the analogy with the extended Vasicek model. This model takes as origin the econometric results on the short interest rate. Indeed we could, as for the zero-coupon bonds that are defined via an "instantaneous" interest rate, define the CPI via an instantaneous inflation rate and think of a dynamic close to dCPI/CPI $= i_t dt$.

Following this idea, it is interesting to notice that the definition of Treasury Inflation Protection Securities (TIPS) coupons favours such an approach. They are defined by the following formula for the coupon paid at time T_k,

$$ c_k = c \left[1 + i_k \left(T_k - T_0 \right) \right] = c \frac{CPI \left(T_k \right)}{CPI \left(T_0 \right)} \tag{2} $$

where c is the coupon rate and i_k is the implicit inflation on the period $[T_0, T_k]$ defined by

$$ i_k \Delta T = \frac{\Delta CPI}{CPI} = \frac{CPI_k - CPI_0}{CPI_0} \approx \ln(CPI_k) - \ln(CPI_0) \tag{3} $$

For (theoretical) short periods (ie, $\Delta T = T_k - T_0$ small) we would arrive to a classical dynamic of $\frac{dCPI(t)}{CPI(t)}$.

However i_k features cannot be modelled directly. Indeed, we are faced with a choice between the discrete instantaneous inflation or the short-term inflation $(i_t)_{t \geq 0}$, as for the short interest rate: it is not stationary. In other words the probability law is variable through time. We therefore model the differentiated inflation $(\Delta i_t)_{t \geq 0}$ (which is stationary) in the integrated multivariate framework. These models uses at the same time, a set of exogenous variables and some of their past realisations . This approach corresponds to the co-integration framework in which a linear conjunction of non-stationary variables reduces the degree of stability of the whole system. The resulting series would be more stationary and thus more "stable" through time. In other words, let us consider a stochastic vector $\vec{X}_t$ whose elements $\{X_t^i, i = 1, \ldots, n\}$, are integrated of order d, ie, they should be differentiated d times to become stationary. A stochastic vector is said to be co-integrated of order b if there exists a vector $\vec{\beta}$ such that the univaried process $\vec{\beta} \cdot \vec{X}_t$ is of the order of d $- b$. This approach has the advantage that it can "guarantee" a long-term equilibrium between the variables.

Jacobson *et al* (2002) have shown the relevance of this category of models to inflation and the simplest case would be to consider a model that is co-integrated of degree 1. Consequently, from the representation theorem (Engle and Granger 1987) through an Error Correction Model (ECM), the inflation X_t could be decomposed at any time t as the sum of stationary processes: its past observations $\{\Delta X_j, j < t\}$ and other variables $\beta \cdot X_{t-1}$. If we consider X_t^1 as the implicit inflation and X_t^2 as the long-term inflation, the relation between them would be written as

$$\Delta X_t^1 = \alpha \left(\pi_1, \pi_2 \right) \left(\beta_1 X_t^2 + \beta_2 X_{t-1}^1 \right) + \eta_t \qquad (4)$$

where π_1 and π_2 are system parameters and η_t is white noise $N(0, \sigma^2)$. By using a similar approach as used previously for interest rates, this equation could be seen as the discretisation of a mean reversion Ornstein–Uhlenbeck process,

$$di_t = a(b - i_t)dt + \sigma_t dW_t \qquad (5)$$

where b is the long-term inflation target, $(W_t)_{t \geq 0}$ represents Brownian motion under the risk neutral probability of the market and σ_t is the deterministic volatility of the inflation (standard deviation per unit of time). We could try to link the CPI process with the instantaneous inflation rate by Equation (3) in continuous time as

$$dCPI(t)/CPI(t) = i_t dt \qquad (6)$$

which implies a geometric Brownian dynamics on the CPI, the instantaneous inflation being Gaussian.

This model for inflation was used internally by several banks and universities to evaluate the swaps and options on inflation.[7] The normality assumption on the inflation and the determinism of its volatility induce the traditional Black–Scholes formulas on options as well as the closed reconstitution formulas of CPI forwards, starting from the swaps of inflation.

However, the calibration step of this model proved to be difficult. We must estimate the parameters (namely, the volatility curve σ_t and the mean reversion a) from one of the "implicit" volatility curves (both of inflation options), zero-coupon or year-on-year, and reconstitute the other. This is hard to realise even by using a structure of correlation on the forward CPIs, because there is a limited set of option prices for floors. The points of the volatility "surface" are not known for all strikes. Furthermore, the bootstrap of the elements of the volatility curve σ_t imply a minimal value for a (as volatilities should be positive) and incoherency between zero-coupon and year-on-year option prices. This is mainly due to the fact that the forward CPI does not behave like a zero-coupon bond: we capitalise by the instantaneous inflation rate when we discount by the short interest rate.

The important issue is that some degrees of freedom are missed due to the model limitation. This means that both the zero-coupon and the year-on-year volatility curves are unable to be fitted concurrently. This corresponds, in the econometrics of a slowly moving smooth process, ie, a process co-integrated of order 1 with one noise on the instantaneous inflation. However, empirically, a local linear model, ie, having the same decomposition "trend–random" composition as in (5) and (6) added to a correlated noise term for the CPI, should be more suitable: CPI (t) is an Itô process with a martingale part and not only a finite variation process. The relation should then be something like $dCPI_t / CPI_t = A_t dt + \sigma_t dW_t$.

This additional noise would keep the CPI log-normal and give more flexibility to the framework to link both the option and the swap (zero-coupon and year-on-year) markets.

We mentioned a possible analogy in the introduction: the CPI may be naturally considered as an exchange rate between the nominal and real worlds. It is therefore natural that the first models developed were in phase with this view: the CPI is an Itô process with a (non-zero) martingale part. More precisely, its dynamic to describe the diffusion of an exchange rate is similar to the Garman–Kohlhagen model.

The exchange rate analogy: the Jarrow–Yildirim model

Among the few published models based on the dynamics of Equation (6) is that of Jarrow and Yildirim (2003). Considered as the traditional and probably the most well-known inflation model, it assumes that the CPI is an exchange rate between the nominal and real yields. This naturally sets a three-factor framework, where the driving factors are the nominal, the real and the inflation rate. A key contribution of the Jarrow–Yildirim model is to provide the non-arbitrage conditions between these three components, along the lines of the seminal Heath–Jarrow–Morton (HJM) conditions for interest rate models. This leads to the following dynamics for the CPIs:

$$\begin{cases} \mathrm{dCPI}_t/\mathrm{CPI}_t = \left(r_t^n - r_t^r \right) \mathrm{d}t + \sigma_t^{\mathrm{CPI}} \mathrm{d}W_t^{\mathrm{CPI}} \\ \qquad \mathrm{d}r_t^k = a^k \left(b^k - r_t^k \right) \mathrm{d}t + \sigma_t^k \mathrm{d}W_t^k, \ k \in \{n, r\} \end{cases} \tag{7}$$

where r^n (respectively r^r) is the nominal (respectively real) instantaneous short-term rate, with the factor correlations $\mathrm{d}\left\langle W_t^k, W_t^j \right\rangle = \rho_{k,j} \mathrm{d}t, \ k, j \in \{n, r, \mathrm{CPI}\}$. The nominal and real zero-coupon bonds are both linked with the forward interest rate through the usual relations. The first equation expresses the CPI as an exchange rate between the nominal and the real rates. The second equation states that each of these rates follows an extended Vasicek (or Hull and White) model (1993).

Jarrow and Yildirim calibrate the initial diffusion coefficients under historical probability P. They impose that the nominal, the real zero-coupon bonds and the discounted CPI are martingales under the nominal and the real risk neutral probabilities. The CPI therefore becomes "driven" under the risk neutral probability by the instantaneous inflation rate as stated in Equation (7). This inflation rate is defined as the difference between the nominal and the real interest rates. We can derive similar expressions for the interest and exchange rates.

Let us notice that this model can be seen as the combination of the Fisher approach in Equation (1) on the long-term inflation and the co-integration approach in Equation (6), as long as both the nominal and real interest rates have close mean reversion: $a_n \approx a_r$.

This model has several advantages. First, the analogy with an exchange rate in the interest rate theory makes it intuitive and simple to understand. Resulting from non-arbitrage conditions, its framework is familiar and easy to implement. It is based on an economical hypothesis and interpretation. Second, in the particular case of Equation (6), it provides closed forms for inflation swap and Black–Scholes formulas for the inflation options, zero-coupon and year-on-year. The implied volatilities include the three factor correlations. Finally, Jarrow and Yildirim provide Greek hedging ratios with respect to the different model parameters.

To calibrate the volatility coefficients and the correlations, Jarrow and Yildirim suggest using historical estimation from the series of the nominal and the real zero-coupon bonds. The mean reversion coefficients are computed numerically using least-squares minimisation between the theoretical values (closed formulas) and the real market data. Not surprisingly, the model shows the traditional problem of the instability of historically estimated parameters. These parameters depend not only on the choice of the data sample but also on the size of this window. Therefore, a large amount of market data is needed to validate the empirical estimates. For example, in the long term, the level of the inflation volatility increases with the sample size while in the short term seasonal effects dominate. These issues make the application of the model easier in the United States than in Europe – the United States has a more developed inflation-indexed bond market, which makes the calibration of the real parameters easier, while in Europe these parameters are less "observable".

One could also choose to stay in the traditional economy framework. Usually in this case, we deduce the real value (ie, in terms of a basket of goods and services) from a cash value by observing the inflation of the current month and the interest rate, the real factor being abstract, whereas in the Jarrow–Yildirim framework we define the inflation from the nominal and the real factors. We can note that the non-arbitrage conditions are defined in the risk neutral market world, whereas the drift describes a relation defined in the historical (economical) world.

Therefore, it is felt that this model is more appropriate for the American inflation market derivatives than for the European market derivatives, especially since its development has been driven by the index-linked bond market, which is in contrast to the European one. The United States derivatives market remains a one-way market where inflation swaps are hedged with bonds, while it is more a two-way system in Europe. This explains why structured swaps can be hedged by zero-coupon swaps (see Chapter 5).

Incentive to move to other models

There are other issues in the dynamic of the inflation markets that have driven the development of other pricing models. For instance, some asset-liability managers are ready to pay more to receive inflation-linked swaps exactly matching their liability structure than for linkers with only a partial match. Therefore, the lack of inflation payoffs have forced investment banks to pay inflation via inflation swaps, recycling inflation from the linkers and consequently baring the mismatched risk. This partly explains why BEI is usually higher (more expensive) in the swap than in the bond market.

Therefore, depending on which instrument is priced by the model, it is important to calibrate on the appropriate hedging instruments, ie, bonds *versus* swaps. The development of structured or hybrid notes has also led to models where inputs are swaps rather than bonds.

For example, in 2003, the French tax exempt saving account, "Livret A", was linked to Euribor and inflation via the following formula for its interest rate:

$$\frac{\text{Monthly average of 3 month Euribor} + \text{Annual inflation rate}}{2} + 0.25\%$$

As a result, a pool of €175 billion of bank liabilities has been linked to inflation. Most of these liabilities are hedged with inflation swaps, with a payoff replicating the "Livret A" formula, and these swaps are becoming a commodity priced within a very tight range. As they have been traded within 1–2 bps maximum, the pricing must be very accurate for these products. Moreover, the rounding effect adds some complexity and must be taken into account, first at the level of the CPI (five digits) and then on the formula rounding at the closest 25 bps.

In order to price inflation derivatives with the Jarrow–Yildirim model we have to deal with a non-observable variable (the real rate). We also have to calibrate swaps on bond prices. This brings up the following issues.

❑ We do not calibrate the model on the most natural curve in the derivatives market (ie, the swap curve). Furthermore, the BEI is different in the bond and swap worlds.
❑ The maturities of the calibrated products do not closely match the maturities of the products that we want to price.
❑ The fundamental inputs of several hybrid products (the Euribor or the Libor rates) are only indirectly known.

Another (standard) issue is the possibility of negative nominal interest rates, as is always the case with Gaussian models. These issues have led practitioners to explore new models. A "natural" way is to adapt the "Libor" models as they are increasingly used in the modelling of the nominal fixed income. Two of these models are now presented.

The BGM model for inflation: the Mercurio model

Based on an extension of the Jarrow–Yildirim framework, Mercurio (2004) offers two new approaches to improve the modelling of inflation and nominal rates in a more consistent way.

In his article, Mercurio keeps the exchange rate analogy, but considers a BGM model on both the nominal and "real" Libor forward rates, linking them with the respective zero-coupon bonds. This result relies on the fact that a BGM model can be derived from the HJM framework. He critiqued the Jarrow–Yildirim approach, arguing the possibility of negative nominal interest rates and the difficulty of estimating historically the real interest rate parameters.

He therefore assumes log-normal dynamics on the nominal and the real Libor forward rates as follows:

$$\begin{cases} dF^k\left(t, T_{i-1}, T_i\right)/F^k\left(t, T_{i-1}, T_i\right) = \sigma_{k,i} dZ_i^k\left(t\right) \\ B^k\left(t, T_i\right)/B^k\left(t, T_{i-1}\right) = 1/\left(1 + \tau_i F^k\left(t, T_{i-1}, T_i\right)\right) \end{cases}, \quad k \in \{n, r\} \quad (8)$$

where $F^n(t, T_{i-1}, T_i)$ (respectively $F^r(t, T_{i-1}, T_i)$) is the value at time t of the nominal (respectively real) Libor forward rate between T_{i-1} and T_i, $Z_i^n(t)$ (respectively $Z_i^r(t)$) is a Brownian motion under the nominal (respectively real) forward payment probability, $\tau_i = T_i - T_{i-1}$ and $B^k(t, T)$ is the value at time t of a nominal (when $k = n$) or real (when $k = r$) zero-coupon bond maturing at time T.

Mercurio advances a better understanding of the model parameters and a more accurate calibration to market data. From the spot CPI dynamics (the same as in the Jarrow–Yildirim model, ie, the first line of Equation (7)), the expected forward inflation process is used to valuate the inflation swap leg. Mercurio uses a result of the Jarrow–Yildirim model: the expected value of a forward inflation ratio can be expressed by only the real forward zero-coupon bond and the nominal zero-coupon bond. This will lead to Equation (10).

Thus, for a maturity, two martingale processes are defined: one under the nominal terminal probability measure of the numerator (used for the first and second approaches) and the other under the denominator's nominal terminal probability (used only in the second approach). The two are expressed with the nominal and the real forward Libor rates. In each approach, only the volatilities of the processes and the correlations between them are used, which are themselves implicit functions of the original parameters of the Jarrow–Yildirim model.

For cashflow maturing at time T_n, in the first approach, the martingale process is analogous to a forward exchange rate,

$$I_i(t) = CPI_t \frac{B^r(t, T_i)}{B^n(t, T_i)} \tag{9}$$

from the non-arbitrage conditions of the exchange approach. Here, $B^n(t, T_i)$ (respectively $B^r(t, T_i)$) stands for the value at time t of the nominal (respectively real) zero-coupon bond, maturing at time T_i.

Thus, the ratio of two of these processes at the same date t is equal to the inflation ratio due to the fact that

$$\frac{I_i(t)}{I_{i-1}(t)} = \frac{1 + \tau_i F^n(t; T_{i-1}, T_i)}{1 + \tau_i F^r(t; T_{i-1}, T_i)} \tag{10}$$

where, as already mentioned, $\tau_i = T_i - T_{i-1}$ and $F^n(t; T_{i-1}, T_i)$ (respectively $F^r(t; T_{i-1}, T_i)$) is the value at time t of the nominal (respectively real) Libor rate between T_{i-1} and T_i.

Note that, as a consequence of the approach followed in the market model (as in the BGM model (1997)), the volatility coefficient of the process in Equation (9) is stochastic, containing the instantaneous deterministic CPIs, the nominal and the real forward Libor volatilities, and the correlation between the CPIs and between the nominal and real forward Libor rates. Mercurio then used an approximation of the Libor rates at time $t = 0$ and a one-dimensional numerical integration to compute every future inflation cashflow. Mercurio argues that this procedure is not cumbersome and time consuming as is typical in a market model, and the input parameters can be determined more easily than those coming from the Jarrow–Yildirim approach.

In the second approach, the proposed process is the same as in Equation (9) but is written under another terminal nominal probability at a future date. This change of probability implies a drift

Table 1 Examples of convexity adjustment deduced from the European year-on-year swap rate

Maturity	Rate with convexity adjustment	Rate without convexity adjustment	Convexity adjustment
1	1.68	1.68	–
2	1.83	1.83	(0.0061)
3	1.90	1.90	(0.0071)
4	1.93	1.94	(0.0088)
5	1.95	1.96	(0.0104)
6	1.97	1.98	(0.0122)
7	1.98	1.99	(0.0151)
8	1.99	2.01	(0.0181)
9	2.00	2.02	(0.0212)
10	2.01	2.03	(0.0245)
12	2.03	2.06	(0.0290)
15	2.05	2.08	(0.0308)
20	2.09	2.13	(0.0369)
25	2.13	2.17	(0.0445)
30	2.16	2.21	(0.0527)

correction of this process, and then a correction to the expected value of the forward inflation ratio from the actual ratio by a deterministic correction called the convexity adjustment. This adjustment is a function of the instantaneous volatilities of the nominal forward Libor rate and the CPI, and also of the correlations between the nominal forward Libor themselves (see the example in Table 1).

For the inflation option values, as in the Jarrow–Yildirim model, the second approach provides Black–Scholes formulas due to the determinism of the parameters. The implied volatilities are a function of the volatilities of the processes defined in Equation (9) and the correlation between them. To calibrate the parameters, Mercurio recovers the real forward Libors from the zero-coupon market. The other parameters are estimated by least-squares estimation between the theoretical values (closed formulas) and the real market data of the year-on-year swap rates, under some constraints to avoid over-parameterisation.

This approach solves parts of the issues raised in the section "Modelling challenge".

❑ The nominal interest rate is positive.

❑ The variables used for modelling (Libor forward rates) are more closely related to the inflation derivatives market. In the European market, the calibration is therefore more direct and the pricing of hybrid products is easier.

Another important advantage of Mercurio's approach is that less parameters are needed than in the Jarrow–Yildirim model. Furthermore, since it is analogous to the interest rate model, it keeps the log-normality of the CPI and thus implies closed formulas for the swaps and floors.

However, there are some drawbacks.

❑ As in the Jarrow–Yildirim model, the inflation is always defined through an economic relation from the real factor, so real rates are not deduced from the inflation.

❑ One does not directly deduce the year-on-year analogy from that of the inflation zero-coupon swaps. However, we must note that the year-on-year swaps are not yet very liquid.

In the end, Mercurio announced that, even though the three models are equivalent in terms of calibration, they can lead to different prices for deep out of the money derivatives like 0% inflation floors.

However, this is becoming an issue as the floor market is moving into a wider range of floor strikes but no market prices are observable. In the absence of a standard model, it is important to obtain a range of models and to understand their differences in order to take pricing decisions. This has been another argument for exploring other approaches. In addition, the development of new products, with the payoff directly involving forward inflation or the forward inflation rate, has changed the inflation traders' perspective. They consider the inflation index or inflation rate as the trading variable. This variable would also be useful to price hybrid structures involving forward inflation swaps. As another advantage, it would be possible to more easily link zero-coupon and year-on-year inflation derivatives. Furthermore, this would be a more direct way to distinguish between two views on CPI: either as a sampling of n different processes (eg, one process for each monthly CPI), or as n samplings of one single process. Taking into account the seasonality might therefore be easier.

The market model for inflation: the Belgrade–Benhamou–Koehler (BBK) model

The forward inflation traded in the market is different from the econometrics forecast of the statistical series. Indeed, the zero-coupon swap market quotes an expected CPI curve, which evolves in its own world, influenced by, but not the same as, the historical world (see Figures 4a and 4b).

We can see from these pictures that shocks tend to propagate more strongly in the real world than in the nominal world. From a

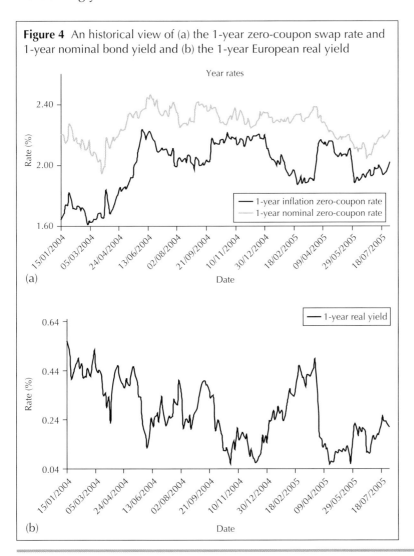

Figure 4 An historical view of (a) the 1-year zero-coupon swap rate and 1-year nominal bond yield and (b) the 1-year European real yield

time series point of view, the CPI may thus be seen either as a single sampling of n different processes observed each at one time or as n samplings of one single process observed at different times. In econometrics, the CPI is considered as heteroskedastic with autocorrelation on errors in the first case, and without autocorrelation in the second.

Belgrade *et al* (2004b) offer to link the zero-coupon and the year-on-year inflation derivatives in the European inflation swap and option markets by means of a market model. As in the BGM model for Libor interest rates, they choose to model the forward values of the CPI. These processes (being tradable) are martingales under their respective nominal terminal probabilities. Moreover, Belgrade *et al* assume that each CPI fixed at time T_i, and seen at time t, is an exponential martingale under each Q_{T_i} (which is the forward probability at time T_i),

$$\frac{\mathrm{dCPI}(t, T_i)}{\mathrm{CPI}(t, T_i)} = \sigma(t, T_i)\,\mathrm{d}W_{T_i}^i(t) \tag{11}$$

with some deterministic volatility term structures $\sigma(t, T)$. The Brownian motions $\{W_{T_i}^i(t), i = 1,\ldots, n\}$ are correlated with an instantaneous correlation given by $\mathrm{d}\langle W_t^i, W_t^j\rangle = \rho_{i,j}^{\mathrm{INF}}\mathrm{d}t$ where $i, j = 1,\ldots,n$, while the nominal zero-coupon bonds are log-normal with deterministic scalar volatilities correlated with those of the forward CPI with the time-dependent structures $\mathrm{d}\langle W_t^i, B_t\rangle = \rho_i^{\mathrm{INF,DF}}\mathrm{d}t$. Correlations are the instantaneous correlations between the forward CPI and the zero-coupon nominal bonds.

Within this framework, Belgrade *et al* show that the forward value of the CPI ratio is simply the ratio of the respective forward CPIs multiplied by a convexity adjustment. This adjustment is an explicit function of the implied volatilities of the forward CPIs, the forward zero-coupon bond and the correlations between them (see the example in Table 1).

In a second step, Belgrade *et al* are able to link the implied volatilities of the zero-coupon and the year-on-year options for strikes other than 0%. They suggest filling up some points of the volatility surface by reconstituting the year-on-year volatilities for strike $K\%$ by an explicit algorithm. The implied CPI correlations in the formula for a strike $K \neq 0$ are the CPI correlations deduced from the same formula as the one used to price 0% zero-coupon and year-on-year volatilities. Hence, Belgrade *et al* can construct a synthetic analogy structure for the inflation options.

The convexity adjustment is dependent on the chosen form of the volatility $\sigma(t, T)$. To reduce the degree of freedom of the framework, Belgrade *et al* assume a homogeneous form of the volatility, given as follows:

$$\sigma(t, T) = fct(T - t) \tag{12}$$

The latter condition provides stability in the volatility term structure, making it attractive. Under this assumption, Belgrade *et al* can state simple relations between the implied volatilities and correlations giving consistency between them. By bounding the covariance, they also provide a range for the zero-coupon and the year-on-year volatilities and the implied CPI correlations (conditionally to the two others).

In addition, under the same framework, it is shown that the volatility of a year-on-year swap rate maturing in n years can be approximated by a weighted average of year-on-year volatilities (Belgrade *et al* 2004a). Naturally, the various weights are functions of the average correlations between the year-on-year swap rate and nominal zero-coupon bonds. The methodology is similar to that used for the usual formula between Foward Rate Agreement (FRA) and swap volatilities.[8]

Belgrade *et al* give closed formulas for the valuation of BEI swaptions and numerical integration for options on real yield by redefining the forward real interest rate as a spread option between the nominal swap rate and a forward year-on-year swap of the same maturity.

Finally, to include the seasonality effect, Belgrade and Benhamou (2005) give two methods for estimating and replicating deterministically the stochastic and non-stationary seasonality component.[9] They suggest correcting the forward value CPI $(0, D_T)$, maturing on the day D_T of the Tth year, by interpolating the annual seasonality through 12 bumps $S(m)$,

$$S(D_T) = S(D_T) - \left((m - m_d) \frac{S(m_u) - S(m_d)}{m_u - m_d} + S(m_d) \right) \tag{13}$$

where m_d (m_u) is the month before (after) the day D_T. By choosing a multiplicative scheme and a deterministic seasonality, they guarantee that the adjustment is the same for the forward and the spot curve. They extract the seasonality bumps from the historical spot CPI data.

As in time series theory, the spot CPI is supposed to be a certain separable function f of hidden components: a deterministic trend Z, deterministic seasonality S, and a random ε:

$$\text{CPI}\,(t, t) = f\,(Z_t, S_t, \varepsilon_t) \tag{14}$$

To recover the regular seasonality S_t from the historical data, they use either a non-parametric method (sequential filtering of the different components) or a parametric method (the Buys–Ballot (1847) econometric model) (see Figure 5).

The market model has many advantages. First, it directly models the observable underlying factors: zero-coupon and year-on-year volatilities and implied CPI correlations. Second, it provides formulas between zero-coupon and year-on-year swap rates and between zero-coupon and year-on-year volatilities. Third, the choice of a homogeneous form for the volatility allows a reduction in the degrees of freedom of the model and enables coherence conditions for each of the implied volatilities and correlations. Finally, it can incorporate a seasonality adjustment for pricing of inflation derivatives and swaptions.

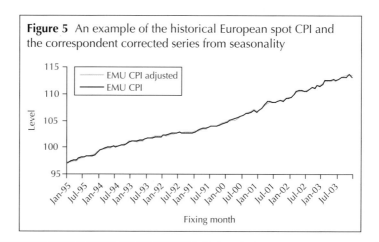

Figure 5 An example of the historical European spot CPI and the correspondent corrected series from seasonality

Table 2 Outlook of inflation models

Model (Year)	Type	Calibration Inputs	Tools	Outputs	Pros	Cons
Jarrow and Yildirim (2003)	Spot	CPI, nominal, real bonds	Historical estimation	Swaps, bonds, floors	Closed formulas Familiarity Exchange analogy	Historical estimation 3 factors
Mercurio (2004)	Forward	Swaps (Convexity Adjustment)	Least Squares	Swaps, bonds, floors, hybrids (inflation – interest rate)	Closed formulas Few parameters Consistency	Multidimensional feature
Belgrade et al (2004a,b)	Forward	Swaps, floors (0% volatilities)	Coherence conditions	Swaps, bonds, floors, swaptions, hybrids (inflation – interest rate)	Closed formulas Observable variables Links the products	Multidimensional feature: a parametric volatility is necessary

On the other hand, the multi-dimensional feature of the model makes the evaluation slower and the calibration is consistently harder for a high dimension of forward inflation structures. Due to the low liquidity of the market, calibration is (as usual) not easy. Also, without a sensible parameterisation of the volatility, the model presents too many degrees of freedom, especially for the implied CPI correlations and the interest rate–inflation correlation structure estimated historically. It is therefore necessary to consider a parametric volatility.

CONCLUDING REMARKS

The early stages of the growing inflation derivative market present, due to its nature, their own particularities, which require specific modelling solutions. However, as yet there is no standard model because of the limited liquidity (the bid–ask on the EMU Harmonised Index of Consumer Prices (HICP) is 3–4 bps) and the necessity to describe both the zero-coupon and year-on-year markets. Historically, the first pricing models were drawn from the quantitative economic theory to explain the inflation or the CPI. Despite the fact that pricing models could be driven by econometric forecasting models, the modelling in finance implies more calibrations and hedging issues. Because of this, most works attempted to derive the modelling from econometric theory and to make an interest rate analogy at the same time.

As market data appeared, the models became closer to existing financial models.

❑ The first inflation-linked products were inflation-indexed bonds and the first models used (directly or not) these bond values as variables and inputs. The models were also used at that time to price inflation-indexed bonds. The first model of Jarrow and Yildirim, published in 2000, proposed using non-arbitrage conditions to define the inflation through the nominal and real interest rates. Even if it gave explicit Greek ratios and closed formulas on swaps and options, it contained many non-observable parameters and used historical estimation. Calibration on bond prices also leaves open the issue of the market distortion between inflation-linked bonds and derivatives (higher BEI for swaps than for bonds).

❏ The inflation derivatives market developed later and allowed a better matching of the liability structure to asset managers. Models then appeared that used these inflation derivatives as variables and inputs. They also aimed at pricing inflation derivatives instead of inflation-indexed bonds.

> ❏ Mercurio (2004) provided two models derived from the two exchange rate approaches in a BGM framework, expressing the forward inflation through only the real factor and thus reducing the number of parameters. These are calibrated on the prices of the year-on-year swap. A simple numerical integration is required in the first approach to compute the swap value, while in the second approach the swaps and the options values are expressed by closed formulas.
>
> ❏ The second model is equivalent to, but independently derived from, the multi-asset approach in the BBK model (Belgrade *et al* 2004a,b). The difference is that the CPI is defined through a volatility-correlation term structure. Furthermore, a specific form of volatility is proposed to define coherence conditions between implied volatilities and the correlations reducing the degree of freedom, linking the closed formulas on the zero-coupon and the year-on-year options and swaps. The seasonality adjustment in the pricing is included in this market model. The model also allows the pricing of the inflation swaption and real yield option.

Challenges for future modelling include the following.

❏ How can the already mentioned distortion between inflation-linked bonds and derivatives be handled? How much will this distortion fade?

❏ The option market needs to become liquid to get volatility information: how long will it take?

❏ Which model will be the standard for pricing vanilla inflation derivatives?

❏ Will this standard model also allow the pricing and hedging of sophisticated callable structure on inflation, in particular the real yield and the hybrid inflation-interest rate derivatives, which are, maybe, the future trend of the inflation market?

ACKNOWLEDGEMENTS

We would like to warmly thank Brice Benaben, Davide Bieber and the anonymous reviewers for their help and most valuable comments and suggestions.

1 E-mail: nbelgrade@ixis-cib.com
2 E-mail: eric.benhamou@pricingpartners.com
3 E-mail: etienne.koehler@nxbp.fr
4 An important remark is that CPI(t) is not exactly the value at time t. For simplification we use the CPI(t) instead of the usual DIR (Daily Indexed Reference). The DIR is a value-interpolated CPI with a 3-month lag and is the value used to index inflation-linked bonds. Let us note, however, that some swaps use the straight method instead of the interpolated method. That means that the swap index is reset once a month, with a lag of 2 or 3 months.
5 One can show that they must be Itô processes, due to the usual computational constraints on these quantities: stability by sum or difference, multiplication, exponentiation, etc.
6 If we note X as the underlying, the term structure is $E^{Qt}[X_t \mid X_s, ..., X_0]$, $s < t$. As the market treats the spot value of the underlying, we have the martingale property: $E^{Qt}[X_t \mid X_t, ..., X_0] = X_t$.
7 See, for example, Koehler and Belgrade (2002) and Beletski (2004).
8 A swap instantaneous volatility is a linear combination of FRA instantaneous volatilities.
9 Bryan, M. and S. Cecchetti, 1995, "The Seasonality of Consumer Prices", NBER Working Paper No.W5173.

REFERENCES

Beletski, T., 2004, "Mathematical models for inflation and pricing of macro derivatives", University of Kaiserslauten, Bonn, thesis presentation, available on http://www.caesar.de/uploads/media/Mathematical_Models_for_Inflation_and_Pricing_of_Macro_Deriv_01.pdf

Belgrade, N. and E. Benhamou, 2005, "Impact of Seasonality in Inflation Derivatives Pricing", *ICFAI Journal of Derivatives Markets*, 2(1). Ixis CIB Fixed Income Quantitative Research Paper, available on SSRN www.ssrn.com

Belgrade, N., E. Benhamou and Y. Khlif, 2004a, "Valuation of Inflation Swap Volatility under a Market Model and Pricing of Real Yield Options", Ixis CIB Fixed Income Quantitative Research Paper, available on SSRN www.ssrn.com

Belgrade, N., E. Benhamou and E. Koehler, 2004b, "A Market model for inflation", Ixis CIB Fixed Income Quantitative Research Paper, available on SSRN www.ssrn.com

Brace, A., D. Gatarek and M. Musiela, 1997, "The Market Model of Interest Rate Dynamics", *Mathematical Finance*, 7(2), pp. 127–55.

Brigo, D. and F. Mercurio, 2001, *Interest Rate Models* (Springer).

Bryan, M. and S. Cecchetti, 1995, "The Seasonality of Consumer Prices", NBER Working Paper No. W5173.

Buys–Ballot, C., 1847, "Les changements périodiques de températures, Utrecht", Publication du Bureau central météorologique de France.

Cleveland and Tiao, 1976, "Decomposition of Seasonal Time Series: A model for the Census X11 Program". JASA, 71, pp. 581–6.

Deacon, M., A. Derry and D. Mirefendereski, 2001, *Inflation-Indexed Securities, Bonds, Swaps and Other Derivatives*, 2nd edn (Wiley Finance).

Engle, R.E., 1982, "Autoregressive Conditional Heterocedasticity with Estimates of the Variance of United Kingdom Inflation", *Econometrica*, **50**, pp. 984–1007.

Engle, R.E. and C.W.J. Granger, 1987, "Cointegration and Error-correction: Representation, Estimation and Testing", *Econometrica*, **55**, 251–76.

Evelyn, G.S. *et al*, 1798, "An Account of Some Endeavours to Ascertain a Standard of Weight and Measure", *Philosophical Transactions of the Royal Society of London*, **88**, pp. 133–82.

Fisher, I., 1930, "The Purchasing Power of Money: Its Determination and Relation to Credit, Interest, and Crises" (New York: The Macmillan Company).

Friedman, M., 1956, "The Quantity Theory of Money: A Restatement," in M. Friedman (ed.), Studies in the Quantity Theory of Money, pp. 3–21 (Chicago: The University of Chicago Press).

Hamilton, J.D. and D.H. Kim, 2000, "A Re-examination of the Predictability of Economic Activity using the Yield Spread", NBER Working Paper No. 7954, October.

Hull, J., and J. White, 1993, "One Factor Interest Rate Models and the Valuation of Interest rate Derivative Securities," with A. White, Journal of Financial and Quantitative Analysis, Vol. 28, No. 2, (June), pp. 235–54.

Jacobson, T., J. Lyhagen, R. Larsson and M. Nessén, 2002, *Inflation, Exchange Rates and PPP in a Multivariate Panel Cointegration Model,* Working Paper Series, Sveriges Riksbank (Central Bank of Sweden), 145

Jarrow, R. and Y. Yildrim, 2003, "Pricing Treasury Inflation Protected Securities and Related Derivative Securities using an HJM Model", *Journal of Financial and Quantitative Analysis*, **38(2)**, 409–30.

Keynes J.M., 1923, "A Tract on Monetary Reform." reprinted in Keynes, Collected Writings, vol. 4.

Koehler, E. and N. Belgrade, 2002, "Evaluation de produits liés à l'inflation", Document interne (internal internship document) IXIS-CIB R&D and Université Paris 1 La Sorbonne.

Lamberton, D. and B. Lapeyre, 1997, "Introduction au calcul stochastique en finance", édition Ellipse.

Mercurio, F., 2004, "Pricing Inflation-Indexed Derivatives", Banca IMI Working paper, available on http://www.fabiomercurio.it/Inflation.pdf

Nelson, D., 1990, "ARCH Models and Diffusion Approximations", *Journal of Econometrics*, **45**, 7–38.

Pigou, A., 1932, "The Economics of Welfare", (London: Macmillan and Co).

Section 2

Asset and Liability Management with Inflation-Linked Products

7

Agence France Trésor's (AFT's) Approach to Inflation-Linked Bonds

Benoît Coeuré and Nicolas Sagnes

AFT

Launching a new debt instrument is both a difficult and intellectually exciting decision. The gains arising from liability diversification have to be weighted against potential fragmentation of the issuance, practical difficulties (such as the exact design of the security, the frequency of issuance or else how to give incentives for primary dealers to trade the new bonds) and of course the willingness of final investors to buy them. Inflation-linked bonds are a case in point. While the rise of the global inflation market is widely perceived as a major success story of modern capital markets, the relevance of issuing inflation-linked bonds remains an issue for discussion in issuers' forums. In this article, we present a brief historical survey of the French Republic inflation-linked bonds programme, as seen from the issuer's point of view. After recalling the theoretical reasons for issuing inflation-linked bonds, we discuss the instruments available to assess their usefulness and present empirical evidence that the consumer price indices OATi/OAT€i have progressively proven to be a cheaper way to finance than conventional (ie, nominal) bonds.

A GROWING MARKET

Issuance of inflation-linked bonds by the French Republic goes back to 1998. It first required an amendment to fiscal legislation, since price indexation of any kind had been forbidden by a 1959 law. This amendment was voted in July 1998, thus materialising political acceptance of the new class of securities. The first OAT

(French government bond) indexed on the French consumer price index excluding tobacco (OATi) was issued in autumn 1998. Three years later, in autumn 2001, France issued the first bond linked to the Euro zone consumer price index excluding tobacco (OAT€i).

At the beginning many investors remained hesitant. The lack of historical track record clouded this new asset class with uncertainty. Also, liquidity was poor compared to nominal bonds due to limited supply, even though all French primary dealers had been asked by AFT (Agence France Trésor) to act as market makers. This contributed to the creation of an illiquidity premium. The average inflation breakeven (that is, the difference between the real yield of the indexed bond and the yield of a nominal bond with similar maturity) at issuance for the first ten auctions was about 1.6% as a consequence of this illiquidity premium and of subdued inflationary pressures. Trading volumes remained limited as supply was only occasional and demand was confined within a limited group of banks and investors.

The introduction in 2001 of the OAT€i indexed on the Euro zone harmonised index of consumer prices excluding tobacco was the real turning point. The decision was taken after a thorough consultation of market participants. It was in accord with the emergence of a truly pan-European bond market and reflected the expectation of a surging liability-driven demand for inflation protection in a number of Euro zone countries.

Domestic demand was then boosted by two regulatory changes. French insurers were allowed to better account for accruing inflation, giving them license to allocate part of their portfolios to the new asset. Demand for OATi was strengthened by a reform of regulated household savings accounts ("Livret A"), with implementation of a fixed formula linking their yield to inflation (excluding tobacco) and short-term interest rates as of 1st August 2004. Almost every retail bank had opened savings accounts following the Livret A rate and some started hedging part of their commitments with index-linked bonds or swaps.

The total amount of OATi and OAT€i had a face value of €70 billion as of the 31st March 2005, with a balance between OATi and OAT€I, since AFT had issued on both consumer price indices, in order to provide liquidity to both real curves. The French Republic was followed by CADES (the body managing French social security debt), the Hellenic Republic and the Republic of Italy in becoming regular issuers of inflation-linked bonds. Also, the German Finance Agency expressed an interest and is generally expected to issue. The emergence of new issuers gave the market additional visibility and opened up demand throughout the Euro zone. In addition, increase in supply stimulated liquidity in the secondary market. The total Euro zone Government inflation bond market now has a face value of €115 billion and has outpaced the United States in terms of yearly issuance.

A good measure of liquidity is the monthly turnover on the secondary market, as reported to AFT by primary dealers, although this figure understates actual volumes since it is limited to trades involving primary dealers. Whereas at the beginning of 2003 the monthly turnover was €15 billion only, it had nearly reached €50 billion by mid-2005 (see Figure 1). The rise in liquidity is also reflected in the strong demand at linkers auctions, where bid-to-cover ratios have been on average one point higher than for conventional bonds at an average of 3. This situation strongly differs from the inception of the programme in 1999, when the bid-to-cover ratio was just a little above nominal bonds.

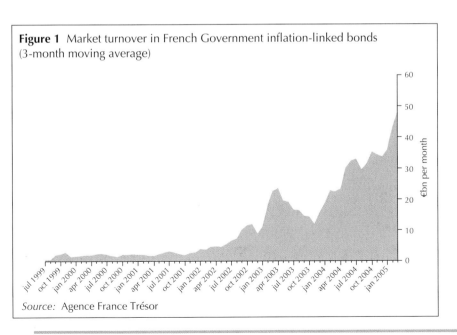

Figure 1 Market turnover in French Government inflation-linked bonds (3-month moving average)

Source: Agence France Trésor

As the inflation market has matured, AFT has done its best to bring its operation progressively in line (size notwithstanding) with the market for conventional government bonds. First, in 2003, AFT issued for the first time via auction (instead of syndication) a new inflation-linked benchmark, the OATi 2013. The same year, AFT started to allocate a minimum share of 10% of its financing programme to index-linked OATs. Since 2004, AFT has applied to indexed bond issues the same monthly issuance calendar as for nominal bonds, with auction dates published in December for the following year. It has thereby expressed its willingness to guarantee the same issuance standards as for conventional bonds: regularity, predictability and transparency. Regular supply is key in a market that remains driven by the inflation receiving side, since only a few economic actors are willing to pay inflation.

In retrospect, the success of inflation-linked bonds can be explained as much by the rising demand for inflation protection to hedge inflation-indexed liabilities, such as pension obligations, as by the unique behaviour of this class of assets whose yield is uncorrelated with nominal bonds. Over time, investors have become more familiar with these bonds and they have used the linkers more extensively to enhance their portfolios. Also, the parallel development of inflation markets in several countries (the United States, then France, Italy, Japan etc) has created opportunities for investors to invest in global inflation portfollios. Strong growth in the cash market has also encouraged a surge in inflation derivatives, particularly inflation swaps, which in turn has generated a stronger demand at linkers' auctions. This is the very kind of positive, market-driven interaction one can expect when a new market has been created.

WHY ISSUE INFLATION-LINKED BONDS?

From the issuer's point of view, issuing inflation-linked bonds can be justified for the following different reasons.

Diversification

First, it makes it possible to diversify the investors' base. Today, the proportion of non-French investors amongst OAT€i holders is 64%, compared with 39% for all French notes and bonds, according to Banque de France data. Even if the gain provided by this diversification is not directly measured, it is key to the strategy of AFT to reach the best debt conditions over time owing to an increase of the investors' base for French government bonds and notes.

Reducing the cost of funding

Another reason is more purely cost-related. Issuing an inflation-linked bond amounts to selling an insurance against inflation. This insurance has a price, the so-called inflation risk premium. Empirical studies estimate this premium to be between 0 and 50 basis points, with no consensus arising on its precise value (see Campbell and Shiller 1996; Shen 1998; Sack 2000; Cappiello and Guéné 2005; Shen and Corning 2001).

An explanation for this lack of consensus is that the premium is only one part of the inflation break-even, along with inflation expectations and liquidity factors, and these three components have proven difficult to disentangle. Theory has developed along two lines.

The first one is the general equilibrium approach, based on a consumption-based asset-pricing model with stochastic inflation (Sarte 1998). This approach provides for a generalised Fisher equation that links the nominal rate to the real rate, the expected inflation and a third parameter, the inflation risk premium, which depends on the correlation between inflation and consumption growth. The magnitude of this premium therefore depends on the covariance between unexpected movements in consumption and inflation. It can therefore be positive or negative depending on the nature of macroeconomic shocks: a supply shock, for example a strong hike in the oil price, will decrease consumption growth and increase inflation, generating a negative correlation in the Fisher formula and a negative inflation risk premium. On the contrary, a demand shock, for example a fall in the households saving rate, will stimulate both inflation and consumption, generating a positive inflation risk premium. This is because households are ready to pay a premium in order to guarantee a real return on their savings and protect their future consumption.

The other model used to assess the inflation risk premium is the Capital Asset Pricing Model (CAPM). The CAPM states that investors will require a premium over the risk-free rate for risky securities whose returns are positively correlated with the return of a market portfolio (Sharpe 1964; Roll and Ross 1983; Burmeister *et al*. 1997). An extension of this simple model allows the identification of additional pricing factors, beyond the market portfolio return, as independent sources of risk and thus as contributions to the implied risk premium. Taking inflation as an independent source of risk, excess returns for stocks and short- and long-term government bonds are explained by the sum of a market risk premium and an inflation risk premium.

Using both approaches on US data for the period 1953–1994, Campbell and Shiller (1996) estimate the inflation risk premium to be in the 50 to 100 basis points range. More recently, the consumption-based asset pricing model of Cappiello and Guéné (2005) results in a mean inflation risk premium of 20 basis points for French long-term bonds in the period 1985–2003 and of 10 basis points for the German bonds.

Managing the inflation risk on the State's balance sheet

An additional reason to issue inflation-linked debt stems from the composition of the State's budget. The theory of tax-smoothing advises one to minimise fluctuations in tax rates over time (Barro 1997). From this point of view and assuming a positive correlation between inflation and taxes, the conclusion is to fully index the debt to inflation. Nevertheless, the optimal structure of debt is probably a mix of nominal and indexed bonds, as the correlation between inflation and taxes can be negative (eg, in the case of a supply shock) and as nominal debt can help the Government to alleviate fiscal pressures when inflation increases.

A fourth reason to issue inflation-linked debt relates to the cyclic nature of the State budget. At the trough of the business cycle, budget deficit tends to hollow out but can be partly compensated for by lower inflation-linked coupons and lower provisions for capital indexation, as inflation generally tends to follow output. This of course depends on the nature of receipts: in France, for example, income tax is more directly linked to inflation than corporate tax. Expenditures are also correlated to inflation but in a more complex way. French State expenditures are currently managed in order to remain stable in real terms, ie, to follow the inflation strictly. However, actual inflation can differ from expected, budget-input levels, not to mention that off-budget social and health expenditures grow at a higher pace than inflation.

In France, the stabilisation effect of inflation-linked issuance is amplified by the provisioning of accrued inflation on future principal repayments in the budget expenditures. This inflation provision has a stronger impact on the budget deficit than the actual coupon payments.

This budget-smoothing effect is partially mitigated by the extra volatility of the debt burden when it is indexed on inflation. The volatility of inflation has decreased significantly over time but it has remained highly persistent.

On the basis of this analysis, AFT is currently working out a risk management model in terms of cost and risk with a view to assessing the optimal share of debt that should be linked to inflation. The model aims to quantify to what extent the budget's smoothing effect can fully compensate the extra volatility that linkers add to the interest cost. Such a model is required to simulate a set of scenarios regarding the macroeconomic variables such as gross domestic product or inflation, the fiscal position and the yield curve. This is done in a consistent way using a Vector Autoregressive Model. A refined version accounts for regime switches, so as to apply the different regimes of interest rates (ie, persistently high or persistently low) observed in the past and likely to occur in the future. A Monte Carlo approach can then generate a great number of environments to compare debt strategies. The final output is an efficient frontier of portfolio strategies, as measured by the average debt burden and its variability. Such an approach was implemented for nominal bonds in 2000 and led AFT to reduce the debt duration through a swap programme.

The last reason for issuing inflation-linked debt has to do with asset and liability management. State revenues are correlated with inflation directly (through indexation mechanisms) or indirectly. According to the French State's balance sheet published by the Ministry of Finance, the "Compte Général de l'Administration des Finances", the assets of the State include primarily real estate and stakes in state-owned companies. Real estate follows long-term inflation and state-owned companies' stock prices are related to their revenues, hence generally to inflation. This asset liability management justification remains mainly theoretical because of the difficulty of establishing the State's accounts and the lack of historical data. A "holistic" approach of the State's balance sheet is currently out of reach and this approach is to be explored further by AFT in the coming years.

WHAT IS THE GAIN/COST OF THE OATi/OAT€i PROGRAMME?

Leaving aside theory, a practical way to assess the inflation programme consists in comparing the cost of past inflation-linked issuance with the cost of counterfactual conventional issuance. An evaluation of the OATi/OAT€i programme has been carried out by AFT for the period running from 1998 to the end of 2004. The methodology applied is globally similar to that of Sack and Elsasser (2004).

The main difficulty occurs in specifying the counterfactual, ie, the issuance strategy that the Treasury would have followed in the absence of OATi/OAT€i. Because the payment flows on nominal and inflation-indexed securities differ considerably, there is no obvious choice of a comparable nominal security. One might be tempted to compare OATi/OAT€i with nominal debt securities having the same cash flows, ie, a hypothetical zero coupon portfolio replicating exactly the back-loaded cash flows of the inflation-linked bonds. It is unlikely that the State would have followed such a strategy in the absence of OATi/OAT€i and it would instead have increased its issuance of on-the-run securities. This is the reason why we have used as comparable on-the-run nominal bonds with the same maturity. This methodology is likely to underestimate the algebraic gain provided by the linkers, in comparison to the use of a synthetic zero-coupon portfolio (that has a higher duration and henceforth a higher rate).

A drawback of the method stems from the fact that the issuance of OATi/OAT€i has enriched the nominal OATs by reducing their supply. Comparing the yield of linkers to existing nominal bonds therefore underestimates the benefits of the former. However, this general equilibrium effect is hard to quantify because of the difficulty of calibrating supply and demand curves for French nominal bonds. We would certainly welcome any further research in this direction.

In practice, the evaluation rests on a cost/advantage analysis for every single OATi/OAT€i auction and syndication. For every auctioned or syndicated bond, the inflation realised so far is compared to the inflation break-even at issuance. The gap between the two is weighted by the issued volume and by the time elapsed since the auction. If inflation exceeds the break-even rate, the OATi/OAT€i will be

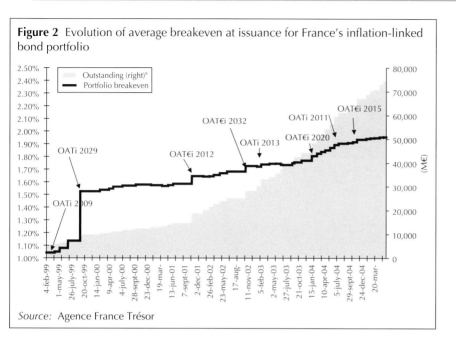

Figure 2 Evolution of average breakeven at issuance for France's inflation-linked bond portfolio

Source: Agence France Trésor

more costly than the nominal security and *vice versa*. The break-even at issuance is indeed the rate of inflation at which the cost to the Treasury of issuing a linker will exactly equal the cost of raising the same amount of funds by issuing the comparable nominal security.

The result is the following. We find that at the end of 2004 the programme has generated a net gain of about €120 million. The result is best understood when looking at the average break-even of the linkers portfolio (Figure 2). As already discussed, linkers were initially issued at a low break-even. Unsurprisingly, this break-even proved lower than subsequent inflation. As a result, linkers in the first few years were costly relative to conventional issuance. It is only since 2003 that the French Republic has been able to spare money through the linkers' programme, owing to higher break-even levels. These gains have grown larger ever since.

Several caveats and comments can be made in relation to this result. First, the relatively modest impact lies within AFT's range of expectation since, as discussed above, the inflation premium is likely to be limited. Second, the direct comparison with conventional issuance understates overall gains. Third, any such cost/advantage analysis should be performed over a sustained period of time as

States being *de facto* permanent issuers may attach less importance to incidental "gains" or "losses" than to the preservation of market access and investors' confidence. These general goals explain why AFT has taken the commitment, since 2003, to keep on issuing a minimum amount of inflation-linked bonds (currently, 10% of the medium- and long-term issuance) irrespective of market conditions. Fourth, this assessment is backward-looking and does not account for future costs. No comprehensive assessment of any inflation-linked issuance can be carried out before the redemption of the security. The result of the first linker issued by France will thus be known for real in July 2009. Any assessment of future costs (or, equivalently, of the fair value of the linkers' portfolio) would require forecasting of the future path of inflation, which AFT will not do since it has a policy not to rely on assumptions other than market expectations. Finally, as a public-interest agency, AFT can to some extent legitimately fund the emergence and/or proper functioning of a new market segment that is likely to involve positive effects for other market participants, although this may certainly not be the main decision criteria since the mandate of AFT is to lower the cost of debt to the French taxpayers over time. These spill over effects are difficult to fathom and remain to be fully studied.

CONCLUDING REMARKS

This exercise tends to confirm another rationale behind the launching of the French inflation-linked programme: the acknowledgment that building an entirely new market is akin to an investment, the rewards of which will be reaped only gradually and cannot be stated upfront. As far as the inflation programme is concerned, AFT is pleased with the outcome, but this is not an adventure on which it will embark too often.

REFERENCES

Barro, R.J., 1997, "Optimal Management of Indexed and Nominal Debt", NBER Working Paper no. 6197.

Burmeister, E., R. Roll and S.A. Ross, 1997, "Using Macroeconomic Factors to Control Portfolio Risk", The Research Foundation of the Institute of Chartered Financial Analysts.

Campbell, J.Y. and R.J. Shiller, 1996, "A Scorecard for Indexed Government Debt", in Ben S. Bernanke and Julio Rotemberg (eds), *NBER Macroeconomics Annual 1996*. (Cambridge: MIT Press), pp. 155–97.

Cappiello, L. and S. Guéné, 2005, "Measuring Market and Inflation Risk Premia in France and in Germany?", European Central Bank Working Paper Series, no. 436.

Roll, R. and S. Ross, 1983, "Regulation, the Capital Asset Pricing Model, and the Arbitrage Pricing Theory", *Public Utilities Fortnightly*, May, pp. 22–28.

Sack, B., 2000, "Deriving Inflation Expectations from Nominal and Inflation-Indexed Treasury Yields", *Board of Governors of the Federal Reserve System Working Paper*. no 2000-33.

Sack, B. and R. Elsasser, 2004, "Treasury Inflation Indexed Debt, a Review of the US Experience", *FRBNY Economic Policy Review*, May, pp. 47–63.

Sarte, P.D., 1998, "Fisher's Equation and the Inflation Risk Premium in a Simple Endowment Economy"., *Federal Reserve Bank of Richmond Economic Quarterly*, Fall, pp. 53–72.

Sharpe, W.F., 1964, "Capital Asset Prices: A Theory of Market Equilibrium under Conditions of Risk", *The Journal of Finance*, **19(3)**, pp. 425–42.

Shen, P. and J. Corning, 2001, "Can TIPS Help Identify Long-term Inflation Expectations?", *Federal Reserve Bank of Kansas City Economic Review*, Fourth Quarter, pp. 67–87.

Shen, P., 1998, "How Important is the Inflation Risk Premium?", *Federal Reserve Bank of Kansas City Economic Review*, Fourth Quarter, pp. 35–47.

8

Active Liability Management with Inflation Products

Stanley Myint

Royal Bank of Scotland

INTRODUCTION

One of the key purposes of active liability management is to optimise the funding cost. These days, many corporates use sophisticated portfolio optimisation techniques borrowed from asset management to decide on the right risk/reward ratio in their liability portfolio. Traditionally, to adjust the risk/reward, corporates choose to issue fixed or floating coupon debt in different currencies and maturities. In addition, where the company's preference for debt parameters is different from that of the investor's, derivatives are used to vary currency, duration, maturity and other parameters of debt. With a growth in inflation-linked products, a company's liability structure can now be optimised along an additional dimension. We will focus on one such example.

OPTIMISING THE INFLATION PROPORTION OF DEBT

In early 2005, a UK company, INFLATCO PLC, whose revenue is explicitly linked to inflation, is trying to determine its optimal capital structure. Its financial projections for the next five years are shown in Table 1.

As INFLATCO is a regulated company, it is allowed to increase prices in line with inflation index, RPI (Retail Price Index), which it normally does, like most of its competitors. Therefore, its income, which is shown in the table as constant at GBP 900 million, is actually expected to increase in line with inflation. The company has a significant amount of cash, GBP 500 million, which is projected to

Table 1 Financial projections of INFLATCO PLC (GBP million)

	INFLATCO financial data				
	2005	**2006**	**2007**	**2008**	**2009**
Fixed income	0	0	0	0	0
Inflation-linked income	900	900	900	900	900
Interest-linked income	500	525	551	579	608
Fixed operating expense	250	250	250	250	250
Inflation-linked operating expense	350	350	350	350	350
Interest-linked operating expense	0	0	0	0	0
Gross debt	2,000	2,000	2,000	2,000	2,000
❏ Fixed proportion of debt (%)	70	70	70	70	70
❏ Floating proportion of debt (%)	30	30	30	30	30
❏ Inflation proportion of debt (%)	0	0	0	0	0
Historical fixed rate (%)	6	6	6	6	6
Credit spread (%)	1	1	1	1	1

increase due to operating profits, and will earn a Libor-based interest. The Company has decided not to use the cash to repay down debt, as it may need extra liquidity for operating purposes. Furthermore, INFLATCO has determined that its operating costs can be roughly split into GBP 250 million per year that are fixed and GBP 350 million that are due to increase with inflation. Company debt is projected to stay constant at GBP 2,000 million, of which 70% is fixed, paying an average interest rate of 6%. The Company currently borrows at a credit spread of 1% over Libor.

The Company is considering what the right proportion of funding should be over the next five years, January 2005 to January 2010. There are two obvious choices.

1. INFLATCO pays fixed debt. Currently, the 5-year GBP swap rate is 4.68%, so the company could pay 5.68% including the credit spread. The apparent advantage of this approach is that the interest cost is fixed and therefore predictable.

2. INFLATCO pays floating debt. 1-year Libor currently stands at 4.88%, so in the first year the company would pay 5.88% including credit spread. However, this coupon can change over time. In fact, Libor rates are projected to fall in 2006 and 2007, as shown in Figure 1. The uncertainty about the future is shown through a 1 Standard Deviation ("SD") range, which under the normal model

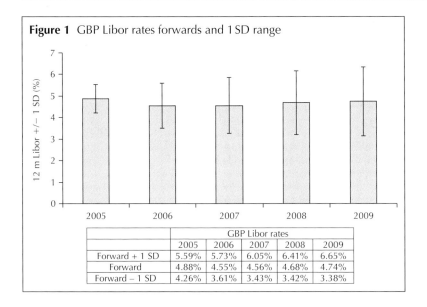

Figure 1 GBP Libor rates forwards and 1 SD range

	GBP Libor rates				
	2005	2006	2007	2008	2009
Forward + 1 SD	5.59%	5.73%	6.05%	6.41%	6.65%
Forward	4.88%	4.55%	4.56%	4.68%	4.74%
Forward – 1 SD	4.26%	3.61%	3.43%	3.42%	3.38%

covers about two-thirds of all cases. For instance, at the start of 2005, the average Libor level, as predicted by the forward rates in 2006, was 4.55%. At the 66% confidence interval, Libor could vary anywhere between 3.61% and 5.73%. The Libor range is implied by the option markets. The apparent advantage of Libor-linked funding is that, in so far as the revenues of INFLATCO are dependent on interest rates, floating-rate debt is a natural hedge.

There are various debt products through which INFLATCO can achieve its funding goals: bilateral and syndicated bank loans, public bonds and private placements, commercial paper, securitisation, etc. On top of that, INFLATCO may overlay derivatives products to change the type of funding. All of these have a slightly different regulatory framework and administrative details. For now, the precise funding mechanism is not important for us as we focus entirely on the fixed, floating or inflation-linked composition. Later we will discuss in more detail how cash *versus* derivatives inflation products are treated by accountants.

So far INFLATCO has relied entirely on these two sources of funding. As mentioned previously, 70% of INFLATCO's funding is in fixed rates. However, recently INFLATCO has had another alternative. Rapid growth of the inflation-linked market means that

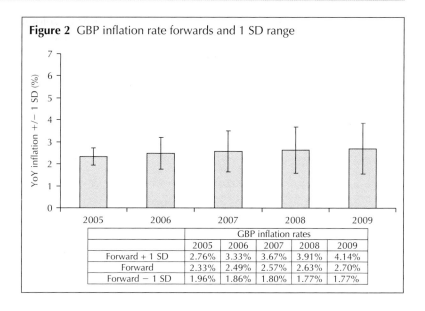

Figure 2 GBP inflation rate forwards and 1 SD range

	GBP inflation rates				
	2005	2006	2007	2008	2009
Forward + 1 SD	2.76%	3.33%	3.67%	3.91%	4.14%
Forward	2.33%	2.49%	2.57%	2.63%	2.70%
Forward − 1 SD	1.96%	1.86%	1.80%	1.77%	1.77%

INFLATCO can also elect to pay an inflation-linked coupon. There are two typical versions of inflation products. Multiplicative inflation bonds normally pay a fixed coupon and principal, multiplied by the inflation rate. Additive inflation bonds normally pay a fixed coupon *plus* inflation. Currently, for additive bonds in the UK, the fixed coupon is about 2.16%. This means that every year for the next five years INFLATCO pays 2.16% of the notional amount plus the annual inflation. For example, if in one year inflation is 2.50%, INFLATCO will pay a coupon of 2.16% + 2.50% = 2.64%. Expected inflation levels together with a 1 SD range are shown in Figure 2. Similarly to the Libor rates, the expected level is implied from the inflation-swaps markets, whereas the SD range is implied from option markets, which are less transparent for Inflation rates than for Libor-based products.

As both revenues and costs have significant inflation dependence, INFLATCO's Treasurer suspects that risk may be reduced by including inflation products in its debt portfolio. In order to determine the optimal debt composition, the Treasurer must decide on the most relevant parameter to monitor risk *versus* reward. After having considered the situation, the Treasurer decides that, for INFLATCO, Profit Before Tax (PBT) is the most relevant and easy-to-understand parameter[1]. Therefore, the Treasurer develops a simple model that links PBT to inflation and interest rates. The objective of the model, whose details are in the Appendix, is to determine the optimal mix of fixed, floating and inflation-linked debt. The model allows our Treasurer to input any debt composition and compare the expected return *versus* the risk. "Return" is defined as expected annual PBT over the next five years and risk as the 1 SD of PBT in that year. The Treasurer can then vary the debt composition and find the best risk/return ratio.

Funding composition can be changed either by buying back debt and re-issuing with a different mix or by keeping the present composition of debt and changing the composition with derivatives. Normally, companies prefer to divorce the funding decision from the optimal debt composition and chose the second of these alternatives. They start with the funding decision based on investor demand and then use derivatives to swap into the right fixed/floating/inflation mix. However, we shall see later that the two alternatives have a drastically different accounting treatment under International Financial Reporting Standards (IFRS). For now we focus purely on the economic aspects.

As a first step, the Treasurer decides to keep the inflation component of debt zero and vary the proportion of floating debt. The expected annual profit and its SD are monitored. Figure 3 shows how the 2005 PBT and its SD vary as we change the level of floating debt, without adding any inflation-linked debt.

We note two interesting phenomena here. First, since the yield curve is inverted, as the proportion of floating debt increases, expected PBT decreases[2] (in 2005 it costs more to borrow floating than fixed). Second, as the proportion of floating debt increases, risk measured by 1 SD first decreases until, at 30% floating debt, the direction reverses and, after that, higher floating proportion increases the risk. This is a typical example of an "efficient frontier", whereby increasing the floating debt above 30% increases risk while reducing the return. This part of the curve is suboptimal, therefore only the rest of the curve, where higher risk is rewarded by higher return, is efficient. Without inflation-linked debt, the company should have no more than 30% of its debt floating. It is precisely at this "turning point" where the company finds itself at the moment.

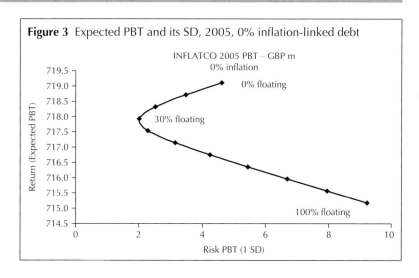

Figure 3 Expected PBT and its SD, 2005, 0% inflation-linked debt

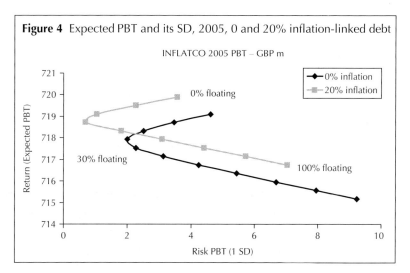

Figure 4 Expected PBT and its SD, 2005, 0 and 20% inflation-linked debt

Everything seems fine for now, but what happens if we consider the inflation dimension? In Figure 4 we add to the previous graph an efficient frontier for 20% inflation-linked debt.

The first observation to make is that the efficient frontier for 20% inflation looks very much like the previous graph for 0% inflation. For both, the optimal part of the curve is at below 30% floating debt. However, what is more interesting is that having 20% inflation is more efficient (ie, return is higher and risk is lower) than having

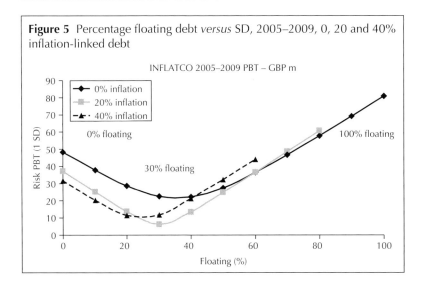

Figure 5 Percentage floating debt *versus* SD, 2005–2009, 0, 20 and 40% inflation-linked debt

0% inflation regardless of the floating proportion. Therefore, the Treasurer is surprised to note that it is more efficient for INFLATCO to have 20% inflation-linked debt than no inflation-linked debt. Isn't the Treasurer glad that he/she looked at this?

Another way of looking at this data is to plot the risk *versus* proportion of floating debt to find the "inversion point of the curve", beyond which higher risk is no longer followed with higher return (efficient frontier). In Figure 5, we show this for a five-year time horizon. We consider cases of 0, 20 and 40% inflation-linked debt. For clarity, we mark the proportion of floating debt on the 0% inflation-linked debt line only. Risk is now shown on the vertical axis.

In this graph, the Treasurer is only comparing risk (ie, SD of PBT) without looking at the reward (ie, expected PBT). What allows the treasurer to disregard the expected PBT is the fact that over the five-year time horizon the expectations of PBT are identical irrespective of whether a company borrows on a fixed, floating or inflation basis. As mentioned before, this is due to the fact that over five years there is no difference of the expected cost, as the fixed rate is given by the discounted average of floating rates and similarly for inflation rates. In practice, this relationship holds well when comparing fixed and floating funding costs but is only approximate for inflation costs, due to the illiquidity of the market.

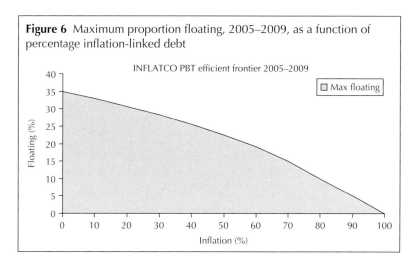

Figure 6 Maximum proportion floating, 2005–2009, as a function of percentage inflation-linked debt

INFLATCO PBT efficient frontier 2005–2009

When comparing different curves in Figure 5, two facts become obvious. First, as we increase the proportion of inflation-linked debt, the inversion point of the curve is slowly moving from 35% floating (at 0% inflation) to about 25% floating (at 40% inflation). In fact, this trend continues as the proportion of inflation-linked debt increases further above 40%. We show this in more detail in Figure 6.

In Figure 6, we focus on the minima of the curves from Figure 5. For example, in the 0% inflation curve in Figure 5, the minimum is at about 35% floating. In Figure 6, we show this at the top left-hand part of the graph, as the point 0% inflation, 35% floating. Below this point we have the efficient frontier for 0% floating. As we increase the proportion of inflation-linked debt, the surface under the line defines the efficient frontier. As just discussed, for 0% inflation-linked debt, it is not efficient to have more than 35% floating. This proportion falls as the proportion of inflation-linked debt is increased.

The other fact that is obvious in Figure 5 is that the SD at the inversion point of the curve for 40% inflation is higher than the SD at the inversion point of the curve for 20% inflation. We plot this in Figure 7.

In Figure 7, the Treasurer plots the SD at the minima of curves in Figure 5 against the proportion of the inflation-linked debt. For example, in 0% inflation curve in Figure 5, the SD of PBT at the minimum is at about GBP 22 million. This is shown as the left-most

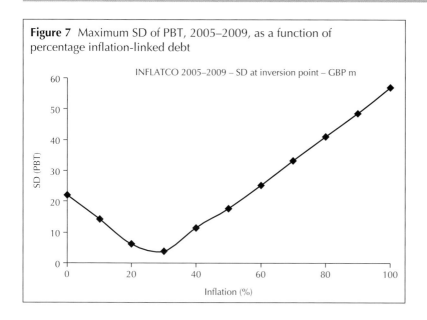

Figure 7 Maximum SD of PBT, 2005–2009, as a function of percentage inflation-linked debt

point on the curve in Figure 7. In this graph we can see that INFLATCO can achieve the lowest SD of PBT at around 30% inflation-linked debt. From Figure 6 we can see that the maximum proportion of floating debt for 30% inflation-linked debt is just below 30%. So the Treasurer finally reaches the end of the optimisation procedure. In order to minimise the variability of its PBT over five years, INFLATCO should have around 30% inflation-linked debt and no more than 30% floating debt. Within those limits, the exact proportion of floating *versus* fixed debt depends on company's risk/return preferences and cannot be determined *via* the efficient frontier procedure.

So far we have focused on how a company can determine the optimal proportion of inflation-linked debt, while only in passing mentioning that there are different products with which to do this. Let us now briefly discuss in more detail some of the possible products that are at the Treasurer's disposal.

MECHANICS OF THE INFLATION MARKET
The UK inflation swaps market has been in existence since the mid 1990s, yet it is only in the past two years that the market has

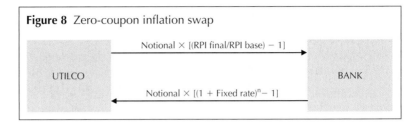

Figure 8 Zero-coupon inflation swap

Notional × [(RPI final/RPI base) − 1]

UTILCO   BANK

Notional × [(1 + Fixed rate)^n − 1]

become established. Over the course of the past two years a larger number of market makers and users have lead to improved liquidity. The supply of inflation-linked cashflows has become more diverse as awareness of inflation-linked products has increased. Simultaneously, on the demand side, institutions have become more derivatives literate and now regularly utilise inflation swaps and options as part of liability-driven investment, recognising the benefits that inflation derivatives offer over traditional cash bonds. Demand from institutions is not only for inflation swaps, but also for inflation options. Most popular options are Limited Price Indexation (LPI)[3] products, since they can perfectly mimic certain pension liabilities. A significant development in the market has been the arrival of Hedge Funds using inflation swaps and options as a method of profit generation. It has to be seen whether this tactical activity will lead to other UK financial institutions also using the inflation derivatives for profit rather than entirely for strategic asset and liability management.

As mentioned previously, there are many ways an inflation product can be structured. A typical product in the inflation swaps market is the zero-coupon inflation swap, shown in Figure 8.

❏ At maturity, UTILCO pays to BANK the notional on the swap multiplied by

$$[(\text{RPI Final}/\text{RPI Base}) - 1]$$

The standard convention for the base RPI is a two-month lag from the start date of the trade. For example, a trade starting on the 27th June will use a base RPI month of April of the same year.

❏ At maturity, BANK pays to UTILCO the notional on the swap multiplied by

$$[(1 + \text{Fixed Rate})^n - 1]$$

where n is equivalent to the tenor of the swap, for example for a 30-year inflation swap $n = 30$.

❑ There is only one net payment at maturity of the swap and deals use an annual 30/360 unadjusted day count.

Inflation swaps offer the same flexibility as interest rate swaps and, therefore, can be tailored to meet an individual's needs. The zero-coupon swap is the most widely used method of risk transfer in the inter-dealer market; however, the vast majority of corporate transactions look completely different. For example, one way for INFLATCO to increase inflation-linked debt is to convert a conventional fixed-coupon bond into a synthetic inflation-linked bond. INFLATCO would enter into a structured inflation swap. INFLATCO would receive bond coupons to match its existing fixed bond and would pay an inflation-linked leg similar to inflation-linked bonds with both coupons and principal payments linked to inflation.

An additional benefit of synthetic inflation-linked bonds over real inflation-linked bonds is that, due to the supply and demand imbalance, the inflation swaps market has consistently offered a premium to anyone looking to pay inflation-linked cashflows in swap form rather than bond form. The premium is a result of demand from both pension funds and life companies outstripping supply of long-dated inflation swap cashflows. The liquidity in the UK inflation swaps market is predominantly at the long end of the market as that is where the vast majority of supply and demand occurs. Nowadays, it is not unusual for trades of GBP 100–200 million to go through the market on a regular basis, whereas this was not the case two years ago. Inflation swaps offer an efficient, flexible method to manage inflation-linked exposures.

HISTORICAL OVERVIEW OF THE CORPORATE IL BOND ISSUANCE IN THE UK

As can be seen in Figure 9, the sterling inflation-linked bond market had its peak between 2000 and 2003. This is due to several reasons. First, a lot of the existing issues were issued in a relatively small number of sectors, mostly Healthcare and Utility, which therefore naturally stifles the supply side in the years immediately thereafter. Second, as investors are becoming more sophisticated,

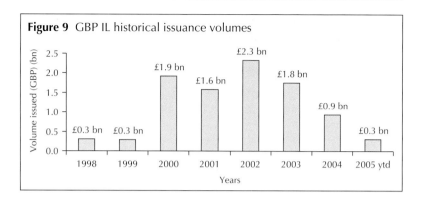

Figure 9 GBP IL historical issuance volumes

they tend to source inflation-linked revenues through the IL swap market, as it is more liquid and flexible. Moreover, IL investors are usually not concerned about the onerous accounting treatment accorded to inflation derivatives, which we discuss later. Also, the inflation risk premium (which is a rough measure of potential savings to IL issuers, if the inflation performs as expected) has come down in recent years. Finally, as the bond market has been relatively illiquid so far, it is difficult to diversify between the issuers, which is a fundamental problem for credit investing. The asymmetry between cash and derivative markets is further evidenced by the premium paid by investors for derivatives. In Europe, until the June 2005 issue by Veolia Environnement, most of the issuance has been by government agencies and supra-nationals. One of the reasons for this is the non-homogeneity of the European market in terms of inflation indices. A corporate issuing an IL bond has to chose whether the underlying index is linked to its home country or the wider Euro-zone inflation. Choosing its own market reduces the potential investor base, while choosing the Euro-zone inflation can be bad from both the economic and accounting perspectives. If corporate revenues are linked to their own market, then there is a basis risk if a corporates issue is linked to a Euro-wide index. Also, there is a potential problem with the accounting treatment – as discussed later – there may be a penalty to be paid in terms of mark-to-market volatility if a corporate issues an IL bond where the underlying inflation is not related to its home country. Veolia decided to issue an IL bond linked to the Euro-zone HICP index. It is possible that this landmark transaction will act as a catalyst for the other Euro-land corporates to issue IL bonds, perhaps in the utilities and/or toll-road sector. However, due to similar issues as in the UK, the swap market is, for now, equally likely to remain the main source of corporate inflation-linked cashflows. The problem with this is the accounting treatment of inflation derivatives, which we discuss in the next section.

ACCOUNTING IMPLICATIONS

Treatment under UK generally accepted accounting principles

Traditionally, under UK generally accepted accounting principles (GAAP), UK companies have been able to use RPI-linked bonds and RPI-linked swaps as economic and accounting hedges for (implicitly or explicitly) index-linked revenue streams. RPI-linked bonds were generally accounted for on an amortised cost basis in the books of the issuer under accounting standard FRS4, similarly to the conventional bonds. Uplifts in the bond notional known at the reporting date were generally taken as part of the finance charge through the Profit and Loss (P&L) account. Regarding inflation-linked swaps, the practice in the UK was to account for derivative hedges in a manner similar to the item they were hedging and so for a fixed (or floating) to RPI-linked swap an accruals basis was normally adopted. Therefore, under UK GAAP, irrespective of whether the proportion of inflation-linked debt was adjusted *via* RPI-linked bonds or RPI-linked swaps, it was not likely to attract negative accounting treatment under UK GAAP. Under UK GAAP, life was easy, but how the things have changed under IFRS!

Treatment under International Financial Reporting Standards

While the interpretation and application of IAS 39 differs between accounting firms, the general consensus on how to account and report for hedging activities involving inflation-linked swaps is currently less than desirable. For one thing, you can have dramatically different reported results for something that is practically economically identical. Under International Financial Reporting Standards (IFRS) the accounting treatment for a UK issuer of RPI-linked bonds will remain largely the same using an amortised cost approach. However, UK companies may have difficulty replicating the accounting treatment that has been available under UK GAAP for the synthetic index-linked bond under the "new" IFRS rules.

Take, for instance, inflation-linked bonds. These fall under the "Embedded Derivatives" section of IAS39. Paragraph 11 states that an embedded derivative shall be separated from the host contract and accounted for as a derivative (ie, it has to be marked-to-market) unless its economic characteristics and risks are "closely related" to the economic characteristics and risks of the host contract. In the case of inflation-linked bonds, the embedded derivative would be an inflation swap and the host derivative the bond. The Standards do not specify how to determine what "closely related" is, so in general, it is left to the auditor to determine this. However, under Application Guidance AG33 f, it is explicitly stated that an embedded derivative in a host lease contract (and, therefore, it is generally assumed in other kinds of debt instruments) is closely related to the host if it is an unleveraged inflation-related index, which relates to inflation in the entity's own economic environment. Therefore, for the most part, the inflation coupon is considered economically closely related to the bond and, therefore, does not have to be split out from the bond (what some people refer to "bifurcation") and accounted for separately on a mark-to-market basis as a normal free-standing inflation swap would. This accounting treatment allows the issuer the benefits of accounting for the bond on an accrual basis. It should be noted that inflation coupons in debt are not always considered clearly related. When making this interpretation, one key point is to compare the economic area of the inflation the coupon is based on to the interest rate of the currency the bond is denominated in. In the UK, this is not usually an issue, as a UK-wide inflation index covers the same area as GBP Libor (both cover the UK). However, for wider areas, such as the EU, this is not as clear. Take, for instance, a EUR bond that pays a coupon based on French inflation. In this case the areas are not identical (France *versus* the single-currency area as a whole), and the embedded inflation coupon may be required to be split out and accounted for as a free-standing inflation swap.

However, if you use an inflation-linked swap in combination with a fixed-rate bond, synthetically creating inflation-linked debt, the same treatment of the debt is not available. This is because of the requirement to carry all free-standing derivatives on the balance sheet at fair value. Changes in the fair value of the swap are to be reported in current period P&L, which could cause some unpleasant volatility, unless hedge accounting can be applied.

Unfortunately, as IAS 39 is currently interpreted, the application of hedge accounting is not as clear-cut for inflation swaps as it is for interest rate swaps. As such, in practice we have found the use of hedge accounting hard to implement. However, it is still possible in some circumstances to qualify for hedge accounting, and we believe that the use of hedge accounting for inflation derivatives will expand as corporates and auditors become more familiar with their use and concepts. Moreover, the fact that inflation hedging is based on good common sense and economics, does not hurt the case one bit.

Here are a few instances of economic inflation hedging, with potential accounting pitfalls and opportunities for hedge accounting for each.

Swapping floating-rate debt into inflation-linked debt

It is unlikely that the inflation-linked swap can be designated either as a successful cashflow or fair-value hedge for a floating-rate debt obligation. Cashflow hedging implies that currently variable cashflows are effectively being fixed – this is unlikely to be the case as the "new" cashflows are themselves variable and linked to RPI. On the other hand, fair-value hedge accounting is unlikely as the swap does not offset changes in the fair value of the floating rate debt. Therefore, in this case, the hedger should assess the potential changes in the fair value of the inflation-linked swap and determine if the potential reported P&L volatility is acceptable.

Swapping fixed-rate debt into inflation-linked debt

In this case there are two potential solutions but so far we have seen very limited success of these strategies in practice. The first is to designate the swap as a cashflow hedge of inflation-linked revenues, instead of designating the bond as being hedged. The second method is to designate the swap as a fair-value hedge of the bond, where the swap is hedging changes in the fair value of the bond due to changes in inflation rates.

The first possible method of achieving the hedge accounting treatment may be to designate the swap as a hedge of the index-linked revenue streams that the enterprise may have. However, these are usually not contractual and therefore may not be considered to be financial assets, and hence not fit the requirements for a "highly probable anticipated future transaction" under IAS39. Accordingly, the successful designation of such RPI-linked swaps as hedges for the inflation exposures in the revenue stream is uncertain and the required hedge accounting treatment may not be available to the enterprise. Moreover, the swap would be a hedge of highly probable forecasted or contractual cashflows (ie, sales), where the variability in the cashflows from the first X amount of sales would be designated as the hedged item. As the hedged item is not a financial asset or liability, the variability as a whole would have to be hedged, rather than the variability specifically arising from inflation. Provided the hedger can prove that the variability in cashflows is offset by the swap within a range of 80–125%, hedge accounting can be applied. In practice, this is very difficult to do, as many other factors can also affect the amount of cashflows, including, for example, competitive pressures.

Regarding the fair-value hedge, as mentioned previously, the swap would be hedging changes in the fair value of the bond due to changes in inflation rates. This works on a similar concept as a normal interest rate swap, hedging the changes in the fair value of the bond due to changes in interest rates, not taking into account the changes in the fair value of the bond due to credit spread movements (more specifically, credit spreads above swap spreads). The key problem here is that the fair-value hedging implies that the changes in the value of the swap and the underlying conventional bond will be "almost fully offset" – again this is unlikely, since, although one leg of the swap is fixed and mirrors the bond, the other leg is RPI-linked and its value will vary in a GBP LIBOR discounting environment. You would most likely also want to designate the hedged item as a "portion" of the cashflows of the bond, equivalent to what the inflation rate was at the time the bond was issued. However, some accounting firms have not allowed this approach for various reasons, including the belief that, when hedging a portion of the risk, it must be a "benchmark" rate such as Libor. However, as inflation is an identifiable and separately measurable portion of the interest rate exposure, it is expected that accounting firms will look on this approach more favourably over time.

CONCLUDING REMARKS

Economically, it makes a lot of sense for INFLATCO to add infla-tion-linked debt to its portfolio. Its risks will be reduced without a drop in revenues. There are two ways to do this, *via* debt or deriva-tives. Ideally, the funding decision would be made first and deriva-tives could be overlaid subsequently to incorporate the inflation dependence. Unfortunately, as we have just seen, under IFRS it is difficult to get hedge accounting for inflation derivatives. Therefore, INFLATCO has two possibilities. First, it can embed the inflation exposure into its debt. By IAS39 Application Guidance AG33 f, as long as the inflation index is unleveraged and linked to the inflation in its own economic environment, the derivative will not have to be split and the debt instrument will be accounted for on an accrual basis. The second alternative is to achieve the same economic treatment synthetically by overlaying inflation swaps over existing bonds, but then, if the hedge accounting treatment cannot be achieved, INFLATCO will have to show variation in the mark-to-market of the inflation swap through the P&L account. Ultimately, of course, as the economic impact is identical, everyone hopes that IFRS will evolve to the point when the accounting treat-ment is the same.

ACKNOWLEDGEMENTS

I would like to thank Jonathan Chesebrough, Greg MacKay, Stuart Montgomerie, Oskar Nelvin and Andrew Walker from the Royal Bank of Scotland as well as the anonymous referee for the helpful comments and input in writing this chapter.

APPENDIX: THE LINEAR INFLATION MODEL
General assumptions

❑ time is divided into years $t = 1, 2, ..., n$
❑ companies exist in a single currency/inflation zone only.
❑ interest rates and inflation rates follow a correlated normal dis-tribution.

Market parameters

❑ floating rate (Libor) $r(t)$, with expectation $\langle r(t) \rangle$ and SD $SD(r)$.
❑ inflation rate $i(t)$, with expectation $\langle i(t) \rangle$ and SD $SD(i)$.

243

❑ correlation between floating and inflation rates $\rho(i, r)$.
❑ inflation interest rate (real rate) i_r for the period.

Company parameters

❑ fixed income $IF(t)$.
❑ inflation-linked income $II(t)$ (grows with inflation).
❑ interest-linked income $IR(t)$ (grows with Libor rates and may include Cash on deposit).
❑ fixed operating expense $CF(t)$.
❑ inflation-linked operating expense $CI(t)$ (grows with inflation).
❑ interest-linked operating expense $CR(t)$ (grows with Libor rates).
❑ debt $D(t)$ of which:
  – $x(t)$ fixed with $x(0)$, the historical fixed proportion, paying a rate of $R(0)$, while new debt, $x'(t) = x(t) - x(0)$, paying a rate of $R + s$, where s is the constant credit spread.
  – $z(t)$ inflation linked, paying a rate of $i(t) + i_r(t) + s$.

From these assumptions and parameters one can derive the company Profit Before Tax (PBT) in any year (for simplicity, we do not show the time dependence wherever it is obvious):

$$PBT = (IF - CF) + (II - CI) \cdot (1 + i) + (IR - CR) \cdot (1 + r) - D \cdot \{x(0) \cdot R(0) + [x(t) - x(0)] \cdot (R + s) + y \cdot (r + s) + z \cdot (i + i_r + s)\}$$

We can write this as $PBT = \alpha \cdot i + \beta \cdot r + \gamma$, where

$$\alpha \equiv (II - CI) - D \cdot z$$

$$\beta \equiv (IR - CR) - D \cdot y$$

$$\gamma \equiv (IF - CF) + (II - CI) + (IR - CR) - D \cdot \{x(0) \cdot R(0) + [x(t) - x(0)] \cdot (R+s) + y \cdot s + z \cdot (i_r + s)\}$$

If we denote the expectation by $\langle \cdots \rangle$ and the SD by $SD(\ldots)$, then

$$\langle PBT \rangle = \alpha \cdot \langle i \rangle + \beta \cdot \langle r \rangle + \gamma$$

and

$$SD(PBT)^2 = \alpha^2 \cdot SD(i)^2 + \beta^2 \cdot SD(r)^2 + 2 \cdot \alpha \cdot \beta \cdot SD(i) \cdot SD(r) \cdot \rho(i, r)$$

1   Other possible risk parameters to optimise can be: earnings per share, interest cover, interest cost, etc.

2   Over the entire five-year period, there is no difference on the expected basis, as the fixed rate is given by the discounted average of the floating rates.

3   LPI is defined as RPI capped at 5% and floored at 0%. Most frequently, the cap is at 5% and the floor at 0%, in order to mimic typical pension liabilities, but other strikes are traded too.

9

The Active Alpha Framework and Inflation-Protected Securities

Markus Aakko and Bob Litterman

Goldman, Sachs & Co

INTRODUCTION

Evidence from the past five years of financial returns has tested the conventional wisdom in financial markets. Portfolios of S&P 500 pension plans have been inadequately hedged against market movements and they have often been reliant upon unrealistically high return assumptions; consequently, funding levels have plummeted from 30% over-funded to 11% under-funded (Lehman 2005).

Pension plans are also facing demographic hurdles as population in the developed countries ages. Interestingly, with the cost of living adjustment (COLA) of post-retirement benefits pegged to inflation, this can also potentially raise plans' exposure to inflation risk. In the past 15 years inflation has not been a major contributor to plan risk; in fact, the disinflationary environment has pushed yields to their lowest levels in decades.

One of the driving constraints on portfolio structure has been scarcity of capital. Plans have invested in cash bonds in order to match their known liability streams and have aimed to gain additional returns through investments in equities in order to provide a buffer against uncertainty of their future liabilities. Since both investments cannot be made at the same time in the cash securities market, scarcity of capital has forced plans to make a choice between seeking a higher expected return on their assets in exchange for higher surplus volatility from interest rate sensitivity.

We believe that with the onset of deeper markets for less capital-intensive instruments, such as swaps and futures, pension plans

247

have at their disposal a toolkit that enhances their ability to take risks where they can reap the highest benefits from them. Inflation derivatives in particular have given pension plans the ability to tackle the issue of their liabilities' sensitivity to inflation; and in some cases, even to the specific form of inflation such as health-care costs. In other words, plans have the ability to reduce or elimi-nate unwanted risk exposures in exchange for more market risk and actively managed risk.

ACTIVE ALPHA INVESTING

The Active Alpha Investing approach is an application of traditional portfolio theory, addressing practical problems facing pension plans and other investors seeking to maximise the performance of their investments. The basic tenet underlying our approach is to measure unintended risks, hedge them to the extent possible and direct the use of risk capital to its most productive use.

Looking from a risk perspective, the primary risks of any given pension plan can be divided into three categories: (i) interest rate risk; (ii) market risk; and (iii) active risk. The traditional approach to asset allocation has most often focused on the asset side of the balance sheet and ignored the fact that a given pension plan also carries another "portfolio" of risks: sensitivity of the liability pool to interest rates and inflation.

In the Active Alpha Investing approach, the traditional frame-work is expanded by considering a pension plan to consist of three portfolios: (i) the Alpha portfolio; (ii) the Beta portfolio; and (iii) a liability hedge. Given that derivative instruments can be used to convert market risks from asset class to asset class, in our view decisions on market risk (beta) and actively managed risk (alpha) can be separated and optimised as independent portfolios.

The asset side of the balance sheet includes the capital available for investment in both market risk and active risk. Traditionally, active management has been allocated in the same proportion as asset classes defined by desired market risk (beta), resulting in smaller than optimal allocation to strategies with high expected information ratios and often underweight to fixed income markets through a duration mismatch between assets and liabilities.

The liability hedge can be used to hedge the unintended risk exposures of the liability side of the balance sheet, shortening the

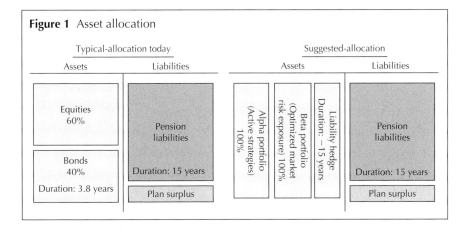

Figure 1 Asset allocation

duration gap between assets and liabilities. Typically, the main risk in liabilities comes in the form of interest rate risk, resulting from the fixed stream of payments to plan participants (akin to outright issuance of bonds). Actuaries can provide a measure of this sensitivity to interest rates and, consequently, it can be hedged using swaps or futures. Similarly, actuaries can measure the plan's sensitivity to inflation, which can in turn be hedged using inflation derivatives. Ideally, a liability hedge should therefore consist of instruments that target each measurable source of unwanted risk.

Since investors are usually constrained by the amount of risk they can take, risk becomes a scarce resource. Without the liability hedge, a typical pension plan carries a substantial amount of surplus variance risk in the form of interest rate risk, as a consequence of the duration mismatch and potentially inflation risk.

In our analysis, a better allocation of risk results in a larger proportion of asset capital available to be distributed to areas with market and active risk and a virtual eradication of the interest rate risk. Using the example in Figure 1, we can look at the risk distribution of both the typical allocation and our suggested allocation (see Figure 2).

With the increasing availability and acceptance of derivative instruments, the toolkit of investors is expanding. These instruments require small capital outlays but provide an effective hedge against unmanaged risks on both asset and liability sides of the balance sheet.

Figure 2 Distribution of risk

Typical risk allocation today	Suggested risk allocation

Market risk: 84%
Active risk: 1%
Interest rate risk: 15%

Market risk: 90%
Active risk: 10%
Interest rate risk: 0%

Estimated excess return	279 bps		Estimated excess return	392 bps
Estimated volatility	11.8%		Estimated volatility	11.4%
Estimated sharpe ratio	0.26		Estimated sharpe ratio	0.4

This typical portfolio is assumed to have 40% bonds, 60% equities, with active managers providing 125 bps of active risk with an information ratio of 0.5. The fixed income portfolio is assumed to have a duration of 3.8 and the plan has a liability structure with a duration of 15 years.

This suggested portfolio is assumed to have hedged its liability interest rate exposure using derivatives. The market risk comes from a 60% allocation to equities. The active risk is assumed to have 350 bps of volatility and an information ratio of 0.5.

Source: Litterman 2003

Once the plan's risks are measured, identified and hedged, we believe the best way to allocate capital is to create a risk budget, for both market risk (Beta portfolio) and active risk (Alpha portfolio). This budget is used to plan the allocation of scarce risk capital to strategies that provide the highest expected returns and functions as a blueprint for the investment committee for implementation of the overall strategy.

INFLATION-LINKED LIABILITIES

As discussed earlier, risks contained in pension liabilities arise from a variety of sources. Most prominent sources of uncertainty come from changes in interest rates, inflation and plan demographics. COLAs, which give rise to inflation sensitivity, exist in both private-sector and public-sector plans, albeit more commonly in a formulaic way in public-sector plans. Non-formulaic one-time increases in private-sector pension plans were prevalent in the inflationary period of 1978–1981, when about 40% of retired pension plan participants received increases (Schmitt 1984), and less so during the subsequent disinflationary period when only 6% did (Weinstein 1997).

Pension liabilities, therefore, contain dimensions of risk that can be further hedged in order to lower the exposure to unintended sources of volatility. Even a partial or an imperfect hedge is better than none. Examples of currently unhedgeable exposures include demographic and industry changes, which may lower participation rates in defined-benefit pension plans. Over time, if the proportion of retired employees to active employees grows, cashflow and under-funding problems for plans may arise. Taking more active and market risk will help counter the negative effects on plan assets, although in some cases additional contributions by the sponsor may be needed.

As one of the hedgeable risks, inflation risk is becoming increasingly manageable. One side effect of demographic shifts is that the higher proportion of retirees versus active participants results in higher sensitivity of plan funding-levels to inflation, provided that the benefit payments are indexed to inflation. Waring (2004) has recently proposed a concept of dual durations; in other words, a measure of not only interest rate sensitivity but also sensitivity to inflation. In his simplified example of the calculation of the present value of pension liabilities, it becomes apparent that inflation risk is potentially a very important risk to "older" plans with higher proportions of retired participants:

$$PV_{liability} = \sum_{t=0}^{T} \frac{CF_{active}(1+i_{wage})^t + CF_{retired}(1+i_{COLA})^t}{(1+i)^t(1+r)^t}$$

Wage increases of active participants (i_{wage}) have less influence over the fortunes of the plan since active participants end up contributing higher payments as a result of their increases. Therefore the proportion of retired participants to active contributing participants becomes important in determining the inflation sensitivity of the plan. Expected future inflation is largely captured in the discount rate (i) but unexpected COLA-related changes in plan liability related to the post-retirement benefits directly influence the economic surplus variance of the plan. The ratio of active to retired participants in private pension plans has had a decreasing trend over the past 30 years (US Department of Labour 2001), increasing the inflation sensitivity of average plans (see Figure 3).

Traditional use of investment asset classes has provided only a partial hedge against inflation. Historically, equities and real estate have been viewed as inflation hedges, but studies (Fama and Schwert 1977) have shown that only private residential real estate is an effective hedge against expected and unexpected inflation. In

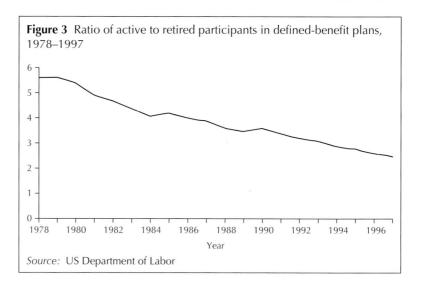

Figure 3 Ratio of active to retired participants in defined-benefit plans, 1978–1997

Year

Source: US Department of Labor

their study, they found that while government debt provided a good hedge against expected inflation, it did not hedge against unexpected inflation. Common stock in their view turned out to be a poor hedge against inflation as from time to time it exhibited negative correlation with both expected and unexpected inflation.

Private residential real estate is certainly not a tradable liquid asset, and is prone to bubbles just like any other market. From a practical perspective, pension funds are unlikely to be able to rely on such an imperfect hedge on their liabilities. Nor are they able to invest large pools of assets into such an illiquid market.

Academic evidence (Litterman 2005) speaks against the ability to use equity instruments as an effective hedge against interest rate risk due to instability of duration and evidence from Fama and Schwert's study shows that equities do not provide stable hedges against inflation. It would therefore seem foolish to rely on these potentially unstable hedge relationships when better instruments are available. For both the interest rate risk and the inflation risk, better hedges can be found in the derivative markets.

USING INFLATION DERIVATIVES IN THE LIABILITY HEDGE
Similar to hedging nominal duration of liabilities through the use of interest rate swaps and futures, inflation-linked liabilities can be

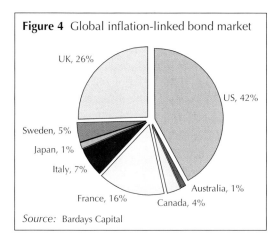

Figure 4 Global inflation-linked bond market

UK, 26%

US, 42%

Sweden, 5%

Japan, 1%

Italy, 7%

France, 16%

Canada, 4%

Australia, 1%

Source: Barclays Capital

hedged using derivative instruments. Until the past few years, the proliferation of inflation instruments since the introduction of the first index-linked issue in the UK in 1981 had been relatively slow. In 1997, the US government entered the market and vastly increased the supply of bonds, and in 2000, the emergence of inflation derivatives brought the ability to more effectively use inflation hedges in portfolios within the reach of institutional investors.

The inflation-indexed global bond market currently accounts for US$708 billion in total issuance. While the market is still dominated by the United States (42%) and the UK (26%), a number of new issuers have recently brought bonds to market. European Economic and Monetary Union countries have issued about 22% of the outstanding issuance, and the rest is created by countries such as Australia, Canada, Sweden and, most recently, Japan (see Figure 4).

The history of the inflation market can be divided into time prior to the year 2000, when the market was primarily dominated by inflation bonds issued by the UK and US governments, and post 2000, when the swap market began to grow and new issuers entered the market. Swap trading volume in Europe has risen from nil to €35 billion in a matter of four years,[1] and as of July 2005 current outstanding notional volume has reached US$100 billion.[2] Medium-term note (MTN) issuance has also grown, as non-sovereign issuers, such as utilities, have entered the market. In 2003, nearly €10 billion of inflation-linked MTNs were brought to the market.

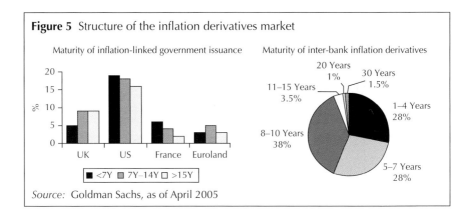

Figure 5 Structure of the inflation derivatives market

Maturity of inflation-linked government issuance

Maturity of inter-bank inflation derivatives

Source: Goldman Sachs, as of April 2005

As discussed earlier, pension plan's sensitivity to inflation depends on the demographics of plan participants and the form of indexation used to adjust benefit payments to inflation. Actuaries can help measure this risk and, with the emergence of inflation bonds and derivatives, it can be also hedged.

Inflation swap markets are an important part of the solution for hedging the inflation risk. Swaps can be customised to better reflect hedging needs of the plan, as well as being linked to an index that more accurately tracks the indexation formula used for adjustments in benefit payments. For example, a Spanish pension plan may need to track COLAs based on Spanish indices even if a majority of the inflation-product issuance in the Euro area comes from Italy and France. Alternatively, a hedge can be linked to an index more closely related to the nature of liabilities, for example a swap might be linked to healthcare inflation rather than core inflation.

Building blocks in the inflation swap market are: (i) zero-coupon; and (ii) year-on-year swaps. Counter-parties to a zero-coupon inflation swap pay a lump sum at the end of the contract, payments going to either the long- or the short-party depending whether inflation exceeded the agreed-upon strike price. Year-on-year swaps pay an inflation-linked coupon annually and ignore the cumulative inflation.

To go back to our example, a liability hedge can be constructed to reduce exposure to inflation through entering into an inflation-linked swap contract. The solution from the swap markets is called

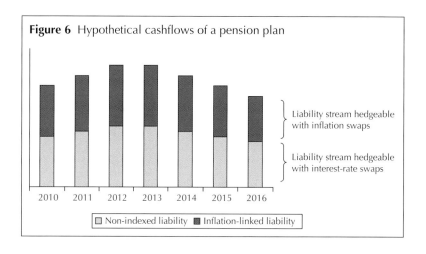

Figure 6 Hypothetical cashflows of a pension plan

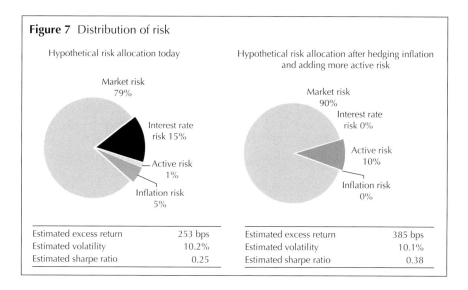

Figure 7 Distribution of risk

a Revenue Inflation swap, which is simply a series of zero-coupon inflation swaps matching the expected benefit payments indexed to inflation (see Figure 6).

Similarly to the example mentioned before, the liability hedge can therefore eradicate the unwanted source of volatility and the plan can increase exposure to active management without taking incremental surplus volatility, resulting in an improved Sharpe ratio (see Figure 7).

Practical considerations may make constructing the liability hedge still somewhat difficult. First, the size of the hedging market in the home currency of the plan may still be too small to be used by larger plans. Currently, the peak monthly trading volume of inflation swaps is approximately €5 billion,[3] amounting roughly to 1% of the inflation cash bond market. Defined-benefit liabilities for S&P 500 firms, on the other hand, amount to US$1.8 trillion (US Department of Labour 2001). Due to difficulties in finding natural hedges, there is a general lack of sellers in the inflation market, although sovereign issuance has created more supply. It is notable, however, that the supply has been rapidly increasing. In case derivative instruments are not available due to regulatory or liquidity reasons, plans may consider using inflation-protected securities in addition to nominal cash bonds.

Second, for the inflation sensitivity to be an accurately hedgeable exposure, it needs to be somewhat stable. Demographics of the plan may change over time in unanticipated ways, and COLAs may be or become discretionary. It seems reasonable to expect, however, that the inflation sensitivity can be at least partially hedged.

It may be tempting to think that other existing assets in pension portfolios already provide some hedge against inflation. Expected inflation is priced in nominal government bonds and thus can be hedged using interest-rate swaps. However, as discussed earlier, unexpected rises in inflation can prove difficult to hedge and can potentially be damaging to plans with a high proportion of retirees to active participants. The only liquid alternative assets with characteristics similar to the nature of liabilities are inflation-linked bonds and swaps.

ACTIVE MANAGEMENT STRATEGIES AND GLOBAL INFLATION-LINKED SECURITIES

Inflation-linked securities and derivatives can also be used for generating alpha in active portfolio management. In essence, the emergence of inflation-linked securities has brought another arrow to the portfolio managers' quiver. Simple correlation analysis shows that inflation bonds can provide an alternative source for investment opportunities. From a US bond portfolio perspective, Treasury Inflation Protection Securities (TIPS) can provide another bond asset class with roughly similar diversification benefit as credit or

Table 1 Correlation of inflation-linked bond indices with other debt indices

	US Treasury	Credit Index	Mortgage Bonds	High Yield	Emerging Debt	US Municipal Bonds	Global Hedged (US$)	Global Unhedged (US$)	US TIPS	Global Inflation Liked
US Treasury	1.00									
Credit Index	0.87	1.00								
Mortgage Bonds	0.87	0.79	1.00							
High Yield	−0.08	0.32	−0.04	1.00						
Emerging Debt	0.16	0.44	0.20	0.61	1.00					
US Municipal Bonds	0.90	0.88	0.79	0.08	0.28	1.00				
Global Hedged (US$)	0.93	0.82	0.79	−0.08	0.13	0.83	1.00			
Global Unhedged (US$)	0.61	0.59	0.52	0.06	0.24	0.58	0.62	1.00		
US TIPS	0.85	0.83	0.69	0.03	0.23	0.79	0.79	0.62	1.00	
Global Inflation Linked	0.66	0.66	0.50	0.08	0.24	0.64	0.66	0.91	0.77	1.00

Source: JP Morgan (Global Hedged and Unhedged Indices); Lehman Brothers (all other indices); July 1997–June 2005

mortgage bonds; and global inflation bonds an even broader set of investments. Consequently, most active fixed-income managers in the United States have adopted the use of inflation-protected securities as part of their tactical allocation in broad-market bond portfolios, known as "Core Plus" strategies. Recently, some firms have also launched "real-return" products, focusing exclusively on inflation-protected securities.

Given that the asset class is relatively new and small, opportunities for out-performance through exploitation of market inefficiencies should exist. Markets may still be too narrow for country-specific funds focusing exclusively on inflation-protected bonds but, as these markets expand, emergence of global inflation investment products should provide opportunities for active management.

While inflation has been well behaved in the world's largest economies, correlations of inflation-protected bond indices have

Table 2 Correlation of Lehman real return bond indices

	US	Canada	UK	Sweden	France
US	1.00				
Canada	0.54	1.00			
UK	0.47	0.48	1.00		
Sweden	0.44	0.55	0.81	1.00	
France	0.54	0.54	0.85	0.85	1.00

Source: Lehman Brothers; July 1997–June 2005

Table 3 Numbers of government inflation-linked issues

	US	Canada	UK	Sweden	Japan	France
Number of issues	17	4	9	4	3	8

Source: Bloomberg

been only moderate, with variance resulting from changes in countries' real yields. Inflation bonds are the only way to directly express views on real interest rate fluctuations (see Table 2).

Inflation-linked bonds can be used for active management in the same way as nominal bonds, for relative value and directional strategies. Since the inflation markets are still relatively illiquid, gains can also be made from exploiting technical supply/demand conditions. However, as mentioned earlier, the number of liquid issues and issuers in many markets is small, resulting in lesser breadth of strategy and lower expected information ratio (see Table 3).

In the United States there is also a small, emerging segment of a municipal inflation-linked market, but the total size of the issuance outstanding, US$682 million,[4] has been too small to attract much interest. As a market it has been primarily interesting to taxable investors, such as US individuals and certain insurance asset pools.

Most inflation-linked active strategies in the US have currently been created as portable alpha strategies; in other words, the outperformance is generated in other asset classes and transferred atop of a portfolio of index-like exposure to inflation-linked bonds. Since these strategies typically rely on generating alpha from a pool of money market, mortgage and short-dated corporate securities, judging from historical evidence, expected excess returns fall short

Table 4 Select performance statistics of TIPS investment products in the United States (gross of fees)

Percentile (%)	Excess return	Percentile (%)	Tracking error	Percentile (%)	Information ratio
75	0.46	75	0.83	75	0.83
50	0.06	50	0.66	50	0.12
25	−0.06	25	0.47	25	−0.23

Source: Wilshire Compass, using Lehman US TIPS as benchmark; July 2002–June 2005

of 100 bps and can potentially be correlated with similar enhanced index strategies. Excess returns represent the economic value added on top of the passive benchmark index return; in other words, the performance generated through active management of portfolios.

In fact, the median manager has outperformed the performance of the Lehman US TIPS index by 0.06% over the past three years. Sample size in both investment products (14 products) and monthly observations (36 months) limits the ability to draw firm conclusions from this, but it is not clear from this evidence that most traditional TIPS mandates have a positive information ratio after fees (see Table 4). The benchmark index chosen here for comparison may not fully reflect the investment strategies of the underlying funds.[5]

From an Active Alpha Investing standpoint, for plans that can use derivative instruments to construct the liability hedge, use of these enhanced strategies may not make sense: the alpha potential of these strategies is low and they are typically capital-intensive as the underlying investments need to be fully funded. It is more efficient to hedge the liability exposure elsewhere and use the available capital in actively managed investments with greater breadth and higher information ratios. We will discuss risk budgeting using both approaches later in this chapter.

With the increasing number of inflation instruments coming to the market, the ability to generate true alpha from inflation markets may increase. In the end, many global macroeconomic managers already forecast inflation trends as part of their investment strategy, and inflation derivatives may prove to provide a more accurate way to express those investment insights.

RISK BUDGETING AND INFLATION-LINKED STRATEGIES

In earlier parts of this chapter, we discussed the need for allocating the scarce resource of risk where it reaps the most reward. In other words, risk budgeting is a process used to maximise the expected information ratio of the entire fund. The risk budgeting methodology that we employ builds from the top down, beginning with asset allocation and ending at the level of individual investments.

Before investments are made, we create a risk budget, which incorporates our expectations for investment risks and correlations in one comprehensive assessment of the deployment of risk. The practice of risk budgeting is a key feature of the way we invest, and would warrant a deeper discussion that is outside of the scope of this chapter. For further reference, a recently published book "Modern Investment Management" (Litterman 2003) provides additional insight into our risk budgeting process.

A risk budget typically includes an overall blueprint for the fund's investment strategy. In the example given in Table 5, we have created a sample risk budget covering three high-level asset classes (US Large Cap, US Small Cap, Fixed Income) and one derivatives-based active overlay strategy. The risk budget includes information on size of investment in each category in both relative and absolute terms (% of Fund and Assets USD (US dollars) columns) as well as a set of targets for both excess return and tracking error. The last column from the left (% of Active Risk) is the active risk decomposition. It shows how active management risk is allocated across investments. It is calculated using targeted tracking errors, weights and correlations for each investment.

The sample risk budget reflects a fund with an asset allocation to US Large Cap (25%), US Small Cap (25%) and US Fixed Income (50%). In addition, we have allocated more capital and active risk to higher information ratio asset classes and strategies such as US Small Cap and Global Tactical Asset Allocation (GTAA) overlay.[5,6] Policy overlay is implemented to bring back the strategic benchmark exposure to 25/25/50. Since policy overlay and GTAA are executed using futures, swaps and forwards and therefore require only a small cash outlay, the majority of the investment capital is deployed in the actively managed strategies.

Without these portable alpha strategies, the target excess return would be 1.75% and target risk 1.37%, resulting in a target

Table 5 Sample risk budget

Asset class	Assets USD			Excess return (%)	Tracking error (%)	Information ratio	% of active risk
	% of fund	MM	Benchmark				
US Large Cap Manager I	10.00	20.00	Russell 1000	2.50	5.00	0.50	11.00
US Large Cap Manager II	10.00	20.00	Russell 1000	2.50	5.00	0.50	11.00
US Large Cap Futures Contracts	5.00	10.00	Russell 1000	0.00	0.00	0.00	0.00
US Large Cap Total	**25.00**	50.00	Russell 1000	**2.00**	**3.87**	**0.52**	**21.90**
US Small Cap Manager I	15.00	30.00	Russell 2000	3.00	4.00	0.75	15.80
US Small Cap Manager II	15.00	30.00	Russell 2000	3.00	4.00	0.75	15.80
US Small Cap Futures Contracts	-5.00	-10.00	Russell 2000	0.00	0.00	0.00	0.00
US Small Cap Total	**25.00**	50.00	Russell 2000	**3.60**	**3.10**	**1.16**	**31.60**
US Core Fixed Income	22.50	45.00	Lehman Aggregate	0.75	1.50	0.50	5.00
US Core Fixed Income	22.50	45.00	Lehman Aggregate	0.75	1.50	0.50	5.00
US Fixed Income Futures Contracts	5.00	10.00	Lehman Aggregate	0.00	0.00	0.00	0.00
US Fixed Income Total	**50.00**	100.00		**0.68**	**1.05**	**0.65**	**10.00**

Portable alpha

Table 5 (continued)

Asset class	Assets USD			Excess return (%)	Tracking error (%)	Information ratio	% of active risk
	% of fund	MM	Benchmark				
Policy Overlay Cash Account	**2.50**	**5.00**	Cash	0.00	0.00	0.00	0.00
Policy Overlay Futures Contracts	−2.50	−5.00	Cash	0.00	0.00	0.00	0.00
Total Portfolio ex-GTAA*	**100.00**	200.00		**1.74**	**1.39**	**1.25**	**63.50**
GTAA Active Overlay	100.00	200.00	Cash	0.50	1.00	0.50	36.50
GTAA Overlay Cash Account	2.50	5.00	Cash	0.00	0.00	0.00	0.00
Policy Overlay Futures Contracts	−2.50	−5.00	Cash	0.00	0.00	0.00	0.00
Total Portfolio	100.00	200.00		**2.24**	**1.65**	**1.35**	**100.00**

information ratio of 1.28. Therefore, implementation of these portable alpha strategies improves expected returns by 0.50%, or US$1 million per annum on the US$200 mm fund. The improvement in expected returns comes from deployment of active risk in asset classes with higher expected information ratios. The portable alpha strategy mentioned here is a practical example of our approach of separating sources of alpha and beta, ie, dividing the risk in the portfolio to the Alpha portfolio and the Beta portfolio.

As discussed earlier, plans that are unable to use the liability hedge for mitigation of the inflation exposure may choose to include inflation-protected assets in the strategic benchmark. Thoughtful risk budgeting can also help increase expected information ratios of inflation-indexed strategies in the same way as in the previous example. Assuming that the benchmark in the previous example were changed to US Large Cap (25%), US Small Cap (25%) and US TIPS (50%), the fund manager could alternatively use the policy completion to bring the fund back to strategic benchmark or deploy the funds in actively managed TIPS strategies. Assuming that there are no constraints in using derivative strategies for completion, the fund should choose the implementation path that yields the highest information ratio.

In comparison with the expected information ratios of 0.23 for a top quartile manager in TIPS mandates, a reasonable information ratio assumption for a broad US domestic fixed income mandate is higher.[7] For merely illustrative purposes, let us assume TIPS managers can achieve an information ratio of 0.25 and broad fixed-income managers can reach an information ratio of 0.50. In addition, assuming that no leverage can be taken in each strategy, let us assume that Core Plus mandates can generate 1.50% of tracking error and TIPS mandates about 0.80%.

Focusing solely on the fixed-income component of the risk budget, the choices for portfolio construction could then be as shown by Table 6.[8]

As can be seen from this example, using a broad fixed-income mandate to generate the excess returns and bringing the benchmark index exposure in line using derivative instrument creates a portfolio with significantly higher expected excess return (0.75% versus 0.20%). The Portfolio B is also taking more active risk but, most importantly, the risk is used more efficiently as indicated by the expected information ratio, which is double that of Portfolio A.

Table 6 Sample inflation-linked fixed income portfolios

Investment	% of fixed income	Excess return (%)	Tracking error (%)	Information ratio
Portfolio A: Inflation-linked fixed income with direct investment in TIPS mandate				
TIPS mandate	100	0.20	0.80	0.25
Total fixed income	100	0.20	0.80	0.25
Portfolio B: Inflation-linked fixed income with portable alpha investment				
US Core Plus mandate	100	0.75	1.50	0.50
Short futures position	−100	0.00	0.00	0.00
Long inflation swap	100	0.00	0.00	0.00
Total fixed income	100	0.75	1.50	0.50

At the present stage, the most effective form of capital deployment in our view is to use other parts of the risk budget to generate alpha, rather than rely on active TIPS strategies. With the onset of new issuers in the global TIPS markets, this may change, especially for funds that have a global real-return policy benchmark.

CONCLUDING REMARKS

Globally, pension plans are facing challenges in meeting their performance objectives in the light of recent financial market returns and demographics shifts. Better budgeting of scarce risk resources and increased active risk can help plans overcome some of the headwind caused by the environment.

With the recent development of the inflation securities market, inflation risk is another area of unmanaged volatility that can be hedged. Subsequently, the lower surplus volatility will provide opportunities for taking additional risk in other parts of the plan either through increased market risk or active risk.

In our view, the prudent course for any pension plan is to carefully evaluate the risk exposures that can be hedged, and to complete a risk budgeting exercise to ensure that their scarce resources are being used efficiently.

1   Source: ICAP.
2   Source: Lehman Brothers.
3   Source: ICAP.

4   Source: Bloomberg.

5   Three-year regression beta of each manager against the index ranges from 0.94 to 1.05, implying that the benchmark is roughly of similar duration as the portfolios in our sample. The annualised index return for the time period is 9.43%.

6   GTAA strategies are actively managed overlay strategies that seek to benefit from relative value and directional trade opportunities using futures, forwards and swaps.

7   Wilshire data of the universe of US broad-market "Core Plus" managers (80 managers) indicates that for the time period of July 2002–June 2005, information ratios were 0.48, 1.01 and 1.60 for lower 25th percentile, median and top 25th percentile managers, respectively.

8   The example assumes that there is no cost or basis risk in the completion strategy, ie, tracking error and excess returns from both short future position and long inflation swap are zero.

REFERENCES

Dickson, C. Henry, and Charles L. Reinhard, 2005, "Latest On Pensions", Investments Strategy & Macro Portfolio Strategy. (Lehman Brothers).

Fama, E. and W. Schwert, 1977, "Asset Returns and Inflation", *Journal of Financial Economics*, **5**, pp. 115–146.

Lax, Y., T. Tyagi, and K. Winkelmann, 2003, "Active Risk Budgeting in Action", *Goldman Sachs Risk Management Series* (Goldman Sachs).

Litterman, R., 2003, *Modern Investment Management* (Hoboken, NJ: John Wiley & Sons).

Litterman, R., 2003, "Active Alpha Investing: A New Paradigm for Today's Challenges", *Goldman Sachs Active Alpha Investing Series* (Goldman Sachs). Available at: http://active-alpha.gs.com.

Litterman, R., 2005, "Equity Duration: Is this a Viable Concept? The Evidence is Examined", Working Paper.

Rudolph-Shabinsky, I., 2000, "Inflation-protected Securities in an Asset Allocation Framework", *Investment Counseling for Private Clients II* (Association for Investment Management and Research), pp. 26–38.

Rudolph-Shabinsky, I. and F. H. Trainer, 1999, "Assigning a Duration to Inflation-Protected Bonds", *Financial Analysts Journal*, **55(5)**, pp. 53–59.

Siegel, Laurence B., 2004, "Distinguishing True Alpha from Beta", *CFA Institute Conference Proceedings*, Challenges and Innovation in Hedge Fund Management, August 2004, CFA Institute.

Schmitt, D. G., 1984, "Postretirement Increases Under Private Pension Plans", *Bureau of Labor Statistics*, **107(9)**, p. 3.

US Department of Labor, 2001, *Private Pension Plan Bulletin 1997*, Number 10, Winter.

Waring, M. B., 2004, "Liability-relative Strategic Asset Allocation Policies", *The New World of Pension Fund Management* (*CFA Institute Conference Proceedings*) (CFA Institute), pp. 43–64.

Weinstein, H., 1997, "Post-retirement Pension Increases", *Compensation and Working Conditions* (Bureau of Labor Statistics), Fall, p. 49.

Winkelmann, K. *et al*, 2003, "Duration Completion: Enhancing Risk and Return in Pension Fund Management", *Goldman Sachs Asset Management Strategic Research Series* (Goldman Sachs).

10

Quantifying and Hedging Inflation Risk for Pension Funds

Stuart Jarvis; Alan James

Barclays Global Investors;
Barclays Capital

INTRODUCTION

A key source of demand for inflation-linked bonds and derivatives comes from the need to hedge real liabilities. In markets such as the UK and Sweden long-term investors own the vast majority of inflation-linked bonds against their real liabilities. In some other markets they are a major feature only of long-end demand. Inflation-linked liabilities are all but unhedgeable using nominal interest rate instruments, while addressing them with illiquid real assets such as property is inherently high risk. Traditionally many investors with a significant percentage of their liabilities in real rather than nominal form held a majority of their assets in equity rather than bonds, but equities do not always provide an effective hedge against inflation, even in the long term. In the UK between 1950 and 1996, the five-year rolling average correlation between the retail price index (RPI) inflation and equity-index returns were always negative. Despite this, UK pension funds were happy to increase the percentage of equities in their overall portfolios from the 1950s onwards, reaching 80% on average by the early 1990s. This increase was sometimes justified by reference to the real nature of fund liabilities, but in truth was driven more by higher expected returns in the equity market. These returns were required to finance discretionary increases to pensions, which used to be targeted by many funds. However, Government regulation effectively turned these discretions slowly into guarantees, so that when the equity bubble was eventually pricked, significant levels of under-funding appeared in UK pension plan balance sheets. These under-lying drivers have combined with increased accounting scrutiny to drive liability management to the fore in the UK and increasingly across the world, with regulation playing a lesser but still impor-tant role.

The need to address inflation liabilities is not new, it was one of the main reasons for the launch of the UK linker market in 1981, but the focus on it is now much more intense. The Financial Reporting Standard FRS17 accounting rules in the UK mean that the value of pension schemes is recognised in full on company balance sheets. The problem is that the combination of equity market losses and unrealistic historical discount factors have left many funds in a situation where holding inflation linked bonds would merely lock in a certainty of having insufficient assets to meet liabilities. Fortunately, the range of tools with which inves-tors can hedge their inflation liabilities has expanded greatly in recent years. Even if they are far from a complete solution, infla-tion-linked derivatives offer the opportunity to reduce the risk from real liabilities without tying up all the capital that is needed to try and achieve sufficient returns to bring a fund back above water.

The UK pensions industry has the most prominent real liabili-ties, with their exposure to RPI being larger than the US$750 billion size of the total global inflation-linked bond market and dwarfing that of the US$180 billion UK linker market. While they own the majority of the UK market as a result, insurance companies own almost 30%. Mainly this is to cover a subset of life insurance poli-cies that have inflation linkages. Life companies have traditionally been more active in assessing their liabilities, partly due to less actuarial uncertainty than for defined benefit pension schemes, but the introduction of the most recent PS16/04 regulations has intensi-fied the pressure for them to address such exposure. With the scale of their exposure becoming much more tractable and the pressure for it to be addressed greater, the UK insurance industry was the major driver of the development of the inflation-swaps market until recently, but their needs are now broadly covered as new inflation-linked policies are not being written.

As discussed in more detail in the next section, liabilities in the UK pension market are much more closely linked to inflation than in other major markets. In addition, the FRS17 accounting conventions are among the strictest in the world, making it difficult to hide the degree of liabilities. Nonetheless, the introduction of IAS19 accounting standards across Europe does put pressure on private-sector-defined benefit schemes to address their broader inflation exposures, but this sector is relatively small and the nature of linkages is diverse. The exception is the Netherlands, which has US$750 billion in defined benefit pension scheme assets, where the separate Financial Assessment Framework (usually known by its Dutch acronym, FTK) takes precedence. The degree of inflation exposure in the Netherlands has been cut substantially by the end of traditional indexation for the vast majority of schemes, leaving most liabilities as nominal. In the United States there is a clear move towards liability assessment, which could impact the allocation of around US$1.5 billion trillion of private defined benefit money, but the larger inflation liabilities lie in the state and local government pension sector that may be under less pressure to address them. The country that potentially has the largest inflation-linked pension liabilities is Japan, but here accounting or regulatory reform that might encourage liability matching is likely to be many years away. While almost every form of Japanese defined-benefit pension is indexed, pension funds cannot easily hold inflation-linked assets while they are considered derivative instruments under domestic accounting standards.

PENSION LIABILITIES

A defined-benefit pension plan accrues liabilities to its scheme members while they are in employment with the sponsoring employer(s). The most common form of defined-benefit scheme is one that is based on the final salary of the member. These liabilities may be:

❑ pensions payable to the employees themselves from retirement age;
❑ pensions payable to dependents (chiefly, spouses) of the employees on the employee's death;
❑ lump sums payable, either on retirement or on death; and
❑ other benefits, in particular many US schemes include health insurance for employees and dependents.

269

Traditionally, these liabilities are split into:

❏ *Pensioner liabilities.* These are the liabilities in respect of members currently in receipt of a pension (including contingent pensions payable on their death, for example to spouses).
❏ *Deferred (or "preserved") liabilities.* These represent members who are no longer accruing liabilities (usually, because they have left employment) but whose pensions are not yet in payment. In the UK, these pensions are normally[1] inflation-protected in the period between leaving employment and retirement.
❏ *Active liabilities.* These are the liabilities to members still in employment. Usually, these members' pensions will still be accruing (that is, the percentage of final pay they will receive increases each year) and their liabilities are also linked to their salary growth.

The certainty of the liabilities for these members decreases in the order shown; pensioner cashflows are much easier to predict than those for existing active members. A particular risk for active and deferred liabilities is that, on retirement, members in private sector UK plans often have an option to commute part of their (taxed) pension for a (tax-free) lump sum. This gives rise to extra uncertainty as the commutation terms often vary over time and the amount commuted will have a significant impact on the cashflow profile of the liabilities. At any point, the actuary's estimate of the cashflow profile associated with a plan's liabilities will be subject to uncertainty, perhaps as much as 4% per annum.

Finally, in addition to the obvious impact of longevity, there is uncertainty around how long members will stay in employment ("withdrawal rates") and when they will retire ("retirement age"). Table 1 summarises these uncertainties for a UK pension fund.

Note that if accrued, rather than projected, benefits were the focus, then the active column would change to become a copy of the deferred column. Commutations only present a risk where they are not on neutral terms.

Market risks embedded in pension liabilities

Pension plans increasingly seek to invest in assets that enable them to meet their liabilities and, moreover, to manage the relative volatility of assets and liabilities. Therefore, in addition to the main uncertainties affecting the cashflow estimates (see Table 1), there is

Table 1 Main uncertainties associated with estimating liability cashflows

Risk	Actives	Deferreds	Pensioners
Longevity	Yes (high)	Yes (high)	Yes (medium)
Price inflation	Yes	Yes	Yes
Salary inflation	Yes	No	No
Withdrawal rates	Yes	No	No
Retirement age	Yes	Yes	No
Commutation	Yes	Yes	No

Source: Barclays Global Investors July 2005.

Table 2 Main uncertainties associated with valuing liabilities

Risk	Actives	Deferreds	Pensioners	Hedgeable
Longevity	Yes (high)	Yes (high)	Yes (medium)	No (see below)
Commutation	Yes	Yes	No	No
Price inflation	Yes	Yes	Yes	Yes
Real salary inflation	Yes	No	No	No
Withdrawal rates	Yes	No	No	No
Interest rates	Yes	Yes	Yes	Yes

Source: Barclays Global Investors July 2005.

also the risk associated with the choice of discount rate to value the resulting cashflow profile. The risks associated with a liability valuation are thus readily obtained (see Table 2).

The final column summarises the areas where asset markets currently provide means to manage a plan's exposures to the risks underlying the liability values.

Longevity is a slightly special case as an insurer can be used to remove the longevity risk from a plan's balance sheet. However, the premium charged is often seen as excessive. This is especially the case for deferred annuities, where the longevity risk, which the insurer will take on, is very large. In recent months a longevity bond has been brought to the market (by the European Investment Bank) – if a sufficiently deep market in longevity were to develop, this may come to be a way to hedge these risks. Governments have been lobbied to introduce longevity bonds in several countries where there are large defined-benefit pension sectors but as their own liabilities to pensioners (both directly in terms of state pension and indirectly in terms of health care etc) are also heavily dependent on longevity they are not natural sellers of this type of bond.

Pension plans are increasingly focused on hedging their interest-rate and inflation exposures. For practical calculation purposes, the remaining risks can be assumed to be uncorrelated to market instruments.[2] Indeed for many practical purposes it usually suffices to treat a particular cashflow projection as being the liabilities of the plan, even when this projection is only an estimate of the actual economic liabilities. This difference is, however, an important feature to bear in mind: solutions that hedge long-term uncertain liabilities with a high degree of precision should be avoided if this precision can only be secured at a high cost.

Inflation linkages

In the United States today, Cost of Living Allowances (COLAs) are not a necessary part of the pension promise made to employees. The most common COLAs are linked to national price inflation, but others are linked to average/sectoral earnings or regional inflation. COLAs tend to be more common within the public sector than the private sector but can vary even for schemes within individual companies. In the Netherlands, inflationary protection has often been paid out of positive investment returns, in a similar way to bonuses in UK life insurance, but without an indexation guarantee if returns fall. More recently the FTK legislation has encouraged Dutch funds to state explicitly whether or not they offer indexation (and whether this is wage or price based) but the majority have chosen to abandon any formal tie.

UK pension plans also used to provide discretionary increases partially contingent on investment returns. However, in contrast to the Dutch experience, UK pension plans have had price inflation linkage imposed upon them by successive governments.

❑ *Minimum revaluation in deferment.* Members who left their pension plan after 31st December 1990 have inflation protection on the bulk of their pension in the period up to retirement (in excess of any "Guaranteed Minimum Pension" which is subject to different revaluation protection). This was introduced in a number of steps, starting in 1985. The inflation protection is that the benefit must rise between exit and retirement by the increase in prices over the period, subject to a 5% per annum cap. This cap is applied just once, to the whole period being protected.

❑ *Minimum increases in payment*. Pension plans have to provide a pension accrued after 5th April 1997 with annual increases at least as good as inflation subject to a 5% per annum cap. This was flagged by a 1993 Act and finally introduced in 1995. It is known as Limited Price Indexation (LPI), or, where more precision is needed, LPI (0,5) – the zero refers to the fact that pensions cannot fall, ie, a 0% floor as well as a 5% cap is applied to inflation.[3]

Some schemes provide inflation protection to other liabilities (eg, pre 1997 pensions) even where this is not required by legislation. For example, this generosity is common in the public and formerly public (privatised) sectors. Inflation-linked liabilities therefore form a large portion of the UK plans' book of liabilities. In other countries, the extent of inflation liability is often a much smaller proportion of the total liability exposure. For a scheme without a COLA, the exposure to inflation is embedded within average salary growth for active members, but the linkage to price inflation is notably less certain for this kind of exposure. Salaries of active members covered by the scheme may grow at a very different pace from average salary levels, especially for highly skilled and specialised industries.

Managing the risks

Interest rate risks and inflation risks in the liabilities can be managed by comparing the exposures of the assets to these same risks. The interest rate risks are well understood and can be managed using government and corporate bonds, interest rate swaps, etc.

The same approach can be used for inflation, but here the range of available instruments is less extensive. Index-linked bonds have been issued in the UK since the early 1980s and since the late 1990s in the US and Europe, but corporations have been reluctant to follow suit. Those corporate bonds that do exist, £11 billion by market value as of the end of 2004 in the UK and far fewer in other markets, are notably less liquid than their nominal equivalents. Inflation swaps are increasingly being used by many large UK plans to manage the inflation risks and have also been used by funds in other countries whose inflation liabilities are explicit. Inflation swaps provide greater flexibility over the inflation exposure to be purchased.

ASSET LIABILITY MODELLING
Framework
The goal of asset liability modelling is to establish which strategies will best enable the pension plan, or the corporate sponsor, to meet its pension liabilities. Different strategies can be compared using the usual two metrics:

❑ *Return*. The expected return of the fund assets.
❑ *Risk*. The relative volatility of the assets against the liabilities is the key measure for comparing alternative investment strategies.

Note that it is only the volatility of the assets *relative to the liabilities* that is important, not the absolute volatility. With this important twist, the usual mean/variance framework can then be imported wholesale to aid the comparison of different strategies.

Measuring the risk
Until relatively recently, the bond/equity split of a pension plan was thought to be a sufficiently good statistic to give a feel for a portfolio's overall risk. However, as maturities, bond proportions and modelling capabilities have increased, and interest rates have fallen, the "duration" of the assets and liabilities (the sensitivity to small parallel shifts in interest rates) has come to be seen as a key measure.

It is well known that duration only accounts for a proportion of a bond portfolio's volatility. Care must therefore be taken that the volatility measure also captures changes in the slope, curvature and other (less significant) movements in the term structure. Portfolios of identical duration can then be compared.

In the next section we describe how the fixed income universe can be analysed to ensure that the volatility calculation includes these different volatilities. They then appear, with appropriate weights, in a common framework.

Constructing a fixed-income covariance matrix

The risk calculation is, in principle, a simple one, where all assets provide fixed cashflows. These cashflows can be compared and the differences applied to a covariance matrix:

$$\sum_{s,t} \left(Cashflow_{Asset}(s) - Cashflow_{Liab}(s) \right) Cov(s,t)$$
$$\times \left(Cashflow_{Asset}(t) - Cashflow_{Liab}(t) \right)$$

Here $Cov(s, t)$ is the covariance between investing in a (zero-coupon) bond of maturity s versus one of maturity t. The objective is therefore to construct this covariance matrix.

This formulation is simplified for two reasons.

❑ First, there are two yield curves, for nominal and inflation-linked cashflows, and these must be accounted for separately.
❑ Second, the inflation linkage in the liabilities may be subject to a floor and cap (see the section "Inflation linkages", eg, LPI pension increases). In theory, the impact of these on the risk of a strategy is subtler than can be measured by a covariance calculation; the LPI linkage is often path-dependent and a calculation based on stochastically generated scenarios is needed. In practice, splitting the LPI liabilities into (notional) real and nominal components gives a sufficiently accurate calculation. A stochastic model effectively determines the proportions used to make this split.

To keep things tractable, a small number of maturity points t must be used, and then any cashflow mapped into different maturity points. For example, the points we use are:

❑ cash;
❑ 0.5, 1, 2.5, 5, 7.5, 10, 15, 20, 25, 30, 35, 40, 45, 50 for fixed interest;
❑ 0.5, 1, 2.5, 5, 7.5, 10, 15, 20, 25, 30, 35, 40, 45, 50 for index linked.

For example, a cashflow at time 26 will be allocated 80%/20% into the maturity points 25/30 for the purposes of the tracking error calculation.

To evaluate the covariance matrix, we calculate monthly returns from investing in zero-coupon bonds of the differing maturities and calculate the covariance of these series. The comparisons later in this chapter are based on prices of (notional) zero-coupon bonds for month-ends from June 1999 onwards.

Full mean/variance framework

This risk covariance calculation for fixed-income assets extends in the obvious way to other assets, the risk calculation in general is just

$$\sum_{i,j} \left(Asset_i - Liability_i \right) Cov\left(i, j\right) \left(Asset_j - Liability_j \right)$$

Here i and j run over all assets, and $Liability_i$ is only non-zero for bond instruments i. This covariance matrix can be constructed just as for the fixed income matrix, using historic asset returns.

Finally, to help assess alternative solutions and determine optimal ones, a return vector is also required. This can be determined by a combination of reverse optimisation and user inputs (for example, using the Black–Litterman methodology to interpolate between the two). A (surplus) mean/variance efficient frontier can then be determined in the usual way (cf Waring 2004).

Aside: corporate finance approach

There is one important caveat to liability modelling for pension schemes. A firm specific pension plan is, from an economic perspective, a subsidiary of the sponsoring employer. For example, since the sponsor is ultimately responsible for making up any deficits that arise, the financial exposure of the sponsor (and therefore of any shareholders, if appropriate) is the same as if the plan's assets and liabilities were held directly on the corporate balance sheet. Therefore, it is reasonable to argue that the machinery of corporate finance should be used instead of portfolio and optimisation considerations. In fact, this is both controversial and counterintuitive: most schemes operate at arm's length from the sponsor and UK sponsors were until recently able to wind up plans and walk away paying only part of the deficit. (This changed in June 2003 when the Government effectively removed this default option from solvent employers.)

Corporate finance is different because a company is essentially a package of investment decisions. The company is not the final investor and care has to be taken that financial decisions make sense for the ultimate investors, ie, shareholders, bondholders and plan beneficiaries. The needs of these competing factors ought to be relatively well balanced if the market effectively prices the firm's exposure to the pension scheme but historically this has not been the case. More recently the change in accounting practices coupled with renewed corporate activity, ie, takeovers, buy-outs etc, has started to align the various stakeholders more tightly by more actively valuing the state of pension exposures within equity and bond prices.

If this employer-centric view is the correct one then the asset mix of the scheme is only part of the picture. The sponsor's owners (eg, shareholders) can arrange their other investments to offset any particular investment strategy of the scheme, and therefore the investment strategy is, to first order, irrelevant to the value of the entity as a whole. Instead, second-order effects determine the optimal mix that maximises value. Chiefly, these are tax, the value of the sponsor's option to default and the frictional costs caused by the management time taken up in dealing with pension finance issues.[4] Where the option-to-default can be ignored or when its value is to be minimised (eg, for investment decisions taken by trustees) the tax situation is most important. In the UK and the United States, for a typical shareholder, it is more tax efficient for the scheme to hold bonds rather than equities[5] and, furthermore, management costs will be reduced if asset/liability volatility is reduced.

In practice, decision makers routinely ignore this corporate finance point of view. Indeed, the trustees or plan managers making the asset allocation decision will focus on maximising fund assets while minimising the risk of the liabilities not being met. So far only a small number of firms have to date taken a wider firm-centric or shareholder-centric point of view.

STRATEGIES ADOPTED IN PRACTICE
Range of approaches
As stated previously, detailed attention has only recently started to be paid to the structure of fixed income portfolios and much of this is based around duration as the main metric. For many years

asset/liability modelling tended to focus on returns rather than risk, for example by defining the objective function in terms of contribution rates and focusing on the middle 90% or less of stochastically generated scenarios. Pension plans' strategic-asset allocations have, in the UK particularly, often had significant equity weightings and low bond weightings.

The poor returns, yield falls and increased accounting transparency have highlighted the true risks. Among the responses have been:

❑ the development of liability proxies, eg, a "liability benchmark portfolio", which adequately reflects the investment risks embedded in the liabilities, (this has helped plan advisers and managers to increase their understanding of liability risks very rapidly);
❑ moves to increase the duration of bond holdings to be closer to that of the liabilities;
❑ moves to increase the bonds' duration so that the scheme is immunised from parallel shifts in yield curves;
❑ increasing willingness by managers to manage portfolios against a liability benchmark, expressed either as a (nominal and real) duration target or as a series of cashflows.

Impact of accounting rules

In theory, peculiarities of accounting rules should not affect companies' investment decisions; any economic profit or loss must come through in the accounting numbers at some point. In practice, of course, accounting rules can defer recognition for very long periods, and this does affect the behaviour of managers who are focused on this year's numbers.

SSAP24, the previous UK pension accounting rules, allowed the use of actuarial discount rates, off-market asset values and other smoothing mechanisms, resulting in a wide scope within which underlying profits and losses could be readily obscured. FRS17 provided much of this by applying a mark to market value of liabilities at a high quality (AA-rated) corporate bond yield for the discount rate. The equivalent US standard, FAS87, occupies a position intermediate between these two UK ones.

Consequently, moves to hedging liabilities only gathered pace in the UK once companies were forced to disclose their FRS17 positions. There is some volatility arising from the difference between AA bond yields and gilt or swap yields, but this risk is small compared to the equity-related risks to which funds often continue to be exposed. It is therefore the swap or gilt value of liabilities that is hedged in practice.

A further related issue is the use of "expected rates of return" on fund assets in companies' profit and loss accounts under FRS17 (and FAS87). Such a rate is also often used within actuaries' funding reviews (known as valuations). Although reducing equity exposure should have a positive impact in reducing risk, it can reduce the accounting profit and increase contributions in the short term. Discussions with the actuary and the fund sponsor are therefore a key component of the discussions in advance of any decision to reduce risk within a pension plan.

Products used

As funds have moved from increased bond allocations through duration benchmarks to more complex liability benchmarks, so the range of products used by pension plans has expanded by moving through the following list.

❏ Government and corporate bonds, eg, measured against an iBoxx benchmark.
❏ Bond futures. Futures on long-duration bonds can be used to extend the duration exposure of a plan's assets, bringing them closer into line with the liabilities.
❏ Corporate index-linked bonds. There are very few issues of these, partly because they remain an unusual form of debt and partly because a higher premium will tend to be demanded (in addition to their rarity, they have a longer duration than a conventional bond of identical maturity).
❏ Interest rate and inflation swaps. These are used where increased precision is required, eg, where the specific liabilities are being monitored, perhaps via a liability benchmark consisting of annual cashflow projections.

Inflation swaps offer particular attractions.

❏ They offer a form of inflation linkage with a small amount of risk and may offer a small pickup relative to gilt linkers.

❑ Inflation-linked corporates can be constructed synthetically by overlaying an inflation swap on a corporate bond.

❑ The liquidity in UK LPI (0,5) swaps is almost as good as that available in RPI and the cost is lower than hedging the cap and floor separately. Bank counterparties are prepared to provide LPI based on whatever RPI month is required. Other flavours of LPI are also available. Swaps therefore enable a better hedge for the pension liabilities to be constructed (compared to using physical instruments).

❑ In conjunction with interest rate swaps, they can be used to hedge in full the long-term nominal and real interest rate risks of the liabilities, without having to allocate explicit capital. Effectively, if the prevailing strategic asset allocation is retained and swaps overlaid on top, the long-term interest rate risk embedded in the liabilities is replaced with short-term interest rate risk (the floating leg of the interest rate swaps).

Comparison of strategies

For funds with a low allocation to fixed income, or plans that have not yet adopted a liability-driven approach to managing their assets, it remains the case that the typical profile has the following features.

❑ The duration is very short compared to the liabilities. For example, in the United States, the Lehman Aggregate is very often used as a portfolio benchmark. Similarly in the UK, typical benchmarks reflect the propensity of corporates to offer short-dated debt rather than the long-dated liabilities.

❑ The inflation exposure is low. In the UK, the lack of non-Government index-linked issue and the perception that real yields are anomalously low lead to low allocations.

Lengthening the duration and increasing the inflation exposure (using any of the products previously described) therefore represent two "quick wins". Where there are significant non-fixed income assets within the portfolio (eg, more than 50% of the assets), going further may not result in any significant reduction in the risk of the assets against the liabilities.

To give an idea of the scale of reduction possible when the fixed income allocation is significant, consider the following four strategies (compared to a typical liability profile with a duration of 22 years) where the allocation is 100% to fixed income.

❑ *Short duration*. As described above, this is the typical situation for many plans. The expected tracking error of the assets against the liabilities (ie, the standard deviation of assets minus liabilities) is around 11% of the liabilities per annum.

❑ *Barbell*. The portfolio is effectively split into two pieces: a short- and a long-duration piece (eg, 40 years' duration) in order to give the same duration as the liabilities. This strategy provides an effective reduction in risk, reducing the tracking error to around 3% of liabilities per annum.

❑ *Optimised barbell*. By slightly lengthening the duration of the short-duration portfolio (which can be readily done within the typical range of physical instruments that would be used) and then reducing the duration of the long-duration portfolio (which will probably involve synthetic instruments) a better solution can be found. Although duration is effectively the primary principal component of yield curve volatility, hedging duration only removes the exposure to parallel yield curve shifts. More complicated yield curve shifts are expressed in the tracking error numbers we have been using – the next most important factor is convexity, effectively the spread of the exposure across the yield curve. Liabilities have a large spread (the amount paid out in one year is very similar to the amount paid out the next), but the convexity of the assets in the "barbell" solution above is often even greater. By reducing this spread at the margin, the tracking error can be reduced to around 1.5% of liabilities per annum.

❑ *Cashflow matched*. Finally, of course, interest and inflation swaps can be used to remove all these yield curve risks – either in a 100% synthetic solution or more commonly by overlaying a "cashflow timing" onto an underlying physical bond portfolio. The tracking error can then be reduced very far indeed (eg, to below 0.2% if five-year buckets are used for the cashflow matching).

Note that reducing the tracking error much below 1% may not be sensible.

❑ The cost may start to increase as the tracking error is reduced further. This is primarily due to moving into areas where the market is less liquid, such as complex inflation exposures or very long duration – hedging the payments in annual buckets is not prohibitive. The cost of transacting a swap with a complex schedule of payments is very similar to one with a simplified schedule.

❑ The liability cashflows provided by the fund's actuary are only ever estimates. There is considerable uncertainty around these – retirement ages and withdrawal rates etc, are subject to estimation error just as is longevity – and therefore precise hedging is inappropriate. This can easily contribute 2% to our tracking error numbers above.

Dynamic versus static view of the plan

The tracking error measure used above is a "static" measure of the risk embedded in the pension scheme assets. In practice, unless the fund has sufficient assets to fully hedge the liability risks with cashflows, the asset strategy is more dynamic. Plan managers must take the dynamic aspects of any solution into account when choosing their strategy.

❑ *Cashflow timing can have a leveraging effect on the asset returns.* Consider, for example, a fund that is paying out 5% of its assets per annum. It may expect to remove its deficit if it achieves outperformance relative to the liabilities of 2% per annum over the next 10 years. Yet, the incidence of the actual performance matters: receiving a 4% outperformance over two years then 0% for the next two years would leave the scheme 1% better off than if the returns occur in the opposite order. Put another way, it is the money-weighted rate of return that matters more than the time-weighted rate of return.

❑ *Partial cashflow matching implies an evolution of the asset allocation strategy.* In order to remove the short-term dependence on the incidence of asset returns, and to reduce the target required to get to full funding, some plans have chosen to match the cashflows expected to arise in the first 10–30 years. The remaining assets are then notionally hypothecated to the remaining liabilities. Commonly, these assets would be invested in equities. Over time, the short-term cashflows will be paid and the percentage allocation to equities would naturally increase. This increased risk-taking may well be different to what the plan is seeking to achieve.

Another important aspect of matching only the first n years' cashflows is that this period is often not where the largest risk resides. The impact of interest rate and inflation movements on the first years' cashflows is not great; while hedging these cashflows thus provides a good amount of short-term certainty, it is not going very far towards hedging the pension plan's risks.

Conversely, if only the long-term cashflows are hedged, then equities may need to be sold to meet the short-term cashflow needs, and the equity percentage allocation will decrease over time. The target return required of the fund's non-fixed income assets will be correspondingly larger.

A compromise between these two strategies is to cashflow match a slice of the entire liability profile. This enables the asset allocation strategy to remain roughly constant over time (subject to actual returns achieved) and gives the plan some comfort that at all times a certain percentage of the liabilities are covered. Each plan is different, however, and an open plan that is cashflow positive (ie, contributions from the sponsor and members exceed the outgo to members) can afford to be less concerned about short-term cashflow matching. This is often the case in the Dutch market, for example.

What the future holds

Inflation liability hedging is set to be the major feature dominating the UK linker market over the next decade but most of this will be for liabilities already in existence. Benefits that start accruing from April 2005 are subject to an RPI capped at 2.5% rather than the previous 5%, unless the specifics of a scheme have a higher minimum level. With this cap below the market break-even level the resultant growth of new inflation liabilities is limited. In addition, whereas in 1995 there were over five million active members of private-sector-defined benefit schemes, by April 2004 the Government Actuary's Department estimated that there were 2.3 million, of which 1.4 million were in schemes still open to new members. Public sector active members are now larger than those in the private sector. Here the move away from defined-benefit to defined-contribution schemes has been much slower but the accounting and regulatory pressure for real liabilities to be addressed is lower.

The closing of many private defined-benefit schemes and the natural running down of the percentage of active members that has resulted has increased the certainty with which these schemes can assess their liabilities, as uncertain wage drift and length of employment terms have become less important elements to consider. Thus, while ultimately the end of defined-benefit schemes will dry up liability-related demand for linkers, at present the trend is, if anything, hastening the move towards liability matching. Coupled with the change in the RPI cap this means that inflation liabilities drop off sharply after 2045 (assuming longevity does not increase dramatically), with the liabilities after this date relatively small. Thus it is likely that the 2055 index-linked gilt launched in September 2005 will remain the longest issue on the curve for the next 20 years. For liability managers the bond is likely to be more important in helping to define the shape of the inflation swap curve than for direct investment.

Across Europe the need for liability hedging is coming increasingly into focus. In the Netherlands there is little incentive for most pension funds to hedge their previous implied indexation obligations, but if equity markets rally and bond yields rise sufficiently then many funds may choose to lock in this real return element. It is likely that individual country consumer price index (CPI) swaps will develop further, but absent issuance by governments of different inflation-based liquidity will remain focused on the French and the euro. Specific country inflation is likely to trade at shorter maturities where the co-integration with euro area prices is a less powerful force.

Few US private defined-benefit schemes are likely to go down a full liability-matching route using inflation swaps. While legislative and accounting reform is likely to encourage the use of nominal derivatives, it is only for schemes with explicit CPI indexation for deferred members and pensioners that have sufficient certainty to use inflation swaps for matching purposes as their liquidity develops. There is a strong case for any active scheme to hold Treasury Inflation Protected Securities (TIPS) within their general asset allocation to offset the real element of wage rises, but the extra cost of using inflation swaps is not justified given the higher uncertainty. The pressure on state and local government funds to address their liabilities is less at this stage, and it may also be more difficult to obtain approval to use inflation swaps in size even though the linkages to liabilities are generally clearer than for the private sector. Thus it is likely that the majority of public sector fund-inflation asset exposure will be in TIPS, but it is likely to be moving away from a market index target to one based on the nature of liabilities, ie, skewed towards much longer durations.

ACKNOWLEDGEMENTS
The authors are grateful to Doug Graham, Andy Harrison, Moyeen Islam, Kate Jones, Vincent de Martel and Tarik Ben-Saud for helpful discussions during the writing of this chapter.

1   Inflation protection became compulsory in the mid 1980s. The inflation protection is the cumulative increase in RPI over the period between exit and retirement, subject to a maximum of 5% per annum. Since this maximum is applied cumulatively and since inflation has been well below this cap in recent years, the maximum is usually ignored. Inflation protection is not statutory in the United States – which leads to a more marked difference between the accumulated benefit obligation (ABO) and projected benefit obligation (PBO), which incudes future salary escalation, in the United States.
2   There is room for debate here: eg, some UK equities have large exposure to longevity via final salary schemes and there is likely to be correlation between prevailing economic conditions and commutation rates. However, the linkages are much weaker than for inflation and interest rates, where, if the other risks did not exist, the exposures could in principle be offset very precisely by appropriate asset allocation.
3   Legislation does not mention this 0% floor, although it is presumed to exist. It is no coincidence that inflation was, or had recently been, high at the time that these inflation guarantees were passed by the UK parliament.
4   This is of course just the "Modigliani Miller" irrelevancy proposition applied to pension plans. Black (1980) and Tepper (1981) are early examples of this argument, which has been repeated more recently by numerous authors, eg, Cooper (2003).
5   The analysis is not straightforward. For example, the light tax treatment of bonds compared to equities should increase shareholder value if a plan switches to bonds, and so result in a capital gain, but this capital gain is taxed, reducing the original enhancement. See Gold and Hudson (2003) for worked examples under the US tax code and Ralfe *et al* (2004) for a UK version.

REFERENCES

Black, Fischer, 1980, "The Tax Consequences of Long-Run Pension Policy", *Financial Analysts Journal* **36**, 21–28.

Cooper, Stephen and David Bianco, 2003, "Q-series: Pension Fund Asset Allocation", *UBS Investment Research*, September.

Gold, Jeremy and Nick Hudson, 2003, "Creating Value in Pension Plans (or, Gentlemen Prefer Bonds)", *Journal of Applied Corporate Finance*, Fall. Available at http://www.sternstewart.com/content/gentlemen_prefer_bonds.pdf, pp. 51–57.

Ralfe, John, Cliff Speed and Jon Palin, 2004, "Pensions and Capital Structure: Why hold Equities in the Pension Fund?", *North American Actuarial Journal*. July, pp. 103–113.

Tepper, Irwin, 1981, "Taxation and Corporate Pension Policy", *Journal of Finance* **36**, 1–13.

Waring, Barton, 2004, "Liability-Relative Investing II", *Journal of Portfolio Management,* **31**(1), September.

11

From Conditional to Full Indexation: A Discussion of Liability Solutions used in the Dutch and UK Pension Funds

Theo Kocken, Jeroen van der Hoek; Adam Michaels; David Bieber

Cardono Risk Management; Lane, Clark and Peacock LCP;
ABN AMRO

INTRODUCTION

In an ageing society, the pension issue is heading towards the top of the agenda for many world leaders – if not today, than at least in the next few years. This goes for both pay-as-you go systems that will put a heavy financial burden on society, as well as funded capital systems such as defined contribution (DC) and defined benefit (DB), (also known as final salary schemes). The problems with DB are the most imminent, due to the fair value system that makes future obligations – and so shortfall – directly visible. This has occurred at a time when the benign inflationary environment currently being enjoyed by the western world has convinced many that inflation risk is under control. Very few schemes have hedged all of their inflation risk.

There are two different DB variants in Europe that currently receive a lot of attention, where the regulators and pension funds have approached the crisis in different ways:

❏ the conditionally indexed system of the Netherlands, where inflation compensation is conditional on the coverage ratio of the pension fund; and
❏ the capped indexed system of the UK where inflation compensation is now limited to an upper level, determined by the regulator.

The ageing of society in these countries – and the rest of the western world – has dramatically changed the ratio of the economically active to the inactive. This renders the contribution rate instrument – varying contributions to adjust fluctuations in the funding ratio – ineffective. In the past, this was one of the most powerful tools to stabilise funding ratios.

To make matters worse, the combination of falls in equity markets and falls in long-term interest rates have put most pension funds in a far from prosperous condition. Following these developments, the pension regulators have tightened their policies on solvency requirements and recovery actions. New rules require fair value calculation for the liabilities, which for many pension fund trustees has radically changed the perception of risk.

All this has made it clear that pension funds' health is, *on average*, far from good, and that increasing contribution rates will not solve the problem. A question that emerges is how to cope with this sequence of developments that has swamped the pension community. This chapter will not focus on these specific developments, such as regulation, but rather on the nature of inflation risk and indexation risk. Furthermore, we will discuss how pension funds can reduce this risk in a both effective and efficient way.

STRATEGIC HEDGING OF EMBEDDED INFLATION OPTIONS IN DUTCH PENSION FUNDS
Risk Management changes in the Netherlands
Pension funds in the Netherlands, with assets totalling about €500 billion, have initially reacted on the developments in the early years of this millennium by intensifying the use of an effective policy instrument that is already in use by a large number of pension funds: conditional indexation. In case of stormy weather and therefore a low funded ratio, indexation is temporarily suspended. As the value of (full) indexation in a pension fund's liability can easily reach 30% up to 50% on top of nominal liabilities, this is quite an effective measure. This policy comes in many forms and will be elaborated on in the following sections. This embedded option can provide relief for the solvency level, but is only an emergency measure, since the objective is to pay a fully indexed pension to the members.

Real improvements should come from advanced risk-return innovations. One main source of risk-return improvement stems

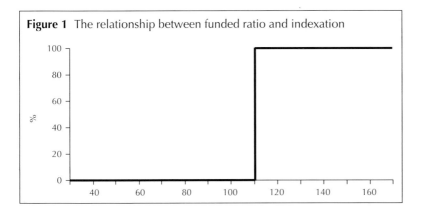

Figure 1 The relationship between funded ratio and indexation

from the move to fair value, which has revealed a lot of interest rate risk – both real and nominal – implicitly present in the pension funds. It has become clear to pension funds that they run interest rate risks within the long-term at the best zero (and more realistically, negative) risk premiums.

This chapter will focus on how to arrive at strategically optimal solutions to hedge complex conditional indexation features, without necessarily changing the asset allocation. This will be split into theoretical considerations followed by practical Asset Liability Modelling (ALM) with hedging based on the currently available financial market instruments.

Embedded indexation options

Let us assume a pension fund that grants indexation simply as follows. In case the funding ratio exceeds 110, full indexation in line with the consumer price inflation index is awarded that year.[1] In case the funded ratio falls short of 110, no indexation is granted that year. The year after, again the funding ratio is examined to determine whether indexation can be awarded that year. Figure 1 shows this all-or-nothing relationship.

What is exhibited in Figure 1 is a pay-off from an option termed a digital option (also "binary option" or "all-or-nothing" option). It is an option that pays either zero or a pre-agreed amount, depending on the stochastic underlying "variable", in this case the funding ratio of the pension fund. The digital options available in the markets often pay a fixed amount in case it expires in the money. In the pension fund indexation case, this amount equals the inflation at the end of the period. So the pre-agreed amount is also a stochastic variable: its level is not known exactly in advance.

A conditionally indexed pension fund is a string of digital options maturing 1, 2,..., 50 years from now.[2] The question for risk management application is, what is the value of these options and how this value influences the optimal hedging strategy.

To get some feeling for the situation, it is useful to investigate upper and lower bounds of the value. In the case of a very low funding ratio, most options will have zero value and the whole set of options is worthless. In case of a very high funding ratio, the participants can expect full indexation. In this case, the value of the options is the present value of the liabilities, discounted against the real interest rate curve, minus the present value of the liabilities discounted against the nominal interest rate curve. For an average Dutch pension fund, this average is currently 35–40% of the nominal liabilities.

Digital options happen to have some very specific characteristics. Like all options, the value of the indexation option is determined by (amongst others) the volatility of the "underlying stochastic variable". In the case of indexation options, this variable is the funding ratio. For normal options (plain vanilla call and put options) this implies that the higher the volatility of the underlying variable (funding ratio), the higher the value of the option. A digital option is different. If the option is out of the money, the value increases as volatility increases. This is simply because the probability of ending up in the money – and consequently receiving inflation – increases with higher volatility. However, when the option gets in the money (where indexation becomes more likely) higher volatility will increase the probability of a much lower funding ratio, with the risk of no indexation. There are no further benefits as when the option is in the money, the maximum pay off is reached. In this case the value decreases with rising volatility. So the exposure to volatility (known as *vega* in option terms) is positive in the case of low funding ratios and negative in the case of high funding ratios. This mechanism is illustrated in Figures 2 and 3.

Figure 2 shows the probability distribution of a high- and low-volatility pension fund compared to the indexation level. Note that the area of the probability distribution on the right-hand side of the

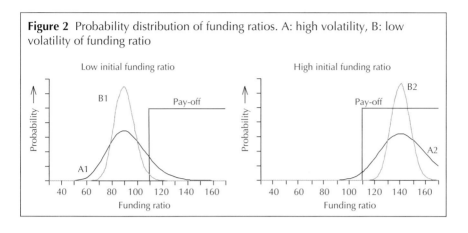

Figure 2 Probability distribution of funding ratios. A: high volatility, B: low volatility of funding ratio

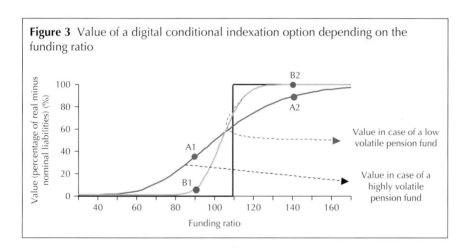

Figure 3 Value of a digital conditional indexation option depending on the funding ratio

funding ratio level of 110, the level at which indexation is granted, represents the probability of indexation. Figure 3 shows the value of the indexation option for low- and high-volatility pension funds.

In practice, sometimes the digital – the all-or-nothing version of indexation – is replaced by a funded ratio-dependent strategy that pays out complete indexation at very high funded ratio levels, partial indexation in the case of a medium funded ratio level, and no indexation at very low funded ratio levels.[3] However, the principle remains the same with respect to finding a (nominal and real) interest rate hedging strategy.

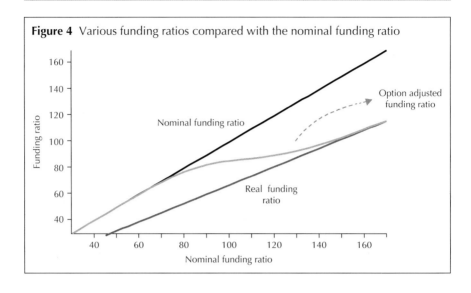

Figure 4 Various funding ratios compared with the nominal funding ratio

So the value of the indexation option depends on the level of funding ratio and the volatility of the funding ratio. Since the funded ratio is defined as the assets divided by the (nominal) liabilities, and the indexation option value comes on top of the nominal liabilities (or alternatively, subtracted from the real liabilities), a good way to make the indexation option comprehensible is by comparing real, nominal and "option adjusted" funding ratios. Take a funding ratio with the liabilities calculated by just discounting the (nominal) obligations by the nominal yield curve (say the swap curve). This is referred to as the Nominal Funding Ratio (NFR). The funding ratio discounted by the real interest rate curve is the Real Funding Ratio (RFR), which represents the value of the liabilities in the case full indexation takes place at any time. It is assumed that the "real curve" corresponds with the inflation compensation of the pension obligations. The third funding ratio is defined as the "true approximation": the Option Adjusted Funding Ratio (OAFR). This is the funding ratio calculated with liabilities based on the nominal yield curve but with the indexation option added to the liabilities.[4]

As can be seen from Figure 4, when the nominal funding ratio increases (due to the conditional indexation scheme), indexation becomes more likely, and the OAFR moves more towards the RFR. The indexation option becomes apparent in this picture. When the

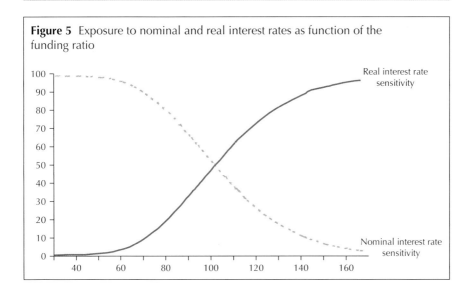

Figure 5 Exposure to nominal and real interest rates as function of the funding ratio

funded ratio severely decreases (eg, due to huge crashes in the markets), the slope of the OAFR at a certain point is almost horizontal. In this "horizontal" area, the participants absorb all of the risk. At a certain low level of the funded ratio, no future indexation is to be expected and further declines in the funded ratio also directly impact the OAFR since participants cannot absorb more risk.[5]

From this view of the value of the indexation option, the sensitivity of the pension fund's liabilities for changes in nominal and real interest rates can be determined. At levels where the indexation option has no value there is only sensitivity to nominal interest rates. Since the value of a digital option can be interpreted as the (risk neutral) probability of ending up in the money (times the pay-off), the value in fact is an indicator of the ratio between nominal and real interest rate sensitivity. This effect is illustrated in Figure 5.

Figure 5 shows the dynamic nature of (relative) exposure to nominal interest rates *versus* real interest rates. The exposure to the nominal interest rates moves gradually from 100% to 0% as the funding ratio increases, the exposure to the real interest rate moves in the opposite direction. This has significant influence on the optimal hedging structure of a pension fund. It implies that real hedges should gradually replace nominal hedges as the funding ratios increase.

In practice, the observed behaviour differs from the previous theoretical foundation given above. For example, the smooth shift towards 100% real interest rate sensitivity does not imply that this is also the optimal hedge ratio to hedge liabilities. Often, the hedge takes place with an inflation-linked product linked to a different index to that used for indexation of the liabilities. In this instance, the Dutch wage or price inflation in the liabilities has to be hedged by the closest proxy that is available in the financial markets, the European harmonised price inflation. A correlation much below one implies a lower inflation-linked hedge-optimum.

Due to the complexity of pension funds, their dynamics and various embedded options, the only sound way to find the optimal hedge is by means of asset and liability models with simulations over the long-term. This is the subject of the following concise ALM case.

A brief ALM analysis of a Dutch pension fund

In general, a pension fund strives for a balance between ambition and risk management constraints. For the participants, indexation is one of the most important objectives (ambitions) as many consider this to be the very nature of a proper pension offered by a pension fund. However, regulators require a pension fund to guarantee at least the nominal value of the liabilities with a high probability. In addition to regulation requirements, constraints may also stem from participants or the sponsor. Participants, for instance, may wish to avoid a policy with an expected high indexation level but with a non-negligible probability of no indexation at all during the consequent years of an economic downturn. Although a thorough analysis focuses on both short (1–5 years) and long (10–30 years) horizons, this simple example is constrained to the 10–30 year time horizon, as the case only serves for explanatory reasons. In the analysis below, the probability of under-funding (in NFR terms) is taken as the risk constraint. The average funding ratio (in NFR terms) is taken as the return measure.

Results and analysis

The pension fund in the current case has an initial funding ratio of 110%. Indexation policy, in line with general practice based on the NFR, grants indexation above 110 and nothing below 110.[6] First we

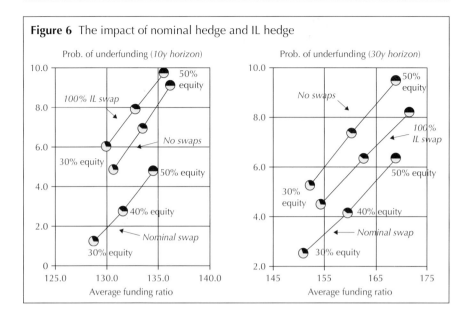

Figure 6 The impact of nominal hedge and IL hedge

construct two liability hedges: a nominal and an inflation-linked (IL) hedge. The latter hedge consists of instruments linked to the European inflation. The real interest rate is modelled with a correlation of 0.8 with the real interest rate linked to Dutch inflation. We have simply applied a small set of swaps with maturities ranging from 10 to 30 years that minimises the risk.[7] For explanatory reasons, the volume of the hedge is not the risk-minimising hedge (which depends on the exact asset allocation), but the interest rate hedge that brings the basis point value gap between assets and liabilities to 0. These hedge constructions are evaluated in an ALM model.[8]

Figure 6 shows the results of both hedges for two time horizons. Both show the risk of under-funding (vertical axis) *versus* average NFR (horizontal axis). Each circle on the line shows a different asset allocation: the percentage of equity is increased from 30% to 50% of the total assets in steps of 10%.

For the 10-year horizon, the inflation hedge performs considerably worse than the nominal hedge when it comes to (nominal shortfall) risk reduction. The risk of shortfall is even increased when compared to the unhedged situation. This poor performance

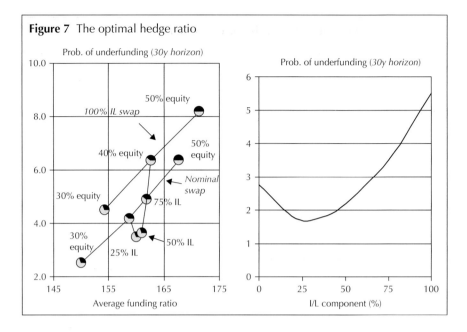

Figure 7 The optimal hedge ratio

is partly explained by the relatively high over-hedge in combination with a hedge that is not even close to the actual sensitivity of the indexation option of the fund.

However, on a long-term horizon of 30 years the performance of the IL hedge is much better, though still not as good as the nominal hedge. The better performance of the IL hedge can be contributed to the increasing (expected) funding ratio over time.[9] The higher the funding ratio on average, the more the indexation is in-the-money, the higher the real interest rate sensitivity.

It should be noted at this point that the results are partly under-valuing inflation-linked contributions because the analysis focuses on the NFR, where the OAFR should be theoretically optimal, closely resembling reality. The reason for using the NFR is that it is the standard funding ratio used in most recent regulatory frameworks.[10]

Given these NFR based objectives, the optimal hedge ratio (ratio between the nominal and inflation-linked component) can be determined (for a given horizon). Figure 7 shows the results over a 30-year horizon.

It appears that a hedge with an inflation-linked component of about 25% is optimal for the measures and horizon considered.

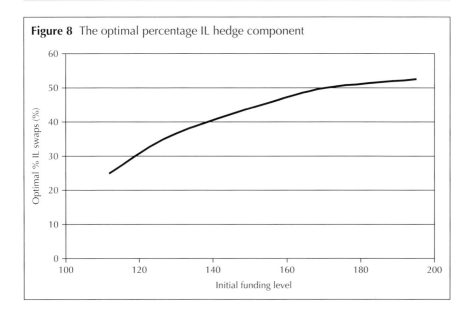

Figure 8 The optimal percentage IL hedge component

Following the theoretical explanations above (especially Figure 5) a growing percentage of inflation hedge is expected as an optimum when the funding ratio of a pension fund increases. The results for this case are shown in Figure 8.

The results are in line with the theory, though the percentages are slightly lower. Though many complex factors are involved, part of the explanation is the limited correlation between the inflation in the hedge and that used in the liabilities. A lower correlation always implies a lower hedge ratio. Again, the use of NFR instead of OAFR as a risk (shortfall) measure also biases the inflation portion.

Unfortunately, this chapter is much too concise to discuss the interesting conflict between the aims of indexation *versus* the risk of nominal funding ratio shortfall. For example, in the present case, the risk of shortfall in the NFR was set against the average funding ratio (as the "return" measure). In the case when the average funding ratio is replaced by, for example, the average amount of indexation shortfall or the risk of significant amounts of cumulative indexation shortfall, the optimal ratio between nominal and inflation-linked hedging changes in favour of inflation-linked hedging.

Furthermore, robustness analysis is crucial but not part of this brief overview. Parameters, such as the correlation between real rates (European *versus* Dutch) and between nominal and real rates, are crucial for the optimal solution analysis and research has to determine how sensitive the solution is for shifts in the parameter.

MANAGING THE INFLATION RISKS OF UK OCCUPATIONAL PENSION FUNDS
Inflation risks in the UK pension fund environment
In recent years, inflation has become an increasingly important issue for UK private sector pension funds and, by extension, for their corporate sponsors. The link between scheme benefits and inflation means that funds are exposed to inflation risks – the risk posed by inflation of a decline in the scheme's solvency position.

Scheme members expect an income in retirement that will keep pace with changes in the cost of living. This means that, historically, inflation has been a key factor for UK pension funds. However, its importance has increased significantly in recent years owing to regulatory change and, perhaps, greater to awareness of the risks.

Inflation was reasonably benign during the 1950s and 1960s, with annual increases in the Retail Price Index (RPI) averaging just over 4%. During the 1970s, the average annual increase in the RPI was over 13%. Just as trustees might have been beginning to forget this inflationary period, Sterling's exit from the Exchange Rate Mechanism contributed to inflation exceeding 9% in 1990.

As well as the risk posed by high inflation (where investment returns may not keep pace with increases in retirement incomes), there are also risks posed by low inflation or deflation. In particular, benefits will not be reduced in the event of deflation but investment returns for many assets may well be negative.

Pension schemes need to be concerned not only about current inflation, which affects the level of pension benefits, but also about expectations of future inflation. These expectations affect the assessed current value of the benefits that must be paid in future.

Before considering the recent history of the UK pension fund environment, it may be worth outlining the various types of inflation that may be relevant to UK schemes.

❑ RPI is a measure of price inflation. State pensions, public sector pensions, and some company pensions are increased in line with changes in the RPI.

❑ Limited Price Indexation (LPI) is generally taken to mean the lower of 5% and the annual increase in RPI. There are variants of this, using a different ceiling such as 2.5%.

❑ Wage inflation drives the level of salary-related pensions (the individual's wages, rather than national wage increases).

❑ Members' expectations for retirement income may be driven by changes in the true cost of living for pensioners, which may be quite different to changes in the RPI (eg, the RPI includes an allowance for the cost of mortgage payments, and many pensioners own their homes outright).

❑ Consumer Price Inflation is the measure targeted by the Monetary Policy Committee of the Bank of England.

It is worth noting that there are a number of different types of inflation that a pension scheme needs to consider.

Regulation drives the increasing importance of inflation for schemes

In 1971, the typical pension fund provided a pension at retirement that was related to final salary and that was increased on a discretionary basis only, if at all. Short service benefits did not have to be increased prior to retirement in nominal terms. This package of benefits reflected employers' wishes to retain key staff and to motivate staff to achieve promotion. Defined contribution arrangements were rare.[11]

In 1970, pension scheme assets were invested predominately in equities, with a small allocation to property. Index-linked gilts did not exist as an asset class. Fixed-interest bonds constituted a significant part of pension scheme investment.[12]

In the last 20 years, the provision of pension benefits in the UK has become much more tightly regulated. A number of legislative changes have formalised the link between pension benefits and inflation.

❑ The Pensions Act 1995 introduced a requirement for schemes to increase pensions (excluding Guaranteed Minimum Pensions and Protected Rights[13]) in line with LPI in respect of benefits accrued after April 1997.

❑ The Social Security Act 1985 and Social Security Act 1990 require that the level of deferred pensions for defined-benefit schemes should be revalued in line with the increase in RPI from exit to retirement age, capped at 5% pa.

Recently, it appears as though the government is backtracking on the increasing formalisation of the link between pension benefits and inflation. The Pensions Act 2004 has relaxed the required level of pension increases for defined-benefit schemes from RPI capped at 5% to RPI capped at 2.5%, and has removed this requirement for the members of money purchase arrangements altogether.

At the same time as schemes have been forced to provide inflation-related pension benefits, the focus on scheme solvency has sharpened.

The Pensions Act 1995 introduced the Minimum Funding Requirement (MFR) for defined-benefit schemes. This required schemes that were under-funded on a prescribed valuation basis to make good this deficit over a certain timescale. The Pensions Act 2004 has replaced the MFR with a scheme-specific funding measure, which again requires employers to make up deficits over a defined period. Since 11th June 2003, a solvent employer is responsible for making up any shortfall if a scheme undergoing wind-up is not able to fully buy out the benefits with an insurance company.

Accounting regulations (such as FRS 17 and IAS 19) mean that high inflation may feed through to a reduced ability for the corporate sponsor to pay dividends to shareholders, via an increase in the assessed value of scheme liabilities.

These developments have increased the importance of inflation risk to pension schemes and their corporate sponsors.

In 2004, defined benefit arrangements were still the dominant form of provision, but many have been closed in response to the increasing burden of regulation. Defined contribution arrangements have become an important form of provision. All defined-benefit schemes must provide increases of at least LPI on benefits accrued since April 1997, and the majority of members receive no more than this.[14]

Equities were very much the dominant asset class for pension schemes, with a small amount invested in property. Fixed-interest bonds made up a relatively small part of pension scheme assets. Investment in index-linked gilts has increased steadily from the first issue in 1981.[15]

In respect of pension schemes' investment in different asset classes, the key change since 1970 has been the fall in fixed-interest bonds and cash, from 38% to 17%. It appears that schemes have acted to reduce their inflation risks by investing increasingly in real assets and in index-linked gilts.

The role of benefit design in limiting inflation risk

One of the ways in which schemes seek to manage their inflation risk is through benefit design. The level of retirement income awarded by the scheme, including the annual increases, defines the extent to which the value of the liability is affected by inflation. However, changes in benefit design will often only affect the future accrual of benefits, and so it may take some time for the effects to be felt. For schemes that are closed to future accrual, such changes would have no effect.

Final salary benefits are linked to wage inflation. There are other models of provision that may entail less inflation risk.

❑ In a Career Average scheme, the pension is calculated with reference to the average salary over the worker's period of employment. Wage inflation is less significant.

❑ Career Average Revalued schemes are similar, but in the calculation of average salary past earnings are revalued in line with price inflation. Compared with final salary schemes inflation is still a risk, but the link to wage inflation is partially replaced with price inflation.

❑ In a Defined Contribution scheme, the employer bears no inflation risks. These are borne by the member. However, the employer may be affected by staff dissatisfaction if members receive inadequate incomes in retirement.

In defined-benefit schemes, the risk posed by wage inflation can be controlled through the definition of pensionable salary. In many schemes there is a maximum amount of salary that will be considered as pensionable, and controlling this can reduce the impact of wage inflation for those close to this cap.

Another option is to limit the increase in pensionable salary so that, for example, pensionable salary is defined as the lower of actual salary and starting salary revalued by 3% pa. Depending on the scheme rules, it may be possible to cap the growth in pensionable salary in respect of benefits already accrued.

On an informal basis, employers can control the increase in pensionable salary by making payments in non-pensionable form, for example via bonuses that do not affect pension entitlement. This relies on the definition of pensionable pay in the scheme rules not including bonus payments.

The pension increases paid by the scheme also influence the degree of inflation risk. Paying increases on a discretionary basis only when the scheme can afford to do so clearly reduces risks, but schemes now have to pay increases of at least LPI.

A scheme awarding LPI increases is less exposed to inflation risks than a scheme awarding full RPI increases and, in particular, the impact of a year of very high inflation is greatly reduced. Schemes offering a fixed annual increase in pensions are exposed to the risk that inflation is lower than expected, since this would mean that benefit increases are higher in real terms.

Case study

One of LCP's clients had a final salary pension scheme with a deficit of 40%. Significant deficit contributions were affecting corporate profits, although the company was committed to meeting the scheme's benefit promises.

The scheme provided benefits that were generous in the context of the UK market: an accrual rate of 1/50th, and guaranteed increases for pensions in payment of 5% pa.

The scheme changed the pension increases for the future accrual of benefits to LPI, reducing the ongoing pension cost from 23% of pensionable salary to 18%.

In addition, the definition of pensionable salary was changed, so that future annual increases were limited to LPI. This lessened the impact of future wage inflation on benefits already accrued, reducing the past service liability by 7%. It also limited the sponsor's exposure to wage inflation with respect to future accrual.

Managing inflation risk through investment strategy

Another important way in which inflation risk can be managed is through investment strategy. To the extent that the value of the assets responds to the level of inflation in the same way as the assessed value of the liabilities, then the solvency position of the scheme is protected from changes in inflation. A change in investment strategy to better align the inflation sensitivity of the assets with that of the liabilites can reduce the inflation risk with respect to past service benefits, as well as in respect to future service benefits. This makes it a more important tool than benefit design.

There are a number of assets that respond to inflation in broadly the same way as scheme liabilities.

Index-linked bonds
Index-linked gilts pay coupons that are explicitly linked to changes in the RPI, and are generally considered to be the best matching asset for inflation-linked pensions in payment. However, there are a number of disadvantages.

❑ The expected return available from government bonds is low, which may be a particular problem given that so many schemes are currently in deficit.[16]
❑ The demand for index-linked gilts from pension schemes and others (including institutions with long-term inflation-linked liabilities such as insurance companies) has been very high.[17] Many schemes do not find current prices attractive.
❑ Index-linked gilts provide no protection against the extent to which wage inflation outstrips price inflation.
❑ Coupons would decrease in the event of deflation, but schemes would not be able to reduce the level of pensions.
❑ Even for RPI-linked liabilities the match is not perfect, as the coupons are linked to RPI with an eight-month time lag. There is no inflation-linkage in the eight months before the gilt is redeemed.

Even where a scheme can afford to lock into the current low yields by matching the projected liability cashflows, it can be difficult to achieve accurately using index-linked gilts. There is a very limited supply of gilts at longer durations, the investment income is concentrated around the redemption date rather than being paid evenly over time, and the limited number of available gilts limits flexibility. For large schemes, more sophisticated approaches are available that combine gilts with swaps. These approaches are discussed in more detail in the next section.

A number of overseas governments have issued inflation-linked bonds, amongst which the largest issuers are the United States and France. Compared with those index-linked bonds issued by the UK, overseas issues provide a less good match for UK pension fund liabilities: the coupons are linked to overseas inflation rather than domestic inflation; and they carry currency risk, though this can be hedged.

Corporate issuance of index-linked bonds has been limited in the UK. As of January 2005, the proportion of outstanding corporate debt that is index-linked rather than fixed coupon was very small.[18]

In 2001, Tesco issued £160 million of long-dated LPI-linked debt. There have also been a number of smaller issues of LPI-linked bonds, mainly by utility companies. These bonds may provide schemes with an improved match for pensions with LPI increases. However, the small size of issues and of the market as a whole means that there are significant liquidity problems. The LPI-linked bond market is expected to remain small.

There is almost no overseas issuance of index-linked corporate bonds.

Real assets

Real assets are assets that provide returns that are broadly linked to inflation, which includes quoted equities, property, private equity, infrastructure assets and commodities.

These investments confer rights to part or all of the income generated by physical assets or property, and this income is expected in the long-term to broadly keep pace with inflation. Therefore, real assets should, in theory, provide some hedge against inflation. In practice, however, the evidence for this is mixed.[19]

Equities may be thought of as providing protection against wage inflation. Corporate earnings, and hence dividend payments, should increase broadly in line with growth in national income, although the evidence for this is weak.

Typically, however, an unexpected increase in inflation might be expected to drive equity markets down. "Cost push" inflation is likely to lead to reduced corporate profits, as companies may not be able to pass on higher input costs to consumers.

In contrast, commodity prices would be expected to respond to an unexpected increase in inflation. Commodity investment is, however, currently rare amongst UK pension schemes.

Real assets are expected to provide a higher return than index-linked gilts, as they are riskier. Returns are unpredictable in the short term, and there may be periods where these assets fall in value in real terms. Pension schemes invest over relatively long time horizons, which may enable them to accept the volatility associated with these assets to a certain extent.

Future contributions from the corporate sponsor and from members can be seen as a real asset. Regular contributions are usually expressed as a proportion of salary. The company's ability to make additional contributions in the future to rectify any current deficit is related to company earnings, which would be expected to keep pace with inflation.

Structured solutions
There are a number of more sophisticated approaches that are still relatively new to pension funds.

Many of these use inflation swaps to manage the scheme's inflation risks. Swap contracts are very flexible and the market is large and liquid, but they are not familiar investments for scheme trustees. There are high costs associated with education and advice, and there is only limited experience of their actual use in the industry to provide trustees with reassurance.

Swaps can be held directly to reduce inflation risk. Holding a combination of fixed-interest bonds and inflation swaps is broadly equivalent to holding index-linked bonds. Indeed, the existence of LPI swaps allows schemes to synthesise LPI-linked bonds.

High minimum fees and the costs of advice and education mean that holding swaps directly may not be practical for smaller funds.

The asset management industry has responded to the difficulties faced by schemes investing in swaps by constructing approaches that reduce the systems and operational burdens.

In January 2005, State Street Global Advisors launched a series of liability-matching funds, and Barclays Global Investors launched a similar range in March 2005. These pooled funds combine holdings of cash with interest rate and inflation swaps in order to target a given set of expected future cashflows with a reasonably high degree of certainty. Within the suites of funds offered by both managers, some have returns linked to changes in

Figure 9 Liability driven investment structure

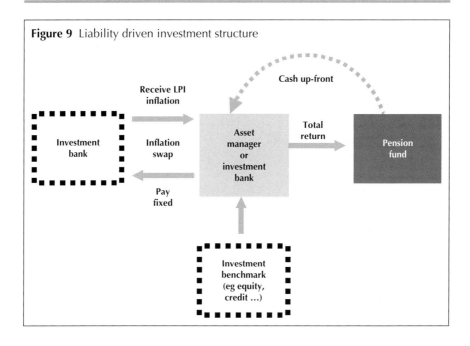

RPI, some are linked to changes in LPI, while others are fixed in nature.

"Liability-driven" investment approaches (see Figure 9) aim to target a level of outperformance over the assessed value of the liabilities; for example, liability plus 2% pa. This outperformance, if achieved, would allow schemes in deficit to improve their funding position. These approaches often invest in a range of real assets, and may use swaps to manage interest rate and inflation risks.

Dynamic switching strategies are another kind of approach that can be used to target a certain level of outperformance relative to the value of the liabilities. Such an approach might involve holding a risky, real asset such as equities and progressively switching these into index-linked gilts. For defined contribution schemes, traditional lifestyle approaches switch assets at pre-defined times in the period before retirement, irrespective of the relative attractiveness of markets at that time. LCP's DCisive™ is an approach that switches assets as outperformance emerges, targeting a level of outperformance over index-linked gilts with a greater degree of certainty than for lifestyle approaches.

Case study

One of LCP's clients is a pension scheme that had a deficit of 35%. The scheme's assets were invested along traditional lines: 15% in fixed interest gilts, 20% in index-linked gilts and 65% in equities.

Pension payments increased in-line with LPI, and the scheme had a significant exposure to inflation, particularly if equity returns failed to keep pace with inflation. Although the gilts were invested against long-duration indices, the scheme was significantly exposed to falls in the level of long-term interest rates.

Like many other, the scheme had suffered from the significant falls in equity markets during the years 2000–2002. During this period, the real interest rate (used by the Scheme Actuary to assess the value of the liabilities) also fell slightly. As a result of these factors, the scheme had moved from surplus into deficit in a reasonably short period.

The trustees and the corporate sponsor were both keen to reduce volatility in the funding level. Investing entirely in bonds would increase the Scheme Actuary's assessment of the deficit, and would also increase the ongoing costs of accrual.

The trustees decided on a liability-driven approach that greatly reduces exposure to equity market volatility, using derivatives. Manager outperformance, isolated using "transportable alpha" techniques, is combined with absolute return funds to give an overall return above a cash benchmark. Swaps are then used to eliminate interest rate and inflation risks.

The assets are expected to give a reasonably stable 3% pa of outperformance relative to the assessed value of the liabilities. The assets should respond to inflation in the same way as the liabilities, as a result of the inflation swaps.

Which approach is most suitable?

Schemes that are trying to reduce their exposure to inflation risks are likely to consider both benefit design and investment strategy.

Investment strategy is generally a more powerful tool than benefit design, as this can address risks in respect of both past and future service. Benefit design often only affects the future accrual of benefits.

Scheme rules may restrict the extent to which benefit design can be used to manage inflation risk. Reducing the value of future benefits is likely to be unpopular with staff.

Changes in investment strategy will have less impact if the scheme is under-funded, as under-funding limits the scope of the assets to match the overall sensitivity of the liabilities to changes in long-term inflation.

The changes in pension provision and in pension scheme investment discussed in Section 3.2 indicate that some of the most common ways in which UK defined-benefit schemes are managing their inflation risks include: closing the scheme to new members or to future accrual, and offering defined contribution benefits instead; and investing more in real assets and index-linked gilts at the expense of fixed-interest bonds and cash.

THE USE OF DERIVATIVES WITHIN ASSET LIABILITY MANAGEMENT

In the previous section we addressed the specific issues affecting the Dutch and UK pension funds, in particular the role of conditional indexation. However, for many pension funds these sector issues are only part of the solution for the overall pension scheme design. For instance, in the Netherlands, a corporate pension fund sponsor might wish to offer fixed indexation between 0% and 100% dependent on the funded ratio while in the UK, many pension funds have 100% indexation on their liabilities. In these cases a pension fund manager knows that inflation products play an important role in hedging inflation risks and yet the same questions arise. What is the benefit of purchasing real yields at such low levels for an under-funded scheme-locking in a low investment return? Is there an investment framework that can control the inflation risk while ensuring that the fund can benefit from any potential performance advantages?

ALM in the broad context of pension fund management aims to answer these questions and thereby reduce the probability of under-funding and high contribution rates. There are three available tools that can be used to control these risks; namely pension scheme policy (thus liabilities), contribution design, and investment policy. In this section we discuss this last topic and the role of inflation derivatives as a new tool in a pension manager's armoury that enables the best control of ALM risks for the broad sector issues.

Typically there are two main approaches to guide this process; precise matching of the projected cashflows, and broad matching of the overall sensitivity to changes in interest rates or inflation (known as duration matching). Both of these approaches lock in the ALM risk by ensuring that both assets and liabilities move in the same way. These are not new subjects but growth of the inflation derivative market has created the next generation of ALM solutions which go above and beyond these simple solutions of the 1980s and start to address the need to target excess return using non-matching assets (ie, equity, real estate, etc). Although these solutions are significantly more effective at controlling the future coverage ratio and contribution rates of the pension fund, their uptake has been limited. Pension fund trustees historically have viewed derivative products with suspicion but perceptions are changing. The Myner Report 2001 states that derivatives should not be a prohibited asset class and acknowledges that strategic asset allocation decisions should find the best solution to the pension fund (including inflation derivatives). Indeed, medium to large funds are very capable of implementing tailor-made derivative strategies though for smaller schemes the barrier to entry can be high. In a recent report by Greenwich Associates on the UK pension fund industry around 40% of funds with assets over £2 billion are either considering or planning to implement ALM solution with derivatives (see Table 1).

In the following sections we outline how inflation derivatives are used within the global market and a new way of approaching the classic duration management techniques.

Cashflow matching

Since the growth of the inflation-linked bond market, it has been possible to incorporate the inflation element into cashflow matching. The strategy is to split the pension fund liabilities into nominal and inflation-linked payments and use a combination of nominal and index-linked bonds to match the future payments. Though highly effective in controlling the duration and convexity risk in principle, such solutions have their own associated problems. The global supply of inflation-linked bonds does not satisfy the demand within the industry, so full immunization is not possible. For example, of the ten index-linked gilt securities only seven

Table 1 Greenwich survey of UK pension fund managers

Action	Implemented (%)	Plan to implement (%)	Considering (%)	Considered and rejected (%)	Have not considered (%)	No answer/not sure (%)
A/L matching through derivatives/LDI	4	5	35	13	28	14
Absolute return strategies	9	6	32	12	25	17

have maturities of more than five years which creates significant re-investment risk and high transaction costs necessitating a rebalance of the portfolio when the bonds mature. Even if cashflow matching were possible this could be an unwise move given the significant uncertainty in projected cashflows relating to actuarial assumptions, while the default risk of the bond portfolio could destroy the carefully constructed matching of the scheme. Finally, there is little flexibility in available investment choices and this locks in the performance of the fund.

The use of inflation derivatives has now created more flexible solutions. Today these strategies offer a new way to reduce ALM risk while allowing chunky allocation to other asset classes, rather than locking in the under-funding. To implement these flexible cashflow matching strategies an investment manager must choose an asset class which it is believed will have a higher return than inflation-linked/nominal bonds, or which offers opportunities through active management (eg, credit products, Collateralised Debt Obligations (CDO), and Constant Proportion Portfolio Insurance (CPPI)). The returns from such a portfolio are then asset swapped into a set of cashflows that match the liabilities of the scheme. Crucially, the flexibility of the derivative market makes it possible to exactly match the inflation liabilities, such as LPI exposure. Sometimes inflation liabilities have significant uncertainties but these strategies can still be used either by cashflow matching the short-term liabilities only, or by creating broad buckets of liabilities which can be cashflow matched using forward-starting inflation swaps (see Figure 10). A challenge to the derivative market is how to price forward-starting and at-the-money LPI inflation swaps while capturing path dependency characteristics. These issues are discussed elsewhere in this edition.

Even these approaches are not devoid of risk. There is no easy way to incorporate the additional ALM risk of using other asset classes (such as equity) – the risk is that an underlying asset class may not perform as expected and will create under-funding for the scheme. Also, these approaches can be expensive, since inflation and nominal exposures are treated separately and this creates double hedging of risks, which is discussed later in the chapter.

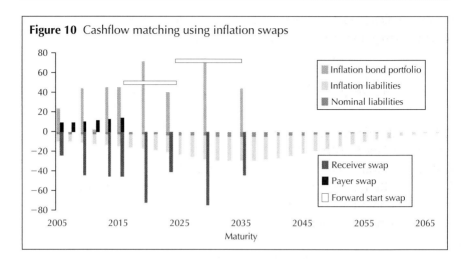

Figure 10 Cashflow matching using inflation swaps

Duration management

The second method of reducing inflation risk, often combined with cashflow matching, is duration matching. In this case the total durations of the liabilities and assets are calculated and if a mismatch exists (which it invariably does) the fund uses swaps/bonds to close the gap and reduce convexity risk.[20] The obvious advantage of using swaps over bonds is that there are significant maturity gaps within the global supply of inflation-linked bonds, so inflation derivatives are used to bridge the gap. Zero-coupon swaps have a longer duration than the corresponding bonds and can be used to boost the duration of a portfolio significantly. Banks can use their trading book to provide another option and offer 50-year inflation structures to sophisticated pension funds. Again, derivatives offer an investment manager the flexibility to diversify into other products while ensuring that the duration risk of the fund is minimised. In reality, the industry uses a combination of overlay solutions (cashflow matching at the short maturity, forward-starting and zero-coupon swaps) to best handle the ALM risk.

Such techniques undoubtedly help but they are not a full solution, and significant risks remain. A subtler risk that has only just started to be recognised by the industry, is the ambiguity of what the exact duration of a portfolio is with both nominal and inflation-linked assets. Typically, duration is defined as the per-centage change in price for a change in the nominal interest rate

$$P = \frac{Z}{(1+i^{nom})^T} \quad \text{and} \quad D_N = -\left(\frac{1}{P}\right)\frac{\partial P}{\partial i^{nom}} = \frac{T}{(1+i^{nom})}$$

This is well defined for a nominal instrument, but what about an inflation-indexed instrument? One approach is to use future infla-tion expectation to calculate the nominal duration of the inflated flows. An alternative is to calibrate a model for the movement of real against nominal rates – this enables a duration calculation for a given movement in real rates (and, the model, from nominal rates)

$$i^{real} = \beta \cdot i^{nom} + \alpha$$

In this model the correlation between the rates is known as the beta and an obvious requirement is that this parameter is stable. However, if an historical analysis of beta is performed, it is found to be significantly unstable (between −20 and 90% in the UK, see Figure 11). In many other markets beta is not a well-behaved para-meter but for ease of risk monitoring the industry convention has been to assume $\beta = 50\%$.

What does this mean for the duration matching of a fund? If real yields move down relative to nominal yields, the value of the lia-bilities will increase. But in nominal-duration management this risk is not hedged. The problem is compounded in the current environment where an increase in beta has increased the duration gap of many funds. The standard solution would be to shift the timescale of the portfolio to longer duration, which can be a costly exercise. Alternatively, both nominal and inflation liabilities could be treated separately by matching nominal duration with nominal liabilities and real duration with inflation-linked liabilities. All these strategies work better if constantly assessed in an active man-agement strategy so that changes in projected liability cashflows (due to increases in average life expectancy) or duration (due to market dynamics) can be quickly addressed.

However, intuitively it should be possible to hedge inflation risk, at least in part, with nominal instruments. This is because real rates and nominal rates appear to be correlated in the very long

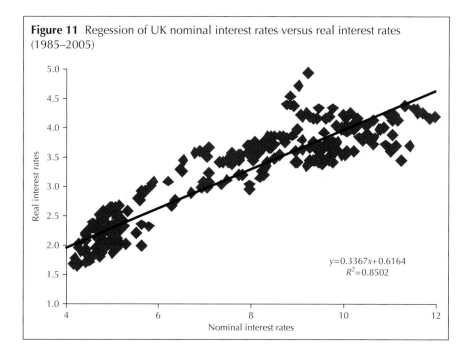

Figure 11 Regession of UK nominal interest rates versus real interest rates (1985–2005)

$y=0.3367x+0.6164$
$R^2=0.8502$

term and therefore need less active management. In a recent paper, Siegel and Waring (2004) suggested an approached that addressed these issues. They highlighted that both assets and liabilities can be decomposed into two durations, and if both are used in a duration-matching frame much of the undefined risks are avoided.

The values of any forecast cashflows are discounted by the nominal rates. However, using the Fisher equation, these nominal rates can be decomposed into real and inflation rates

$$(1 + i^{nom}) = (1 + i^{real})(1 + i^{inf})$$

Therefore, three different types of duration measurements are possible:

❑ D^N: Nominal duration – the percentage change in price for a change in nominal yields;
❑ D^R: Real duration – the percentage change in price for a change in real yields;

❏ D^I: Inflation duration – the percentage change in price for a change in expected inflation.

It is the real and inflation duration that Siegel and Waring suggested should be matched in their dual duration approach. In this framework, nominal instruments have approximately the same real and inflation duration. This means that a nominal investor is unable to bet separately on changes in real and expected inflation. In contrast, with inflation-linked instruments the inflation duration is nearly zero, as the inflation term cancels out in instrument valuation. This means that an investor in inflation-linked bonds can bet independently on changes in real rates, that is, without simultaneously betting on the expected inflation rate.

$$P = \frac{Z(1+i^{inf})^T}{(1+i^{real})^T\,(1+i^{inf})^T}$$

A similar analysis for equity, assuming the valuation as a series of discounted dividends, finds it has similar characteristics to inflation-linked instruments, having a long-maturity real duration and shorter inflation duration (Campbell and Vuolteenaho 2004). Finally, the present value of a typical defined benefit liability (also known as "final salary", where the payout is proportional to the employee's final salary at retirement) the real duration also plays a prominent role

$$P = \sum \frac{CF_{active}(1+i^{inf}+i^{wage})^t + CF_{retiree}(1+i^{inf})^t}{(1+i^{real})^t\,(1+i^{inf})^t}$$

In this case wage inflation in the numerator, cancels with core inflation in the denominator to the extent that the two inflation rates are correlated; besides, the impact of inflation is moderated because an increase in wage inflation will also mean higher contribution rates. On the other side of the equation, retirees have pensions linked to inflation and, similar to inflation-linked bonds, the cashflows are exposed to long maturity real duration.

An insight into the possible combinations of dual duration products can be gained by graphing their duration universe (as seen in Figure 12 if only nominal bonds or swaps are available for

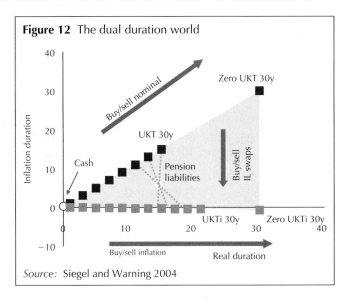

Figure 12 The dual duration world

Source: Siegel and Warning 2004

which the inflation and real durations are the same, the only available assets lie on the *xy* 45° line. In contrast, inflation linked products have zero inflation duration, so these products lie along the *x*-axis. Portfolios of nominal and inflation-linked products, however, may be anywhere in the space bounded by the *xy* 45 line and *x*-axis. Pension liabilities likewise lie somewhere within this bounded dual duration universe, so by careful construction it is possible to find a combinations of assets that matches the liability in both durations (where the dotted lines intersect the pension fund liabilities).

A typical pension fund has nominal, real, and inflation durations of 12.0, 14.9, and 7.8 respectively. In Table 2, it can be seen that for single duration matching the asset allocation might assign 66.7% to a 13-year nominal duration swap and 33.3% to a 10-year inflation swap, but in this mode there are an infinite number of possible solutions. However, the most obvious failing of this allocation is that movements in real yields are not fully hedged in nominal duration matching. In the dual duration world the situation is different – a larger proportion of the portfolio is allocated to the inflation-linked products to reflect the increase in real durations. Also, it has been possible to incorporate equity due to the more sophisticated risk framework.

Table 2 Single- and dual-duration asset allocation

Nominal duration of bonds	Nominal bond holding (%)	Duration matching real duration of inflation bonds	Inflation bond holding (%)	Equity holding (%)	Breakdown nominal: inflation (%)
Single duration matching					
11	200.0	10.0	−100.0	0.0	200:−100
12	100.0	10.0	0.0	0.0	100:0
13	66.7	10.0	33.3	0.0	67:33
14	50.0	10.0	50.0	0.0	50:50
15	40.0	10.0	60.0	0.0	40:60
16	33.3	10.0	66.7	0.0	33:67
17	28.6	10.0	71.4	0.0	29:71
18	25.0	10.0	75.0	0.0	25:75
19	22.2	10.0	77.8	0.0	22:78
20	20.0	10.0	80.0	0.0	20:80
Dual duration matching					
11	40.9	−352.0	−0.9	60.0	102:−2
12	37.5	128.0	2.5	60.0	94:6
13	34.6	59.4	5.4	60.0	87:13
14	32.1	40.7	7.9	60.0	80:20
15	30.0	32.0	10.0	60.0	75:25
16	28.1	26.9	11.9	60.0	70:30
17	26.5	23.7	13.5	60.0	66:34
18	25.0	21.3	15.0	60.0	63:38
19	23.7	19.6	16.3	60.0	59:41
20	22.5	18.3	17.5	60.0	56:44

Ultimately, targeting dual duration (instead of single duration) reduces the volatility of the fund coverage ratio and ensuring a stable contribution profile due to the closer ALM matching while still offering the flexibility to diversify into other asset classes. However, in reality the solution does not consist of one single technique but a combination of cashflow matching, duration management, and diversification into alternative asset classes in order to best manage a pension fund's inflation risk. For smaller pension funds, derivative solutions are still possible using the structured "liability driven" investment solutions offered by banks and asset managers. These use a combination of derivative and cash products to create a duration-weighted asset (both in the nominal and inflation worlds) where the derivative is held on the financial institutions balance sheet.

SUMMARY

Factors including low funding ratios, the fair value approach to valuation, and tighter solvency regulations have forced pension funds into more sophisticated, often derivative based, hedging strategies. Both the specific conditional indexation characteristic of the Dutch pension funds and the capped indexation system of the UK has led to investment strategies that are a mix of nominal and inflation-linked products. The exact mix depends on the indexation policy, the funding ratio of the pension fund, and the attitude to risk of the trustees and sponsor, amongst other things.

Given the complex dynamics of a pension fund, optimal investment strategies have to be determined in an ALM context. Such tailor-made strategies can substantially help to meet both the regulator's requirements and the ambitions of the pension fund. Therefore, a thorough understanding of the mechanics of indexation combined with the increasingly mature markets for inflation-linked products will contribute to adequate risk management for pension funds.

1 The funding ratio is the one valued in nominal terms, without valuing the embedded option of the indexation as discussed below.

2 50 years is taken as an example, in practice the precise liability structure of the pension fund including actuarial assumptions determine the maturity of the pension obligations and thus the indexation options.

3 In practice, the conditional indexation structure is often set up in such a way, that below a certain level (eg, 110), there is no indexation, above a certain (much higher) level (say 150), there is full indexation, and in between, the partial indexation is proportional (eg, 25% at 120). In option terms, this can be seen as a "call spread".

4 So in fact, the option is the value of the "expected" inflation compensation, calculated based on arbitrage-free option pricing calculations.

5 That is, not directly. Indirectly, they have to assume the risk of the pension fund not performing on its nominal obligations.

6 There is also a three year period in which deferred indexation can be made up if the funding ratio exceeds 110.

7 Shorter maturities are not necessary since the (nominal and inflation-linked) bond portfolio already provides an adequate hedge for interest rate risk of the liabilities in short time buckets. Swaps with maturities of over 30 years are not used since liquidity is still limited for these maturities.

8 For a more detailed description of this ALM model, see van Capelleveen *et al* (2004).

9 This effect is due to risk premiums and contributions, which on average increase the expected funding ratio over time in this model, certainly in a low funding ratio environment with little increase in liabilities due to limited indexation at these low levels.

10 By applying long horizons, part of this objective-driven bias is reduced.

11 The Government Actuary's survey "Occupational Pension Schemes 1971" found that 79% of scheme members were in final salary pension schemes, 30% of members were provided with no increases at all after retirement, and around 50% of members were provided with

discretionary increases only. Less than 5% of scheme members were in defined contribution arrangements.

12 According to UBS's "Pension Fund Indicators 2005", the average pension scheme's assets were invested 52% in equities, 10% in property, and 38% in fixed-interest bonds and cash.

13 Guaranteed Minimum Pensions and Protected Rights are hypothecated parts of the total pension provided by schemes that "contract out" of the State Second Pension. Schemes that contract out receive a rebate on the National Insurance contributions, in exchange for providing benefits of equivalent value to those from the State Second Pension.

14 The Government Actuary's survey "Occupational Pension Schemes 2004" found that 25% of members were in defined contribution arrangements, 35% of members were in closed final salary schemes and 40% were in open final salary schemes. Of those members in final salary schemes 67% provided only LPI pension increases.

15 According to UBS's "Pension Fund Indicators 2005", the average pension scheme's assets were invested 67% in equities, 7% in property, 9% in index-linked gilts and 17% in fixed-interest bonds and cash.

16 LCP's 2005 "Accounting for Pensions" survey found that only 4% of the companies in the FTSE 100 were in surplus on an FRS17 basis.

17 Figures provided by the UK Debt Management Office indicate that since January 2000, the average issue of index-linked gilts has been over-subscribed by 103%.

18 According to Merrill Lynch Investment Managers, there were £13 billion of outstanding index-linked corporate issuance as of June 2005, compared with £346 billion of conventional issuance.

19 Data from the Barclays Equity-Gilt Study 2005 indicates that the correlation between equity returns and inflation for the period 1955–2004 is 22%. The correlation between returns on fixed-interest gilts and inflation over this period is 11%.

20 This is the nominal duration of a pension fund liabilities and typically this is calculated by: (1) assuming a correlation between real and nominal yields; or (2) by assuming a constant inflation rate in the inflation linked liabilities and then calculated the duration of the projected cashflows.

REFERENCES

Campbell, J. and T. Vuolteenaho, 2004, "Inflation Illusions and Stock Prices", *American Economic Review*, **94**, pp. 19–23.

Deacon, M., A. Derry and D. Mirfendereski, 2004, *Inflation-indexed Securities: Bonds, Swaps and Other Derivatives*, 2nd edn (New York: Wiley).

Siegel, L. and M. Waring, 2004, "TIPS, the Dual Duration and the Pension Plan", *Financial Analysts Journal*, **60(5)**, p. 52.

Taleb, N., 1997, *Dynamic Hedging – Managing Vanilla And Exotic Options* (New York: Wiley).

van Capelleveen, H. F., H. M. Kat and T. P. Kocken, 2004, "How Derivatives Can Help Solve The Pension Fund Crisis", *The Journal of Portfolio Management*, **30(4)**, pp. 244–53.

Zhang, P. G., 1998, *Exotic Options*, 2nd edn (World Scientific).

Ziemba, W. T. and J. M. Mulvey (eds), 1998, *Worldwide Asset and Liability Modeling* (Cambridge University Press).

12

Asset-Liability Management of Inflation Risk for Insurers

John Hancock

Swiss Reinsurance Co

INTRODUCTION

The Property and Casualty and Accident and Health insurance industries have sizeable exposures to inflation risk. The US Property and Casualty industry alone has over US$600 billion of inflation-sensitive liabilities. The bulk of this inflation exposure is unhedged. In the past, leaving this exposure unhedged has been very profitable for the industry as inflation rates have fallen. The direct impact of lower than expected inflation on claims on contracts written since 1980 was a windfall profit of approximately US$80 billion.[1] In addition, insurers received sizeable investment gains due to the indirect impact of lower inflation and resulting lower interest rates on asset prices.

Currently, however, inflation expectations are at generational lows. With inflation expectations at low levels, risks for future inflation are somewhat asymmetric, with more room for upside risk than downside. If inflation rates did pick up again, the impact on the industry would be higher than in the past, due to a shift in insurance liabilities towards longer-tail liabilities that are particularly sensitive to inflation risk. Based on the current liability structure of the US Property and Casualty industry, a 1% increase in long-term inflation expectations from the current level of 2.5% would result in a direct industry loss of roughly US$23 billion,[2] the same order of magnitude as the second largest insured loss event to date: Hurricane Andrew. In addition, the bad inflation news would very probably negatively impact share prices, interest rates and credit spreads, leading to further investment losses.

With the increased availability and liquidity of inflation-linked securities, taking inflation exposures is no longer an unavoidable risk of doing business, but is rather an investment choice. This chapter examines the links between insurance liabilities and inflation as well as the potential benefits of investing in inflation-linked securities for Property and Casualty and Accident and Health insurers.

The remainder of this chapter is structured as follows. In the first section we outline the different types of claims inflation that insurers experience and their relation to consumer price inflation. Next we outline an optimal hedge of claims inflation using inflation-linked securities. In the final section we outline the accounting and regulatory impacts of investment in inflation-linked securities.

IMPACT OF INFLATION ON CLAIMS
Price inflation *versus* social inflation

There are a number of notions of inflation for insurers. These notions are defined below.

❑ *Claims inflation*: the rate at which insured losses per insured claim grow.
❑ *Price inflation*: the rate at which prices of goods and services grow.
❑ *Social inflation*: the difference between claims inflation and price inflation.

Social inflation, sometimes called superimposed inflation, is the result of many factors, such as tort reforms and changes in medical coverage, which affect insurance exposures but are not related to changing prices. Social inflation also results from the fact that insurance claims have a higher exposure to certain classes of prices (in particular, medical prices and wages) than economy-wide price indices, such as consumer price indices.

The distinction between social and price inflation is important for several reasons:

❑ social inflation diversifies to a significant extent across geographic regions and areas of business and so is most important at a line of business and country level;
❑ inflation risk does not diversify to a significant extent across areas of business or geographic regions and so is most important at a portfolio level;

❏ price inflation is closely related to investment returns (social inflation is largely independent of asset prices).

Due to these factors, risk management of social inflation needs to be conducted in a different manner than price inflation. In particular, because price inflation is a group-wide issue it should be managed at the group level. It should also be managed simultaneously with investment risk.

Linking claims and inflation

The inflation exposure of property insurance is relatively small simply because the time lag between when coverage is bound and when claims are paid is relatively short. In both Property and Casualty and Accident and Health insurance, however, the lag between coverage and claims payments can be considerable and so relatively small changes in inflation rates can accumulate to cause large changes in claims payments over this period of time.

Both Property and Casualty insurance and Accident and Health insurance claims are not directly linked to overall consumer price inflation, but are instead highly dependent on healthcare inflation due to medical expense claims and, in the case of casualty insurance, wage inflation due to disability and wrongful death claims.

Further links between insurance claims and price inflation arise because in many legal jurisdictions, compensatory awards are factored up to current dollar amounts at the time of the claim payment. In addition, punitive damages are subject to general inflation trends.

In some jurisdictions, such as the French auto insurance market, compensatory awards take the form of inflation-indexed annuities. In this case, the link between inflation rates and claims is not so straightforward due to the link between inflation and interest rates: any change in inflation rates is usually matched by an even larger change in interest rates. Economists call this relationship the "Taylor Rule" (Taylor 1993). In the 1990s, inflation rates in France fell by some 200 bps (basis points). However, the yield on 10-year bonds fell by 400 bps over the same period. The capitalised value of indexed annuities therefore rose during this period of falling inflation.

Over the past 30 years, both medical price inflation and wage inflation have been significantly higher than consumer price inflation in both Europe and the United States, as can be seen in

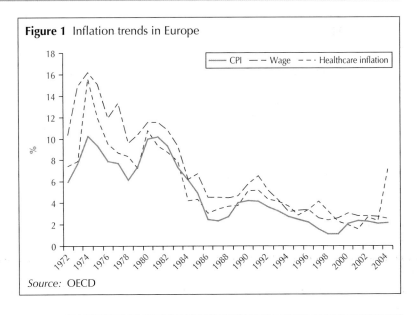

Figure 1 Inflation trends in Europe

Source: OECD

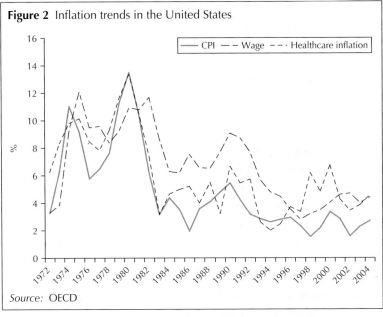

Figure 2 Inflation trends in the United States

Source: OECD

Figures 1 and 2. However, the correlation between both wage inflation and medical price inflation to consumer price inflation is high,
implying that much of the volatility in claims inflation is due to
price inflation, whereas social inflation is relatively stable.

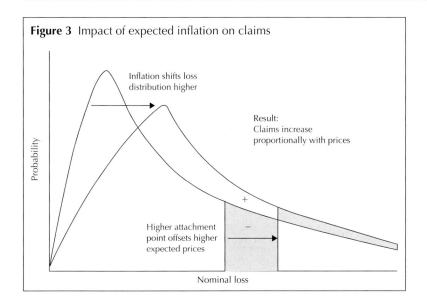

Figure 3 Impact of expected inflation on claims

The close link between consumer price, healthcare and wage inflation is important because index-linked securities that directly hedge the exposure of insurance claims to wage and healthcare inflation are not available. However, securities linked to consumer price indices can still be used to hedge the claims inflation risk embedded in insurance liabilities.

Expected *versus* unexpected inflation

Inflation has a different impact on claims depending on whether the increase in prices was expected and already incorporated into the pricing of contracts or whether the change in inflation was a surprise. Inflation has the effect of shifting the loss distribution of the insured higher by the amount of the increase in prices. If the change in prices was foreseen, then franchises or deductibles (in the case of direct insurance) and attachment points (in the case of non-proportional reinsurance) can be increased to account for the increase in the price level. As a result, an expected change in prices will increase expected claims by a proportionate amount (see Figure 3). In this case, claims have an expected-inflation sensitivity of one, as an $x\%$ expected increase in prices will result in an $x\%$ expected increase in claims.

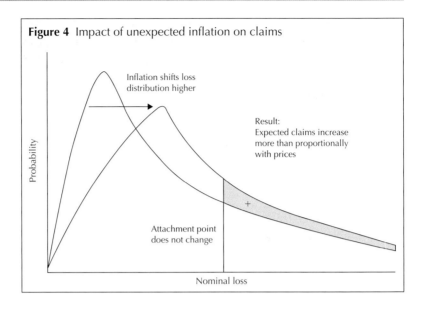

Figure 4 Impact of unexpected inflation on claims

Inflation shifts loss
distribution higher

Result:
Expected claims increase
more than proportionally
with prices

Probability

Attachment point
does not change

+

Nominal loss

If, on the other hand, the change in prices is a surprise and attachment points and franchises are not adjusted *ex post* to the change in prices, then inflation will have a more than proportionate impact on prices (see Figure 4). In this case, claims have an unexpected-inflation sensitivity of α ($\alpha > 1$), as an $x\%$ unexpected increase in prices will result in an ($x \times \alpha$)% increase in the expected value of claims.

In most European countries "stabilisation clauses" are included in reinsurance contracts. These clauses adjust for unexpected inflation by linking attachment points to *ex post* realisations of an inflation index. This adjustment has the effect of reducing the sensitivity of reinsurance claims to unexpected inflation. Primary insurance, however, still has an excess sensitivity to inflation, as franchise or deductible amounts are not adjusted *ex post* for surprise inflation.

Estimating sensitivity of claims to inflation

Measuring the excess sensitivity of claims to inflation surprises is difficult. Historical data on aggregated claims is of little use because in any given year changes in claims due to tort reforms or catastrophes, for example, tend to swamp the impact of changes in inflation rates. The impact of inflation surprises, on the other hand, is spread out over a number of years. It is also difficult to distinguish historical changes in inflation rates that were expected from changes that were a surprise. For this reason, sensitivities must be estimated based on microanalysis of individual exposures. From a theoretical standpoint, the sensitivity of claims to unexpected inflation must be at least one. How much the sensitivity exceeds one depends on a number of factors, including loss distributions and attachment points.

MANAGING INFLATION RISK
Asset-liability management approach
This section outlines a hedge of the inflation and interest-rate risk embedded in insurance liabilities using inflation-linked securities. The hedge can be demonstrated with a very simplified model. This model can easily be generalised to a more realistic framework with some cost in extra notation. However, the basic intuitions remain the same as in the simplified model.

The model consists of one time period. The length of this time period is equivalent to the duration of liabilities. Premiums are either invested in inflation-linked (L) or unlinked (U) zero-coupon bonds with the same duration as the claims payment. The unlinked bond pays a fixed return (r_U) at the end of the period. The return on the inflation-indexed bond is random and depends on the realisation of consumer price inflation rates ($r_L + \varepsilon$, where r_L is the expected yield on the indexed bonds and ε is a random consumer price inflation-rate shock). At the end of the period, the firm must pay claims, which are dependant on claims inflation ($C(1 + \alpha\eta)$, where C is expected claims based on inflation expectations at the beginning of the period, α is the sensitivity of claims to inflation shocks, and η is a random claims inflation shock). The end of period profit of the firm is then

$$\Pi = L(1 + r_L + \varepsilon) + U(1 + r_U) - C(1 + \alpha\eta) \qquad (1)$$

The variance of the profit of the firm can be written

$$V(\Pi) = L^2\sigma_\varepsilon^2 - 2LC\alpha\sigma_{\varepsilon\eta} + C^2\alpha^2\sigma_\eta^2 \qquad (2)$$

The optimal hedge is then simply the level of L that minimises the variance of the profit of the firm. The first-order condition for this minimisation problem is

$$L = C\beta \tag{3}$$

where $\beta = \alpha\sigma_{\varepsilon\eta}/\sigma_{\varepsilon}^2$.

In Equation (3), β can be interpreted in a similar manner to the β in the Capital Asset Pricing Model. It is the ratio between the expected change in claims inflation due to a change in consumer price inflation. In other words, if β has a value of 1, then a 1% change in consumer price inflation is expected to result in a 1% change in claims inflation. If β has a value of 1.1, then a 1% change in consumer price inflation is expected to result in a 1.1% change in claims inflation.

Based on fundamentals, it is not clear that there is a link between social inflation and consumer price inflation: if inflation is higher than expected, there is no fundamental reason why social inflation should be higher or lower than expected. Similarly, if consumer price inflation is lower than expected, there is no reason to expect that social inflation will be impacted. If this is the case, then social inflation and price inflation are uncorrelated and $\beta = \alpha$. This result is important because it implies that, in the absence of a clear link between social inflation and price inflation, the optimal hedge for insurers is to α-match their insurance liabilities with inflation-linked securities, even though insurers' claims inflation exposure is not directly linked to consumer price inflation.

In addition to the first-order condition (Equation (3)), the expected profit of the hedge should be zero:

$$E[\Pi] = L(1 + r_L) + U(1 + r_U) - C = 0 \tag{4}$$

Solving Equation (4) for U and substituting the optimal value of U (Equation (3)), yields a value of the investment in unlinked bonds equal to

$$U = C\frac{1-\beta(1+r_L)}{1+r_U} \tag{5}$$

If $\beta(1 + r_L) > 0$, then the hedge actually involves taking a short position in unlinked bonds.

Effectiveness of the hedge

The effectiveness of the hedge can be judged by substituting the optimal level of bond investments (Equation (3)) into the formula for the variance of firm profit (Equation (2)):

$$V(\Pi) = C^2 \alpha^2 \sigma_\eta^2 \left(1 - R^2\right) \quad \text{(index-linked hedge)} \quad (6)$$

where R^2 is the coefficient of determination in a regression of price inflation surprises on claims inflation surprises. In simpler terms, it is the percentage of the variance of claims risk that can be explained by inflation risk. It is also the correlation coefficient of price and claims inflation risk squared.

Note that there is no perfect hedge unless: α or $\sigma_\eta^2 = 0$, in which case there is no inflation risk and duration matching with non-linked securities can then be used to hedge the interest rate risk; or if $R^2 = 1$ in which case claims inflation is perfectly correlated with price inflation.

To put the effectiveness of this hedge into perspective, the profit variance of the indexed-linked hedge can be compared with the profit variance of a duration matching strategy with non-linked securities

$$V(\Pi) = C^2 \alpha^2 \sigma_\eta^2 \quad \text{(non-linked hedge)} \quad (7)$$

The index-linked hedge results in a reduction of risk by a factor of R^2, compared with a duration matching strategy.

Model risk

The ability to implement this hedge depends on the ability to identify the parameter of the model, β. In practice, these parameters can only be identified with error. It is therefore important to consider the potential impact of this error. If the estimate of β is off by $x\%$, then the variance of firm profit will be

$$V(\Pi) = C^2 \alpha^2 \sigma_\eta^2 \left(1 + x^2 - R^2\right) \quad \text{(indexed hedge with errors)} \quad (8)$$

The necessary and sufficient condition under which the indexed hedge outperforms duration with non-indexed bonds in the presence of hedging errors is

$$x^2 < R^2 \tag{9}$$

Based on theoretical arguments alone, the possible values of β can be narrowed down to a fairly small range. In addition, the relationship between claims inflation and consumer price inflation is fairly strong (R^2 is large; see Figures 1 and 2); it is fairly unlikely that duration matching with inflation-linked bonds would actually inadvertently increase the risk of the insurer even given the uncertainties in estimating β.

ACCOUNTING AND REGULATORY IMPLICATIONS
US GAAP
Under US GAAP, interest rates and the rate of inflation in the currency in which an inflation-linked bond is denominated are considered to be clearly and closely related. In practice, this means that non-leveraged inflation-linked securities should not have the inflation-related embedded derivative separated from the host contract and marked to market as is standard practice for derivatives covered under FAS 133. Instead, inflation-linked securities are designated at initial recognition as held for trading (fair value on balance sheet, change in fair value recognised in earnings), available for sale (fair value on balance sheet, change in fair value not recognised in earnings) or held to maturity (amortised cost basis).

Recognition of income from inflation-linked securities that are designated as held to maturity is covered by EITF 96-12 "Recognition of Interest Income and Balance Sheet Classification of Structured Notes". EITF 96-12 requires the use of the retrospective interest method, under which the amortised cost is updated to reflect changes in past actual and expected future cashflows.

In the retrospective interest method, the internal rate of return (IRR) from the date of initial recognition is calculated for each period based on updated assumptions for cashflows. The amortised cost balance for the current period is then set equal to the net present value of future expected cashflows using the IRR as the discount rate if the IRR is positive and using a discount rate of zero if the IRR is negative. Current period cashflows plus changes in amortised cost are recognised as income.

Application of the retrospective interest method results in some sensitivity of current earnings to future expected inflation: higher expected inflation results in higher current earnings. However, this inflation sensitivity tends to offset the negative impact of higher inflation expectations on future claims reserves. Overall, the US GAAP earnings volatility is therefore reduced by investment in inflation-linked securities.

IFRS

The treatment of investments in inflation-indexed bonds under IFRS is not clear. Under IAS 39, separation of the embedded derivative from the host contract only occurs if all of the following criteria are met:

❏ the economic characteristics and risks of the embedded derivative are not closely related to the economic characteristics of the host contract;
❏ a separate instrument with the same terms as the embedded derivative would meet the definition of a derivative;
❏ the combined instrument is not measured at fair value with changes in fair value recognised in profit or loss (IAS 39 gives the option of measurement at fair value, with changes recognised through income, provided certain criteria are met).

The US GAAP has provided guidance that inflation and interest rates are considered to be clearly and closely linked. However, no such guidance exists currently for IAS (Amblard 2005).

Current regulatory regimes

Most current capital adequacy assessments for insurance companies are based on factor models that apply percentages to accounting-based exposure information to determine both required capital and available capital. These capital adequacy calculations are sometimes augmented with stress test scenarios.

In Europe and the United States there are currently no factor-based models for determining required capital for insurance companies that make a distinction between inflation-linked and non-linked securities. Similarly, there are currently no implemented inflation stress scenarios that consider a link between claims risk and asset risk. However, there may be some restrictions on the accounting of inflation-indexed bonds in the calculation of available capital, for example in France (Amblard 2005).

Solvency II

With Solvency II, insurance regulators will be moving to the use of internal economic risk models for determining capital adequacy. As using inflation-linked securities to hedge the inflation risk embedded in insurance liabilities reduces the overall risk of the insurer, investment in inflation-indexed bonds should, in principle, reduce capital requirements under Solvency II. In practice, though, any capital relief will depend on whether or not inflation risk is reflected in the risk models used.

To date, there are two models for future implementations of Solvency II: the Individual Capital Assessment tests of the UK Financial Services Authority and the Swiss Solvency Test of the Swiss Federal Office of Private Insurance. In both cases, modelling inflation risk is not an explicit requirement. However, it appears to be understood by the auditors that inflation risk should be modelled. In general, inflation risk is a primary driver of solvency risk for insurers and it is likely that inflation risk modelling will be a requirement of future implementations of Solvency II. Investing in inflation-indexed bonds will therefore probably result in capital relief under Solvency II.

CONCLUDING REMARKS

Although insurance claims inflation is not directly linked to consumer price inflation, the indirect links are strong. The increasing availability and liquidity of securities linked to consumer price inflation indices present new opportunities for insurers to reduce their net asset–liability risk with an appropriate investment position in this asset class. The potential reduction in risk is significant. The eventual implementation of the Solvency II regulatory framework will further add to the attractiveness of inflation-linked securities.

---

1   Based on actual industry claims data from Best's Aggregates and Averages, actual *versus* expected inflation data from the Philadelphia Federal Reserves Bank and an assumption of a claims sensitivity factor α, discussed in the following, of 1.1.

2   Based on claims patterns estimated from Schedule P of Best's Aggregates and Averages (average duration of claims of 3.5 years) and a claims sensitivity factor $\alpha = 1.1$.

REFERENCES

Amblard, G., 2005, "Inflation-linked Products in the Euro Area: An AMTE Working Group to Standardise, Develop and Promote the Asset Class".

Taylor, J.B., 1993, "Discretion Versus Policy Rules in Practice", *Carnegie–Rochester Conference Series on Public Policy*, p. 39.

Siegel, L. and M. Barton-Waring, "TIPS, the Dual Duration, and the Pension Plan", *Financial Analysts Journal*, **60(5)**.

Index